FRENCH-SPEAKING

AFRICA

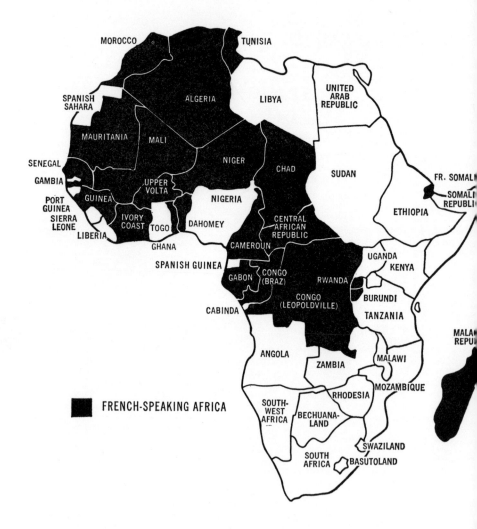

FRENCH-SPEAKING AFRICA

The Search for Identity

Edited by

WILLIAM H. LEWIS

WALKER AND COMPANY
New York

Preface

POPULAR Western opinion recently has turned sharply against Africa in a dramatic shift away from the almost universal euphoria and optimism that attended Africa's independence movement. Independence was attained relatively painlessly—with the notable exception of Algeria—and mutual protestations of friendship and compatability appeared to portend a generation of felicitous relations between Africa and the West. Harmony and hope were reflected in the activities of the Caisse de Coopèration Economique and in the implementation of the Fonds d'Aide et de Coopèration in the French-speaking areas, in British subventions for Ghana and Nigeria, and in rapidly proliferating American technical-assistance programs for a number of African states.

Within the brief span of four years, however, the West apparently has become baffled and frustrated in its hopes and expectations. Events since 1960 have confounded those who expected that the dispensation of dominion and sovereignty to Africans would quiet racial animosities, reduce atavistic nationalist forces to reasonable proportions, and confine the African dialogue with the West to questions involving economic relationships and development planning. These expectations have been dashed in the welter of contentious issues that have emerged since independence: The situation in Congo-Leopoldville has retrogressed; opposition to multiracialism by the "white redoubtists" in southern Africa has exacerbated racial animosities all over the continent; the continued Western military presence has become a *cause célèbre*; and the activities of the Soviet and Chinese Communists have given impetus to indigenous revisionist, radical, and revolutionary forces.

The present generation of African leaders inherited from the colonialists a plethora of problems. The overwhelming majority of African states are highly brittle agglomerations drawing together mélanges of peoples having weakly formed networks of mutual needs, obligations, and responsibilities.

v

Trained, technically competent elites are thin, both in numbers and in experience. Moreover, those Western-oriented emporiums that have been installed in Africa's coastal cities and towns, plantations, and mining complexes are, in many instances, unable to sustain the demands placed upon them for employment, effective administration, goods and services, and revenues for development planning. Surrounded by seemingly parasitic peoples and and communities, many of these new meccas are barely able to sustain themselves at pre-independence levels. Compounding the difficulties of African leaders are the inherent weaknesses of their nascent economies: ill-formed internal markets, low per capita income, costly social overheads, narrowly based infrastructures, inadequate domestic savings and investment, and the embryonic nature of indigenous entrepreneurial classes.

The dimensions of Africa's problems may be better appreciated if we recall that the average per capita income for the continent as a whole is approximately 30 cents per day; that there is only one doctor per 17,000 people; that infant mortality in sub-Saharan areas exceeds 250 per 1,000 live births, or almost 10 times the U.S. rate; that industrial productivity per capita in Western nations is more than 25 times higher than in Africa; that only 15 per cent of the continent's more than 275 million people are literate, and only 40 per cent of school-age children are presently receiving primary-level instruction; that the average African farmer has a productive efficiency which is but 30 per cent that of his American counterpart. Add to this a population growing at a rate of 3 per cent each year, the economic problems faced by nations dependent on one or two primary export products, and the limited revenues available to embryonic regimes, and we have an idea of the range of difficulties confronting Africa's present generation of leaders.

That such difficulties foster instability and disorder is vouchsafed by the lengthy catalogue of crises that have seized Africa recently. Coups and coup-plotting have occurred in more than half of Africa's independent states—most notably Zanzibar, Ethiopia, the Sudan, Tunisia, the Ivory Coast, Congo-Brazzaville, Upper Volta, and Gabon. Assassinations or planned assassinations have taken place in Togo, Ghana, Tunisia, Algeria, and Nigeria. Army mutinies have erupted in Senegal, the Somali Republic, Ethiopia, Kenya, Tanganyika, and Uganda. Tribal and ethnic dissidence has threatened the viability of the Sudan, Nigeria, Ethiopia, and Mali. And insurgency has been prevalent in Cameroun, Congo-Leopoldville, Algeria, and Sudan.

Western interests, of course, have not been unaffected by these outbursts. Many African regimes, in attempting to consolidate themselves, have responded to popular demands for early Africanization of government services. Under the impetus of centrist planning, local Western investors have been subjected to stringent controls. Missionary groups increasingly have been placed under severe inhibitions, and some of their leaders in West Africa have been expelled summarily for "blatantly intervening" in local problems. Where Western nations, particularly France and Great Britain, have sought to retain strategically important military installations, they have been badgered to evacuate. Finally, even the economic networks established by the former métropoles have been accused of perpetuating colonial ambitions and relationships.

Perhaps most distressing, however, has been the eruption of racist passion at a time when illumination and understanding in this area seem imperative. In the December, 1964, debates on the Congo conducted before the United Nations Security Council, the joint Belgian-American Stanleyville paratroop rescue effort, which had clearly been predicated upon humanitarian considerations, was labeled by the Africans as aggression and racist aggrandizement. The Belgian and American representatives charged the Africans with irresponsibility, racially grounded feelings of inferiority, and ill-founded emotionalism. That only a very few African states rose to defend the motives of the rescuers signified the widespread concord on the subject among the Africans.

Hopefully, December, 1964, was a low-water mark in African-Western relations. The bizarre proceedings before the United Nations demonstrated the paucity of understanding between the main protagonists. Nevertheless, the incident still may yield productive and mutually beneficial consequences. At any rate, U.S. innocence concerning things African is being replaced by an awareness of the great complexities and sensitivities that obtain in Africa's body politic. We are becoming increasingly aware of the gulf that exists between cultural heritages and of the issues that obtain in the African's quest for civilization, personality, and identity, and for national prestige, dignity, and status at a time when he is far from certain of the continuing viability of his new nation. The African looks at the external world with a mixture of anticipation and anxiety, pride and peevish sensitivity. He sincerely desires a place for himself in the international communty of nations, and is wary of the knowledge and values of Western civilization and the gratuitous advice of Western technical advisers and economic planners.

Thus, as Africa and Africans seek to establish their "place in the sun," we may anticipate occasional displays of irritation. Even when liberally borrowing from the West, Africans are likely to insist on interpreting what they borrow in an African light. As Professors Friedland and Rosberg have pointed out, for instance,

The ideology of African Socialism differs radically from that of the West. The view of human nature underlying African Socialism rejects the individualistic philosophy of the West. The African Socialist holds a view of human nature which, he believes, rests on the fundamental characteristics of traditional society: classless, communal, and egalitarian. What is common to these characteristics is the concept that only inside a given society can the individual fulfill himself, that the society gives him shape, form, and cohesion. Further, the society takes on a collective animus of intentions, aspirations, and fears, and the failure of any individual to adhere to this animus gives to the society the right of compulsion to force the individual to be free. Unlike the Western majoritarian conception of democracy, the African Socialist rejects the "will of all" or the will of the majority and adopts the language of Rousseau: the "general will," the "will of the people." In fact, many of the leaders of the independent nations of Africa see themselves as filling the role of Rousseau's "Legislator."[1]

The seeming incongruities and inconsistencies in this posture epitomize the paradox of Africa today. The African has adopted the slogans of Western socialism, but interprets them in a "traditional" manner to achieve "modern" goals. Within the Western tradition, an innovational role for the individual is held essential for the process we characterize as "modernizing." By contrast, the individual within African society is expected to be passive but mobilized, oriented toward the communal society, not apart from it, and subject to traditional relationships but willing to evolve away from them. Moreover, since many African states are made up of discrete collectivities that are barely able to establish a consensus, reference to a "general will" seems almost illusory. The average Western observer wonders how real advancement can be achieved by adhering to values that lack universal vigor, appeal, or acceptance.

The principal problem posed by the rationale for African socialism as discussed by Friedland and Rosberg is the absence of any clear distinction between the concepts of "community" and "society." Within the Western context, society is perceived as a means to an end, whereas a community is an end in itself. As pointed out by Tönnies, a modern society tends to be founded upon self-interest and mutual trust, whereas a traditional community demands subordination and induces fear of innovation. A truly modern society tends to be open-ended, pluralistic, innovation-oriented, and mobile. For most contemporary African leaders, however, pluralism is a tribal and ethnic Pandora's box, innovation threatens to unleash political forces that are destabilizing precisely at a time when order is needed, and social mobility is a distant ideal given the continent's limited economic resources and mounting population pressures.

It is not my purpose here to assume an argumentative posture concerning African ideologies and political beliefs. Indeed, there are many Western ideas that deserve close scrutiny, not the least of which is our tendency to see in social change opportunities for the reshaping of underdeveloped societies in our own image. We tend to assume that change is unilinear and that Western experience is the sole effective guideline for the nations of Africa,

Latin America, and Asia. Change, in reality, is multilinear, and there are many paths to it—paths to be followed selectively and prudently.

At a somewhat more sophisticated level, we might note that Western economists have come increasingly to recognize that economic criteria for evaluating barriers to development are incomplete. As Professor Everett Hagen has noted, the assumptions that the income of African populations is too small to make savings easy, that high social-overhead capital, which underdeveloped nations are unable to accumulate, is requisite for growth, and that internal markets are too stunted to induce investment are not adequate barriers to progress. Instinctively, Africa's leaders have come to recognize that the principal barriers are political and social. They are engaged, consequently, in serious efforts to find more realistic paths to meaningful progress.

For the Westerner, then, this should not be a time for skepticism and lamentations, but for flexibility, compassion, and understanding. There are many gaps in our understanding and appreciation of Africa, especially of those factors in the area of social change that are requisite for political development. How, for instance, can we tell that effective integration is being achieved? To what extent are political conflict, competition, and instability a necessary concomitant of advancement? Are we engaging in a gigantic self-deception when we equate political stability with economic advancement? What are the principal sociopolitical networks essential for cohesion and viability? Which functional elites require the greatest encouragement to anchor the political forces at play in African states?

As we seek to develop new conceptual models for understanding social and political processes in independent Africa, some effort must be made to overcome our tendency to restrict our research to English-speaking regions. African studies are of recent origin in the United States, but a widespread reluctance to undertake research in francophonic regions is already having effects. At present, the ratio of Africanists concentrating upon Ghana and Nigeria, as opposed to the eight territories of former French West Africa, is approximately twenty to one. Outside the coastal regions of West Africa, there are only one or two American scholars in each discipline who have engaged in appreciable field research in Mali, Upper Volta, Chad, Central Africa, Malagasy, Niger, or the Congo. As a result, American research in francophonic Africa suffers from a lack of depth, comprehensiveness, or relatedness.

This book emerges from a colloquium conducted in Washington, D.C., from August 17–21, 1964, under the auspices of the U.S. Department of State, The Ford Foundation, Georgetown University, and The African-American Institute. The special program, organized to stimulate greater interest in French-speaking Africa among American scholars, brought together leading specialists from Africa, Western Europe, Canada, and the United States to discuss problems relating to political, economic, and social change. Significantly, this was the first international congress to be convened in the United States that focused exclusively on French-speaking Africa.

A reasonable reservation may be lodged against singling out for special scrutiny a vast area embracing more than 20 nations and almost 50 million people. Incorporating Arabs, Berbers, true Negroids, Sudanic peoples, Pygmies, and Bantu-speaking communities, the area has no homogeneity beyond the coincidence of a shared experience under French dominion. Moreover, historical Arab-African rivalries, slave-raiding between coastal and Sudanic tribes, and a host of related, well-known frictions seem to militate against treating the French-speaking states as a coherent whole.

But is francophonic Africa then simply a fiction? Probably no more or no less so than NATO or the EEC. Although the purist may contend that Africa is only a geographic expression, others point out that among the present generation of French-speaking African leaders a communality of view exists vis-à-vis France. Despite differences in background, experience, style, outlook, and temperament, virtually all these leaders look to Paris with varying degrees of respect, nostalgia, or veneration. The attractions of Gallic culture are well known, as is the appeal of Voltaire, Rousseau, and Montesquieu. The concepts may be African, but the idiom, the slogans, and the patterns of thinking clearly reflect French influence, for the African can no more cast off his French experience and education than he can his African heritage.

This book might never have materialized without the unstinting support of J. Wayne Fredericks, Deputy-Assistant Secretary of State for African Affairs; Melvin Fox of The Ford Foundation; Father George Dunne, S.J., and Dean Rocco Porreco of Georgetown University; Nino Romani, my indefatigable assistant; and Miss Yara Blake and Mrs. Patricia Holland. In addition, the participants in the program, who came from as far afield as Africa, Great Britain, France, and West Germany, must be mentioned. They were totally responsible for the scholarly and provocative nature of both the Congress and this book.

Finally, and perhaps most crucially, I should like to acknowledge the contribution—reflecting patience, understanding, and supreme confidence—made by my wife, Kathleen.

William H. Lewis

Washington, D.C.
January, 1965

Contents

xi

PART I

THE BACKGROUND

1

Independence as a Goal in French West African Politics: 1944–60

MICHAEL CROWDER

BY THE END of 1960 all the states that comprised the administrative federation of French West Africa had become independent. Yet the word "independence" was for long excluded from the public vocabulary of French-speaking African politicians, and the demand for independence was not formally made by any major political party until well over a year after Ghana had become a sovereign state. On July 25, 1958, at its inaugural meeting at Cotonou, the Parti du Regroupement Africain (PRA) was pressured into demands for immediate independence by its more radical members, to the embarrassment of some of its older leaders, particularly Léopold Sédar Senghor of Senegal, who were still committed to the creation of a Franco-African community in which the French-speaking African states would share with France the control of such matters as defense, foreign policy, currency, and higher education. Only the night before the meeting, Senghor had prepared a policy statement in which he had written: "We will be careful not to abuse the word independence, which is a word only too useful for hiding our lack of imagination and our cowardice," and "Independence has no positive content, it is not a solution."

Although the question of independence had been raised within the party, particularly by the Niger and Senegalese radicals, it had seemed that in fact the prevailing view would be Senghor's. It was still the view held by

15

the other major party, the Rassemblement Démocratique Africain (RDA), whose president, Félix Houphouet-Boigny of the Ivory Coast, had sent a telegram to the Congress in which he urged the participants: *"Apportent éléments réalistes construction communauté franco-africaine"* ("Bring realism into the creation of the Franco-African community").[1] Two months later, however, Houphouet's own lieutenant, Sékou Touré of Guinea, led a successful campaign in Guinea against the proposed Franco-African community and declared independence. De Gaulle had put the terms for voting in the referendum bluntly: Anyone could take independence, with all its consequences, by registering a "No" vote to the Constitution of the Fifth Republic. These consequences, it was openly hinted, would involve the withdrawal of all French aid and technical assistance.

Guinea became officially independent on October 2, 1958. By the end of 1960 all the other French African territories had followed suit.

This chapter attempts to trace the rise of the demand for full self-government and independence in French West African politics, to explain the tardiness in its growth, and to assess the strength of the appeal for politicians of the rival goal of membership in the French Union and its successor, the Franco-African Community, during the period 1944–60.

Although the Brazzaville Conference (January 30 to February 8, 1944) was essentially one of administrators, it marks the end of the era when political activity in French West Africa was restricted to the four communes of Senegal. The participants were called upon to make recommendations as to the future relationship of France to her colonies. They proposed an assimilationist framework within which the political development of France's African colonies could take place after the war. René Pleven, Commissioner for the Colonies in the Free French Government, made it clear in his opening speech that France had no intention of prescribing independence as a goal for her colonies, not even in the distant future:

In the Greater France there are neither people to set free, nor racial discrimination to abolish. There are peoples who feel themselves to be French and to whom France wishes to give an increasingly larger part in the life and democratic institutions of the French Community. There are populations which we intend leading stage by stage to a more complete personality and to political freedom, but who will know no other independence than the independence of France.

The Brazzaville Conference was summoned partly as a response to the growing anticolonialist sentiment in the world, which demanded the early granting of self-government to colonial dependencies by the metropolitan powers, and partly in recognition of the debt Free France owed to the colonies in her struggle against the Germans. The Free French Government was based in Algeria and owed much of its success to the loyalty of French Equatorial Africa under Guianese Governor General Félix Eboué. Indeed, at one stage in the war, more than half of the Free French troops were of African origin.[2] However, although Britain was quite prepared to envisage eventual independence for her colonies, the whole colonial tradition of France excluded such a future for her own. Before the Brazzaville Conference, France had never really worked out what political future she intended for her African colonies. The early experiment in assimilation in Senegal had not been followed up elsewhere in Africa, and the dominant policy had become that of *Association,* which in theory was similar to Lugardian indirect rule, but in practice was paternalist, albeit with strong assimilationist traits.

A policy of assimilation carried to its logical conclusion would have involved the cultural, political, and economic integration of the empire with France. This was rejected not only on the grounds of expense but because many French officials were becoming increasingly doubtful as to whether Africans and Indo-Chinese could be successfully absorbed into French culture. In the last analysis, a full-scale policy of assimilation had been rejected, and was never to be put in force, because France, with a population of 40 million, would be dominated by her 60 million colonial subjects, or become a "colony of her colonies," as President Herriot put it so neatly to the Second Constituent Assembly on August 27, 1946. Assimilation was abandoned in favor of a policy that in theory recognized the separateness of African culture and the need for a separate framework of development from France's, but that in practice had strong assimilationist elements, particularly in the field of education and administration.

For our present purposes, the most important features of French administration in the interwar years were its centralization in Paris and its uniformity of application irrespective of territory. The policy followed involved the denial of political rights to all Africans who did not take up French citizenship (which demanded a certain level of education and the acceptance of French civil law) and the classification of those who were not citizens as *sujets,* liable to the *indigénat,* or summary administrative justice, and to the *corvée.*

The Brazzaville Conference stated in clear terms the renewed faith of France in a policy of assimilation, and, in making its recommendations as to the political future of the colonies, it declared that "The ends of France's civilizing achievements in the colonies eliminate any idea of autonomy; all possibility of evolution outside the framework of the French Empire, [and] the eventual establishment, even in the distant future, of *self-governments*[3] in the colonies, is to be dismissed." In pursuance of its assimilationist aims, the Conference advocated the abolition of both the *corvée* and the *indigénat,* and with them the humiliating status of *sujet.* Further, it advocated greatly increased economic development in the colonies, as well as the extension of education, which, true to assimilation, was to be in the French language.[4] However, while the Conference recommended that the colonies be represented in the Constituent Assembly, it was against their representation in the National Assembly. Rather, it proposed a Federal Assembly, in which the colonies would be represented not in proportion to their population, but only on a very restricted franchise. At the Conference, the Sudanese Fily Dabo Sissoko backed up this decision to limit the number of overseas deputies, citing the example of Rome "foundering under the domination of all the barbarians she had wanted to assimilate."[5] All colonials were to be granted citizenship and, at the same time, to retain their *statut personnel,* meaning that they were not required to accept French civil law as a prerequisite of citizenship. What in effect was being proposed was a new type of French citizenship, that of a Greater France, a citizenship different from that obtaining in Metropolitan France, which was automatically accompanied by voting rights. Further departing from the ideals of assimilation, the Conference proposed two electoral colleges for the Constituent Assembly, one for citizens under the old dispensation and one for the proposed new class of French citizens. This would ensure the election of one European delegate for each colony with the exception of Senegal, where French citizens of African origin were in the majority.

From the associationist point of view, the Conference's most important recommendation was the one for administrative and political decentralization. A high degree of centralization in Paris had, as we have already emphasized, characterized the interwar period and was compatible with an assimilationist rather than an associationist policy. Since the Conference was one of administrators, many of whom had had cause to resent directives from Paris that showed ignorance of local conditions, it advocated decentralization, stating:

We also want the colonies to enjoy a large measure of economic and administrative freedom. Further we want the colonial peoples themselves to experience this freedom and to have their responsibilities gradually defined and increased so that they are associated with the conduct of their political affairs in their own country.

Here we find an indication of the dilemma that was to dog French African policy throughout the postwar period. In part, it is the conflict between the traditional universalist approach and the realization that there were differences between cultures; but mainly, it was that France, unwilling to accept a full-scale assimilation policy, was forced to satisfy the Africans' demands for fuller participation in their own affairs by devolving administrative and political control to the territories. But, at the same time, France was not prepared to take this to its logical conclusion of self-government and independence, because of the firm belief in the "republic one and indivisible."[6] French policy then was a constant search for a compromise between these two extremes, for a formula that would conserve the unity of Greater France by retaining ultimate political control in Paris and yet allow a degree of local autonomy both compatible with this thesis of unity and yet sufficient to turn the African politicians' attention away from ideas of independence.

The first Constituent Assembly of 1945 did not meet with the intention of writing a constitution that would envisage independence or even a limited form of self-government for the colonies. Both of the left-wing parties, the Communists and the Socialists, on whose benches the West African deputies sat,[7] were essentially assimilationist in outlook. Yet the Assembly met against the background of revolt in Indo-China, the foundation of Istiqlal, the Moroccan Independence Party, and the demands by Ferhat Abbas for self-government in Algeria—demands that were also being taken up in Madagascar. Independence was becoming popular in the colonial empires. Britain was preparing to give independence to India. France herself had signed the Charter of the United Nations with its liberal sentiments as to the future of the colonies of the Great Powers.

The chief concern of the West African deputies in the Assembly was not independence, or even self-government, a goal openly sought by Ferhat Abbas, but, rather, how to obtain the fruits of France's assimilationist promises, held out at Brazzaville. Thus, they concentrated their energies on securing the abolition of the *corvée* and *indigénat* and on gaining public liberties such as the right to associate, the right to hold public meetings, and the freedom of the press. Their main goal was to obtain French citizenship, which was achieved with the passage of the first *Loi Lamine Guèye* on May 9, 1946. This gave French citizenship to all *sujets,* while allowing them to retain their *statut personnel.* The importance of these series of reforms is emphasized by the joy with which they were received in the colonies.[8]

Right up until 1956 most of the activities of the African deputies in the National Assembly were concerned not with the achievement of local self-government but with squeezing as much juice as possible out of the assimilationist lemon, whether it was in the form of increased aid, or in securing the passage of the Second Loi Lamine Guèye, which established the right of African senior civil servants to equal pay and work conditions with their

French counterparts, and the passage of the Labor Code in 1952, which accorded African workers many of the benefits enjoyed by their French counterparts.[9]

Their second preoccupation was to ensure that that part of the constitution that concerned the colonies be acceptable to them. Here again we must remember that they were operating in an assembly where no party, not even the parties with which they were allied, saw self-government or independence as a possible goal for the colonies.[10] Furthermore, the deputies were, for the time being, intent on making the most of the assimilationist revolution. Nevertheless, there was considerable enthusiasm for the Brazzaville proposals that there be devolution of administrative and political affairs to the colonies and that a Federal Assembly be established for discussion of the affairs of the overseas territories. The Brazzaville solution, apart from being supported by the African deputies, gained greatest support in the Assembly from the left.

As it was, the first constitution proposed for the Fourth French Republic proved an almost ideal compromise between the general desire of French parties to follow an assimilationist policy with regard to the overseas territories, and the desire of both colonial administrators and African politicians for a greater degree of political and administrative decentralization. France and her overseas territories, forming *la république une et indivisible,* together with the associated territories, comprised the French Union *librement consentie.* Contrary to the recommendations of the Brazzaville Conference, African deputies were to retain their seats in the National Assembly. Local assemblies were to be set up in the overseas territories, and these, together with the conseils généraux of the French departments, would elect the Conseil de l'Union.

Although the constitution had important decentralized features, it was ultimately integrationist in character, clearly defining legislative power for the overseas territories as the province of the National Assembly and not of the Conseil de l'Union, as the Brazzaville administrators had hoped it would. Nor was anything like autonomy conceded in the creation of the local assemblies, whose powers were much closer to those of the conseils généraux of the French departments than they ever were to embryonic local national assemblies. However, they were to be elected by universal suffrage and, more important still, nearly one-fifth of the seats in the National Assembly were to be allocated to overseas deputies. Furthermore, the two federations of West Africa (AOF) and Equatorial Africa (AEF) were to be headed not by administrative officials but by secretaries of state responsible to the Assembly. This constitution, associated as it was with the reforms concerning the *corvée* and the *indigénat,* had the support of all the West African deputies, but it was repudiated by the referendum of June, 1946.

The African Deputies who had participated in the First Constituent Assembly joined the Second Constituent Assembly in August, 1946, bitterly disappointed that the Metropolitan majority had rejected a constitution of which they had warmly approved and which, despite the opposition of French citizens originating from France, had gained a majority of votes in the overseas territories. They were also very concerned at the growing influence of colonial interests hostile to the reforms of the First Constituent Assembly. Yacine Diallo summed up this sense of frustration in the debate on the constitution of the French Union on September 18, 1946:

I take the liberty of declaring in my turn that the African peoples have become anxious since the rejection of the Constitution. . . . As far as Black Africa is concerned, I must tell you that the texts which were voted upon on April 19 gave complete satisfaction to all the people. Since the newspapers and radio announced the intention of certain groups to withdraw the rights given to the overseas territories by the first *Constituante,* an immense uneasiness reigns in the territories which we represent.

The powers devolved on African politicians and on the African electorate by the constitution produced by the First Constituent Assembly had been a matter of concern both to the colons and the colonial business houses. To protect their interests in the Second Constituent Assembly, they formed the States General for Colonization. The African deputies retaliated by forming a separate parliamentary intergroup, whereas in the First Constituent Assembly they had, on the whole, worked individually with the French parties to which they were affiliated. The new constitution threatened not only to reduce what little powers the local assemblies had but to introduce the principle of the dual electoral college to ensure sufficient seats for French colonists. This then meant the introduction of a double standard of French citizenship. Their sense of frustration even led the West African deputies as members of the Intergroup to subscribe to a remarkable set of constitutional proposals that bore the stamp of Ferhat Abbas, who proclaimed: "I do not wish to take my seat here [in the Assembly], I want an Algerian state, an Algerian parliament."

The constitutional project presented by the Intergroup was accepted by the Commission for Overseas Territories by a majority of one, and was presented to the Constitutional Commission on July 24, 1946.[11] Its important features were the official renunciation by France of all ideas of "unilateral sovereignty over her colonized people"; the recognition of their *"liberté"* to govern themselves and to run their own affairs democratically;

the postulate that the French Union was composed of nations and peoples who had freely consented to come together; and a stipulation that those states not enjoying the status of *"Etat libre"* could assume it within a twenty-year period. There would be local assemblies empowered to establish their own constitutions, and representation in the Constituent Assembly of the Union would be proportional to population. The project was, of course, not accepted, and its rejection evoked considerable anger among some of the African deputies, led by the Malagasies and the Algerians. Its ideas were to remain the most radical espoused by West African politicians for another decade.

The West Africans, however, with the exception of Sourou Mignan Apithy in Dahomey, seem to have been ultimately lukewarm in their support. Apithy, in a speech made during the final debate on the French Union, was the only West African deputy to pursue the idea of autonomy and possible secession from France. Alluding presumably to President Herriot's speech and the general fears of France's being dominated by the colonies, he declared:

For those who fear the subjection of the mother country by the overseas peoples . . . we must simply but firmly say that our ideal is not to become French citizens. We simply want to enjoy in our countries the same rights and the same liberties as Frenchmen in your country. I should equally like to say that our ideal is not to sit on the banks of the Seine nor to impose ourselves in what are essentially metropolitan affairs, but to regulate the affairs of our own country on the banks of the Congo or of the Niger, free to discuss with the people of France matters interesting the *ensemble* which we form with them.[12]

Houphouet-Boigny calmed any fears France may have had that the West African deputies were being seduced by Ferhat Abbas' secessionist ideas by declaring: "There are no secessionists on these benches."[13]

Although it is very difficult at times to see just what the political objectives of the African deputies were, it does become clear that they all ultimately wanted, as Lamine Guèye of Senegal put it, a "French Union founded not on disunion, but on the loyal support of the French Republicans that we are, with the same rights without distinction as to color, religion or race."[14]

The main concern of the deputies then was to attack the proposal that there should be a dual electoral college not only for the local assemblies but also for the elections to the National Assembly. As it was, there were only forty seats set aside for the overseas territories, and with the introduction of the dual electoral college, this would mean that only half that number would be indigenous to the territories they represented. They also attacked the idea of a double-standard citizenship, one for Frenchmen, one for Africans, which would exclude many of them from the franchise. In short, what they were asking of France was an honest application of her *politique d'assimilation*. Only Apithy and Senghor showed major concern that the political devolution promised by the First Constituent Assembly was being seriously whittled away. Most of the speeches were expressions of disappointment that France seemed to be turning her back on her universalist tradition. Since the Africans who were deputies in that Constituent Assembly are, with two exceptions, important political figures in their countries today and since all played crucial roles in French African politics up to the time of the *Loi Cadre,* it is worth recording those parts of their speeches in which they declare their feelings for France and their ideas on their future association with her. Senghor said:

I think that, in order for there to be a real federation—that is to say, a union of equal Socialist French Republics—it is necessary, first of all, that there be active assimilation on all sides. It is thus that together we shall create a new civilization whose center will be Paris, a new humanism which will be *à la mésure de l'univers et de l'homme au même temps.*[15] . . . If the French Union is to endure, and here I am . . . reiterating the thesis of the Socialist Party, it is essential for it to be founded on liberty and equality, conditions of human brotherhood and of French brotherhood.[16]

Lamine Guèye said:

It is as if we were being obliged to prove by our actions in the future that we are as French, as Republican, as anyone else, while we have shown this by our present and past actions.[17]

Yacine Diallo spoke as follows:

What are the aspirations of the populations that I represent in this Assembly? They demand to be integrated into the French family.[18] . . . We must hope that this French Union will be realized and the French overseas territories will one day become French provinces.[19]

Fily Dabo Sissoko said:

All this proves that when we ask you for pure and simple integration into the French nation, we do not use vague formulae; it is our deep conviction which makes us want to remain French until the end of time.[20]

And Houphouet-Boigny said:

We are not attached to France by its money, by the franc, this poor franc which has lost so much of its value; this essentially material bond would be too fragile. But there remains a powerful bond, capable of resisting all tests, a moral bond which unites us: It is the ideal of liberty, of equality and of brotherhood for those triumph France has never hesitated to sacrifice its most noble blood. It doesn't seem to us rash to say that the French Union will be one day, with the inevitable evolution of the peoples who compose it, a multinational state which will lose none of its cohesion if one can retain within it the sacred love of liberty and equality.[21]

The constitution produced by the Second Constituent Assembly was approved by the referendum of May 5, 1946, and was then implemented as the Constitution of the Fourth Republic. Insofar as it concerned the overseas territories, it was much less liberal than that proposed by the First Constituent Assembly, though in fact all the West African deputies voted for it. The double-college system was retained for elections to the local assemblies. Franchise was extended only to a limited number of citizens within the Union. First, there were to be French citizens who could vote for the first college. (This category included those Africans who already had citizenship under the old law.) Second, there were to be Union citizens with the vote. And, third, there were to be Union citizens without the vote. Representation in the National Assembly was reduced, and the power of the federal and territorial assemblies was restricted, so that the most important focus for African politicians became the National Assembly. The federations of AOF and AEF were headed by a civil servant or governor general rather than by a secretary of state responsible to Parliament. Against this background, the Preamble of the Constitution sounded a little hollow: "France, together with the peoples of its overseas territories, forms a union based on the equality of rights and duties without distinction of race or religion. . . ."

The greatest defect of the Constitution was its failure to create a strong federal assembly. Though an Assembly of the Union was established, it was weak, with few powers, and was certainly not the federal assembly envisaged by the Brazzaville administrators. Moreover, it was situated at Versailles, and was thus removed—some would say significantly—from the main arena of French politics, Paris. Failure to establish a strong assembly where matters concerning the Union could be debated, and the accompanying restriction of African participation in local assemblies (which anyway had almost no power), meant that the demands for political decentralization made by the Brazzaville administrators, and by Senghor and Apithy in the Second Constituent Assembly, were completely frustrated. There was now no way in which such demands could be contained in the future without constitutional revision. As it was, the only place where legislative decisions affecting the overseas territories could be made was in the Metropolitan Assembly of France.

The immediate problem for the African deputies was to organize themselves for the elections to the National Assembly as well as to the local assemblies. Should they continue to ally themselves with the Metropolitan parties or should they form specifically African parties? Lamine Guèye had united Senegalese political groups into the Bloc Africain to elect representatives to the Constituents, but in fact he remained faithful to the SFIO, of which he merely headed the Senegalese branch. On the other hand, Félix Houphouet-Boigny felt there was urgent need for the establishment of an African-based party and to this end invited political leaders, including Senghor and Lamine Guèye, to attend a Congress at Bamako to discuss the question. In any case, neither of them did, at the request of the Metropolitan SFIO, which feared that the new party would be dominated by the French Communist Party. Even Fily Dabo Sissoko, President of the new Congress, seems to have been torn between the desire to establish a purely African party and the need to be affiliated to one of the Metropolitan parties for effective operation in the National Assembly. The other main preoccupation of the conference was over the question of local assemblies. One commission even proposed the establishment of sovereign assemblies with responsible government. The questions of the program and structure of the party and of its relationship with the PCF were referred to a commission that gave its report in Abidjan in early 1947 when the Rassemblement Démocratique Africain (RDA) formally came into being.

The RDA proclaimed itself a specifically African party, but decided to retain its affiliation with the PCF, and its party organization was greatly influenced by Communist theory. Despite the recommendation of the earlier commission that the party demand the establishment of sovereign assemblies with responsible government, the party did not seek further territorial autonomy. It was quite explicit that it did not see its political future outside the framework of the Constitution of the French Union, as Mahjemout Diop stresses in his *Contribution à l'Etude des Problèmes Politiques en Afrique Noire*. He describes the party as the "only anti-imperialist mass movement of consequence which has seen the light of day in this country," but he emphasizes that the main objective of the party was the "struggle for the political, economic, and social emancipation of Africa within the framework of the French Union founded on the equality of rights and obligations (duties)." This faithfulness to the French Union and the proclaimed alliance between the French and African proletariat remained strong right up until 1958, as Diop points out, and was even retained by those who broke with Houphouet-Boigny over his decision to dissolve the alliance with the Communist Party in 1950.[22]

Indeed, the main preoccupation of the RDA from its formation in 1947 until 1951 was its affiliation with the Communist Party rather than with its proclaimed Africanness. For, though official Stalinist policy with regard to the colonies tended to be one of encouraging revolt against the Metropolitan "oppressors," this was far from the attitude adopted by the PCF, which was essentially assimilationist in outlook.[23] From 1934 onward, the PCF was very silent about colonial questions, and, as the largest single party in both the First and Second Constituent Assemblies, it showed no enthusiasm for demands for autonomy on the part of the overseas territories. The Communist deputy, Florimonde Bonte, told the First Constituent Assembly that "France is and ought to remain a great African power."[24] It was opposed to Algerian nationalism, supported repression in Indo-China, and, as David Caute points out, five Communists held ministerial posts in the government in power at the time of the Malagasy massacres. Thus, Communist influence on the RDA was hardly likely to be directed toward encouraging ideas of independence or indeed even of increased devolution of power. Rather, it tried to keep its ambitions within the orbit of the French Union, where, at least in the early postwar years, it had some hopes of playing a dominant role, and laid emphasis on the international role of the proletariat.

Thus, the RDA never proclaimed itself publicly for greater autonomy, let alone eventual independence for the African territories. At its Second Congress, in Treichville in 1949, at the height of Communist influence, it declared (somewhat bizarrely in view of the trend politics were taking over the border in Ghana) that it "expresses its faith in the alliance with the great people of France, who, with the working class and the Communist party at their head, struggle with courage and confidence against American imperialism for their national independence."

The break with the Communist Party, supported by the majority of the RDA, and conveniently justified as in accordance with its declared intention of being a purely African party, came about largely because the party was tired of the persecution it was receiving at the hands of the French colonial administration and saw little further advantage in association in Parliament with the PCF, which, by this time, seemed to have no prospects of acceding to power either in coalition or on its own.

What would be interesting to know is how much the RDA leaders discussed the question of independence in private during the years of their Communist association. After all, this was a time of considerable anticolonial agitation throughout the world and the RDA was itself a self-declared anti-imperialist party. Gabriel d'Arboussier, Secretary-General of the Party in its pro-Communist days, has recently written that the period 1949–50 was the first time in which some members of the Party talked in terms of independence and over this question he was separated from his companions.[25] Mahjemout Diop, an early member of the RDA and subsequently leader of the Parti Africain de l'Independence, a Marxist-oriented party, also writes that within the Party there was much discussion as to why the African territories did not claim their separation from the French Union.[26]

It was left to the more moderate deputies to make the next move toward what retrospectively can be seen to have been independence. In 1948, Senghor broke with Lamine Guèye and the SFIO to form a new party, both because he resented the domination of the Senegalese branch of the SFIO by the Metropolitan mother party, a domination in which Guèye acquiesced,[27] and because he felt the need for a specifically African party, declaring that "assimilation was an illusion in a world where people have become aware of their own personality."[28] In the National Assembly, Senghor and a group of deputies who shared his views formed an interparliamentary group known as the Indépendants d'Outre Mer (IOM), whose aim was to remain independent of any metropolitan group. After the elections of 1951, which were based on a substantially wider franchise, there were enough IOM members to form a separate Parliamentary group. The RDA, on the other hand, allied itself with Mitterand's *Union Démocratique des Socialistes Républicaines* (USDR).

The IOM failed in its attempt to transform its parliamentary unity into the basis of a new political party, but, at its conference at Bobo-Dioulasso in 1953, some revolutionary ideas about the future structure of the Union were introduced. While stressing that they had no separatist ambitions and that their goal was a "symbiose Franco-Africaine," IOM members insisted that the future of the French Union was a federal one in which there would have to be increasing devolution of powers onto the individual territorial assemblies, which should also have responsible governments.[29] This theme was taken up by Senghor, who became the chief advocate of the idea of a federal republic, and it took shape finally in the thesis that only through the federation with France of the two primary federations of French West and French Equatorial Africa could the African voters have any feeling of equality with voters of the mother country. This federal formula was taken up by the RDA, but there was no precision over the structure of the federation, for, although there were those like Sékou Touré who supported Senghor's thesis, the leader of the RDA, Houphouet-Boigny, favored direct federation between the individual territories and France.

The federal formula was revolutionary because it raised the whole question of the unity of the French Republic. The Brazzaville administrators had advocated a federal solution in the form of a Federal Assembly in which France would be dominant; at the same time, they had preserved the unity of the Republic by emphasizing that there should be political devolution, but not self-government. The local assemblies were to be, and in fact did become, merely advisory bodies.

What Senghor was advocating was a true federal formula for the French Union, that is, he was advancing the idea of a *république une et divisible*. He had already raised the possibility of a federation of autonomous republics in the debates on the Constitution of the Union and the distinctness of African culture, but, as we have seen, the Assembly of the Union was a "chimera" and certainly not federal in structure. In it, seventy-six seats were reserved for France and the same number for the overseas territories, which had 20 million more inhabitants than France. The High Council of the Union, which did not even meet until 1951, had as its President by right the French President. The federal formula, which, in retrospect, seems to have been the only one that could have satisfied France's desire to retain the integrity of Greater France and given sufficient rein to the Africans' desires to regulate their own affairs, was assiduously avoided by France, particularly at the very time when it might have worked. In introducing the *Loi Cadre* in March, 1956, France took into account the demand for some form of local responsibility in the overseas territories but did nothing to bring them into a federation, since this would have involved revising the Constitution of the Fourth Republic.

As early as 1954, the Mendès-France government had planned reforms for the overseas territories, but they were not put into effect until 1956, with the passage of the *Loi Cadre,* because of the instability of French governments. The *Loi Cadre,* which allowed for a considerable measure of political decentralization, owed its introduction to the French Minister for the Overseas Territories, Gaston Defferre. In its final shape, however, it was much influenced by Houphouet-Boigny, who had become a Minister without portfolio in the French Government as a result of the great success of the RDA in the January elections to the National Assembly.

The *Loi Cadre* was introduced in response to the changing international situation and the breaking up of a large part of the French Empire. Indo-China had become independent after a bloody war, Morocco and Tunisia had just gained independence, and Algeria was fighting for hers. Ghana's imminent independence had already forced France to concede the principle of autonomy to Togo to satisfy increasing nationalist demands there for self-government. If France was prepared to concede autonomy to Togo, why should she not also be prepared to concede it to the other West African territories?[30] Defferre in his speech on the *Loi Cadre* to the National Assembly made it quite clear that France did not believe that she could isolate her African territories from developments in the world at large. He then went on to record the constitutional progress made by Ghana and Nigeria toward self-government and ultimate independence:

It is not a question for us of plagiarizing the British, but the fact that they have transformed the political and administrative regime of their territories has certainly contributed to the growth of impatience among the peoples of French West and French Equatorial Africa.

The proposed reforms, as Defferre made quite clear, were designed "to maintain and reinforce for many years to come the necessary union between Metropolitan France and the peoples of the overseas territories."[31] The only revolutionary aspect of the *Loi Cadre* was its introduction of the concept of responsible self-government at the local territorial level within the framework of the French Union. Otherwise, it merely effected reforms that had been demanded of France in the Second Constituent Assembly and that were also compatible with a true policy of assimilation. The double electoral college was abolished, and universal suffrage was introduced. The integrity of the Republic was preserved in the person of the respective Governors of the overseas territories. The Governor was also President of the territorial Council of Ministers and had a large number of reserve powers. The effective Prime Minister of the territory was to be the Vice-President, who in turn was to be the political leader commanding a majority in the Assembly. Thus it was clear from the start that a Vice-President with strong electoral support, such as Sékou Touré, would soon push the Governor into the background. It was for this reason that the quip that the *"Loi Cadre est déjà dépassée"* was current only three months after its application.

The logical corollary to the granting of autonomy to the overseas territories would have seemed to have been the conversion of the French Union into the federation which the IOM, followed less enthusiastically by the RDA, was demanding. But this could not have been introduced without a revision of the Constitution, even if the Government had wanted it. One of the reasons put forward by Defferre for introducing the reforms in the guise of a *Loi Cadre* was the great delay that had been experienced in the passage of formal laws affecting the overseas territories, particularly the Labor Code, which had taken four years to enact. Since the *Loi Cadre* also had to make provision for Togo, there was particular urgency for its passage in order that Togo might have autonomy before Ghana became independent. However, it may very well have suited both the French Government and Houphouet, as we shall see, to bring in reforms concerning local self-government, before dealing with the question of federation, about which France had always been reluctant, particularly if it were to be in the form proposed by Senghor. Nevertheless, on May 6, 1956, René Pleven declared at Copenhagen:

The Constitution of France will have to be amended within the next twelve months to allow the adoption of statutes for the union with greater flexibility than those which insist on the traditional conception of the Republic as one and indivisible. We must clear the way toward the conception of a federal republic or of a federation of republics.[32]

For a while the whole issue of federation with France was dominated by the question of what structure the federation would take. It was fundamental to Senghor's thesis of a French Federal Republic that the overseas territories enter into federation with France not as individual territories but in the regional groupings that obtained at the time. It was with considerable bitterness that he denounced France for failing to democratize the Grand Conseils of French West and French Equatorial Africa and endow them with responsible governments. It was clear that in this he was supported by the majortiy of RDA leaders, in particular by Sékou Touré. However, Houphouet-Boigny wanted direct association with France for two reasons: He wanted to avoid the Ivory Coast's having to subsidize a political federation as she was subsidizing the administrative federation; and he feared that a federation with responsible government would be dominated by radicals, who would become increasingly hostile to the more conservative policies he and the Ivory Coast section of the RDA were following.[33]

Senghor accused Houphouet of being the instrument of France in balkanizing Africa. There was certainly no reason why France could not have extended the principle of responsible self-government to the federal level. There were no constitutional obstacles. France was well aware of the hostility she evoked from Senghor, but it was clearly in her own interest to adopt Houphouet's thesis, for there was more chance of maintaining her control over twelve weak states, economically very dependent on her, than over two large federations. Indeed, the French had every reason to believe that the federal formula put forward by Senghor might lead rapidly to demands for independence and national sovereignty. It had, after all, been suggested within the IOM that the federal formula would permit the adhesion of Tunisia and Morocco, both of which were now independent states.

The question of establishing federal executives came into open discussion at the now famous RDA Congress at Bamako in September, 1957. Here it became clear that Houphouet and the Ivory Coast delegation were isolated from the rest of the party in their opinions about the future relationship of the African territories and France. The only support given to his thesis of direct association came from Gabon, whose political and economic position in Equatorial Africa was not dissimilar from that of Ivory Coast in West Africa. So strong was the desire to establish federal executives that the Congress very nearly voted in favor of them, and it was only in deference to their leader, who had sat for three days in a huff in the palace of the Governor (where his status as a French Minister entitled him to stay),[34] that they passed a compromise resolution:

Conscious of the indissoluble economic, political and cultural ties which unite all the territories, and anxious to preserve the destinies of the French Community, the Congress gives a mandate to its elected members to submit the outline of a law tending towards a democratization of the existing federal executive.

Just as important as the discussion of the federal executives was the RDA's attitude toward independence. The other parties, the newly formed Convention Africaine led by Senghor, and the Mouvement Socialiste Africain (MSA), formed from the old SFIO, both set the question of independence to one side and were concentrating on securing the creation of federal executives. The whole problem of independence could not be far from any politician's mind since Ghana had become independent in March, 1957. But there was a tendency, at least in public conversation, to dismiss it as a problem, and by way of justification to point to the internal difficulties Ghana was experiencing.[35] The Convention Africaine, however, at its inaugural meeting in January, 1957, had been quite willing to ask that France acknowledge Algeria's right to independence. In the *Loi Cadre* elections in Senegal, the Socialists actually denounced independence for Senegal as illusory; and Senghor in his campaign seems to have been entirely preoccupied with the threat of balkanization.[36]

However, there was one politician whom a number of observers in France and Great Britain suspected of having as his ultimate goal the independence not only of his own country, but of French West Africa as a whole. Sékou Touré was rapidly acquiring the reputation of the *enfant terrible* of West African politics.[37] The gulf between Houphouet and Nkrumah over the question of independence had appeared quite unbridgeable at their meeting in Abidjan shortly after Ghana's independence, but it was clear when Nkrumah visited Conakry immediately afterward that Sékou Touré was watching the Ghana experiment with close interest.[38]

At the RDA Congress at Bamako, the whole question of independence burst rudely on the participants from the lips of one M. Papiebo, who represented the African students in Paris: "The slogans of Franco-African Community and federalism have been made to deceive the real faithful of Africa. We the students of Black Africa, leaders of tomorrow, who represent five thousand in France, demand independence." This bold demand was received rather coldly by the Africans at the Congress who for the past decade had made it a point of policy to work within the framework of the Constitution of the French Union. A somewhat warmer reception was given the representative of the French West African students in Dakar, M. Ly Baidi, who declared: "No student is *a priori* opposed to the idea of the community of peoples. We want a Franco-African Community founded upon friendship and upon the recognition that the African peoples have the right to make their own decisions about their future, that is, the right to independence."

This thesis of the right to independence was to become common during the coming year. Its enunciation not only by students but by politicians during 1957 really marks the turning point in the march to independence, for many apparently so reluctantly undertaken.

For long, independence had not been considered either a possible or indeed a legitimate goal. But now in 1957 it was becoming recognized as a real alternative to the French Union or what was now being called the Franco-African community. This became clear in the neat formula produced on the subject in the final resolution of the Congress:

The Congress considers that the independence of peoples is an inalienable right permitting them to dispose of their possessions and sovereignty according to the interests of the masses.

The Congress considers that interdependence is the golden rule in the life of a people and manifests itself in the twentieth century by the establishment of large political and economic groupings.

The Congress, believing that the conditions of Black Africa's participation in a large economic and political grouping is a factor for strength and real independence for all members of this grouping, proposes the realization and strengthening of a democratic Franco-African Community based on equality.

For the next nine months political leaders from all the major parties were to side-step the problem of independence with the convenient answer that they wanted to participate in the Franco-African community, provided that their right to independence was recognized. Most of them laid stress on the economic problems involved in independence, particularly if their countries were to take it up individually. In addition, they were all aware that France had, at that time, no intention of granting independence to her overseas territories.

The collapse of the Fourth Republic and the accession to power of General de Gaulle, who promised to undertake the preparation of a new constitution, added urgency to the discussions centering around the question of the establishment of federal executives and the prospects for independence. In the three months during which negotiations over the constitution of the Franco-African community took place, African leaders made hundreds of pronouncements about their political goals, some of which they elaborated, some of which they withdrew or contradicted; indeed, so obscure are some of the arguments that one is almost tempted to suggest that they did not really know what they wanted. Perhaps the moderate Malagasy leader Philibert Tsirinana summed up the dilemma most of his contemporaries faced by declaring, on August 21, 1958, at a press conference connected with De Gaulle's visit to Tananarive: "When I let my heart talk, I am partisan of total and immediate independence; when I make my reason speak, I realize that it is impossible."[39]

This was certainly the dilemma of Sékou Touré and Djibo Bakary of Niger, both of whom were clearly interested in independence. It was the dilemma faced by Modibo Keita of Sudan and Apithy of Dahomey. Some would also say that at that time Ouezzin Goulibaly would have liked to opt for independence. But for Senghor and Houphouet, the problem was not so straightforward. It was not just a question of economic realities. Both, in very different ways, believed in the Franco-African Community, so that their hearts too were divided on the question of total independence.

The only open partisans of independence at the time of De Gaulle's accession to power were student organizations; the important federal trade-union organization, UGTAN, whose President was Sékou Touré; and the small Senegalese-based, Marxist-oriented Parti Africain de l'Indépendance. However, at the Cotonou Conference of the Parti du Regroupement Africain (PRA), formed from the Convention Africaine and the MSA, the demand for immediate and total independence was carried by the Congress, and even acclaimed by conservative leaders like Lamine Guèye, who was either carried away by the enthusiasm of the moment, or, perhaps, wanted to place his cautious colleague and former rival, Senghor, in an embarrassing position. Only Senghor, with considerable courage, in view of the conservative nature of his views on the subject, sounded a note of warning at the close of the conference. Soon, however, other members of the PRA were beginning to question the wisdom of their decision, and during the next two months they indulged in a great deal of verbal acrobatics to make the word independence sound as though it did not in fact mean independence.

Ultimately, the theses put forward during these months were four: The first was for a community that would link France directly with the individual African territories, now transformed into autonomous republics. This was the thesis upheld by Houphouet and the one effectively promulgated by De Gaulle in the final draft of the constitution. The second thesis, upheld by Senghor and the PRA and given open support by Sékou Touré and tacit support by other members of the RDA, was that France should join in a federation or confederation with the two African federations. Each would be endowed with an Executive Council and all would enjoy full autonomy. Some partisans of this thesis envisaged a third and more radical formula whereby the two African federations should declare their independence first and then join the confederation with all the attributes of national sovereignty. This thesis attracted Djibo Bakary of Niger and at times Senghor, who toyed with the possibility of the Maghreb joining in such a Community. This, of course, was coming very close to the Commonwealth idea.

The French were certainly not prepared to contemplate any federal (or confederal) solution to the problem of the Community and were hostile to the idea of establishing primary federations on the grounds that these would almost certainly quickly find themselves strong enough to demand independence. In either a federal or confederal community, unless special position was given to her in the institutions, France would find herself dominated by her former colonies, whose leaders, it was clear, for the most part only wanted to join with her for the economic benefits they would derive. The fourth thesis was, of course, independence, which France rejected as a goal that could be attained in continued friendship with her.

In the face of French intransigence over any solution to the shape of the community other than the one she favored (an intransigence that became only too apparent to those African politicians who had sat on the Constitutional Consultative Committee), most of the African leaders decided to vote for the constitution after two important concessions had been made. First, after much pressure, De Gaulle included the "right to independence" in the final draft of the constitution. He had already made it clear at Brazzaville on August 24, 1958, when confronted by banners demanding immediate independence, that anyone who wanted it could take it. Later, he was to add the threat that it could be taken "with all its consequences."[40] The second major concession was to include a clause that would permit member-states to regroup themselves within the community, so that the hoped-for West African federation could still be realized.

Both the PRA and RDA gave their territorial sections the right to decide for themselves how they would vote in the constitutional referendum. There was no question about Houphouet's decision in Ivory Coast. Nor was there any doubt that Mauretania, who was out of the mainstream of French West African politics, would vote for the constitution, since she depended on France's military aid to deal with her Moroccan-allied rebels. All the other leaders, with the exception of Djibo Bakary, were uncertain about their stand for a long time. For all of them the economic problems of independence were the gravest they had to face.[41] France gave vast economic aid to the overseas territories. For Senegal, who was dependent on France for the subsidy she paid on the groundnut crop, the choice was particularly difficult, especially since it involved alienating the radical wing of the governing party if a decision was made to vote Yes. Senghor, although he emotionally resisted the idea of separating from France, was pressured by the conservative groundnut-producing countryside, led by the *marabouts* or religious leaders, into voting for the Constitution.

Senghor—like Modibo Keita in Sudan—felt that to take independence separately from the other territories would make federation impossible to achieve. It is reported that Houphouet had promised that, if his fellow RDA members voted for the constitution in its present form, he would agree to come together in a federation afterward—a promise that would have weighed seriously with Modibo Keita.[42] But there were other influences on Modibo's decision. Although his party had done well at the last election, securing a substantial majority over the PSS, it was just possible that with French electoral interference he might not be able to secure a majority for a No vote.[43] This consideration certainly was cardinal in Apithy's decision to vote Yes in Dahomey.

Guinea economically had a better basis for independence than any territory other than Ivory Coast, though she did depend on continued French assistance for the construction of the promised Konkoure Dam, which would provide her with enough electricity to process her own aluminum. It seems clear that emotionally Sékou Touré was very deeply attracted by the prospect of independence, but was more hesitant about the consequences than was Djibo Bakary of Niger, who was the first to declare his intention of voting against the constitution. Indeed, Sékou Touré had said that, provided the right to independence was included in the constitution, he would vote for it. However, a day after Djibo Bakary announced his decision to vote No, Sékou Touré followed suit.

The reasons put forward for this decision have been many. Clearly, he was extremely annoyed at the arrogant treatment he received from De Gaulle on the latter's visit to Conakry.[44] Certainly, he was disillusioned by the terms of the referendum and the consequences threatened by France for voting No. But probably as important were internal pressures on him: The students and many of the schoolmasters in Guinea favored independence. The trade unionists, members of Sékou Touré's own UGTAN, had for long declared themselves for independence. Furthermore, the conservative opposition party, affiliated to the PRA, had declared for independence, which made the radical RDA look somewhat foolish in the eyes of those who wanted independence. Finally, it is doubtful whether Sékou Touré ever realized the extent to which De Gaulle would go in demonstrating his anger at Guinea's decision. After all, Sékou Touré's first step was to send De Gaulle telegrams in the warmest of terms asking for the closest association between Guinea and France.[45]

It was with some relief that the other leaders saw one of their number take the plunge. Now they could sit back and watch the Guinean experiment, while those whose internal position was not very secure could be thankful that they had not followed Djibo Bakary's example and incurred the full force of French electoral interference.

De Gaulle's ruthless treatment of Guinea was motivated both by pique and by a desire to demonstrate to the other members of the community that they had been wise to vote Yes. Houphouet was a champion of this approach. If Guinea continued to receive aid, the radical elements in all those states who voted Yes would place their leaders in a most embarrassing position. If Guinea collapsed, as seemed likely, then the lesson would be driven home to all.

In fact, Guinea held together remarkably well. Russia, hoping to gain a foothold in Black Africa, immediately offered assistance, as did a number of other Communist powers. Suddenly Guinea became known all over the world and Sékou Touré became an African hero—young men as far afield as Nigeria wore "Sékou Touré" hats. By December, given moral support by Ghana and the promise of a $28 million loan, it had become clear that Sékou Touré had complete control of his country. Though life in Guinea was difficult, there seemed to be something to his argument: "Better freedom in poverty than slavery in riches." Guinea became like the bad conscience of all those who had voted Yes. In Dakar, it was not Senghor but Sékou Touré for whom the people cheered when his face appeared on cinema screens. What is more, Guinea realized her vantage point in the new African situation and Sékou Touré set out deliberately to persuade other African leaders to opt for independence.

The first efforts of those leaders who had voted Yes was not to discuss the question of independence but to try and salvage what they could of the old federation. One of the regrets expressed by several leaders was that Guinea had effectively broken up the federation by going it alone on the question of independence. Had Sékou Touré been more patient, perhaps they could have forced Houphouet to go along with federation and thus gained "real" independence together. Indeed, it appears that there had been many efforts to persuade Sékou Touré to change his mind, and it is probable that, had Ouezzin-Coulabaly lived, he would have been able to persuade the Guinean leader to stay within the community on the grounds that a more effective group-independence could be achieved at a later date.

As it was, the question of creating a federal executive was quickly raised and studied both within the RDA and in the Grand Conseil before its dismantlement in accordance with the new structure of the community. It became quickly clear that Houphouet was not going to keep his promise about joining a federation—if indeed he had ever made such a promise—and that he was as hostile as ever to it. In this, he was supported by France, who clearly saw that her only hope of maintaining the community—which, like the *Loi Cadre* before it, was beginning to show signs of being "déjà dépassée" before it was even promulgated—was by ensuring the continued balkanization of Africa.

Nevertheless, federalists from Senegal, Sudan, Upper Volta, and Dahomey, with observers from Mauritania, met at Bamako on December 29 and 30 and agreed that they would seek the necessary authority from their individual legislatures to participate in the proposed constituent assembly in Dakar on January 14, which would draw up the constitution for the Federation of Mali. In due course, this constitution was drawn up with the approval of the four countries, and it was agreed that it would be submitted to referendum in each country for approval. Both Upper Volta and Dahomey rejected it, however, and the Federation of Mali finally comprised only Senegal and Sudan. During the federalist deliberations, both France and Ivory Coast brought pressure on Upper Volta and Dahomey to withdraw from the federation.[46] In Upper Volta, it was a question of taking advantage of a very fluid political situation and playing on the differences between the West, traditionally closer to Sudan, and the Mossi-dominated East. France had as its High Commissioner in Upper Volta, the newly appointed M. Masson, who enjoyed a notoriety similar to that of Gouverneur Colombani in Niger when it came to interfering in politics. From his side, Houphouet could play on Upper Volta's heavy dependence on Ivory Coast both for access to the sea and for employment of her migrant labor. The case of Dahomey was equally complex politically, and it is clear that she had genuine fears that she would be cartographically out on a limb in a federation based on Dakar. Most important of all, however, was the threat that France might not finance the projected deep-water port at Cotonou.

Houphouet had succeeded in staving off the federation he detested so much, but he had to come to terms with the fact that desperately poor countries like Upper Volta and Dahomey would find it very difficult to manage on their own and would feel more secure in some kind of alliance. Apithy himself had talked in terms of allying with Togo and forming a Union of Benin States. So, partly in response to this need, partly as a snub to the federalists, and probably also because he wanted to maintain his dominant position in West African politics, Houphouet formed the Conseil de l'Entente, a loose economic grouping consisting of Ivory Coast, Dahomey, Niger, and Upper Volta.

Once the political groupings had been settled, the question of independence, never far from the minds of the more radical political leaders, came to the fore. At the inaugural meeting of the new Parti de la Fédération Africain, formed from the governing parties of Sudan and Senegal, with members from federalist parties from other West African states, it became clear that independence was now the paramount issue in French African politics. The meeting, held in Dakar on July 1–3, 1959, declared that Mali would seek independence and join with France in a confederation. The young federation would thus hope to take advantage of that clause in the constitution of the community that allowed states to become independent and still remain associated with the community. From then on the community was split between those who saw it as a rather more tightly organized French-style commonwealth and those who wanted to retain it in its existing form. The proponents of a commonwealth-type arrangement were led by Modibo Keita and Senghor of the Mali Federation and Tsiranana of the Malagasy Republic, who had an active pro-independence opposition to contend with. Ranged against them were Houphouet-Boigny and the other leaders of the Conseil de l'Entente. Houphouet was quite explicit in his rejection of a French-style Commonwealth and in his desire to establish a tight community with federal institutions. He was also scathing about independence. When interviewed about the All-African People's Conference held in Accra in December, 1958, he described it as destined only to produce idle talk and demands for illusory independence.[47]

As far as France was concerned, her last chance to save the community came when Mali demanded its transformation into a tightly organized commonwealth.[48] Even had she been willing to do this, she still would have had a hostile Houphouet to deal with, and right up until the last he was adamant that the only type of community that he was interested in was the one for which he and the Ivory Coast had voted.

France refused to recognize Mali's existence, and, when De Gaulle eventually came round to the fact that Houphouet's position was no longer tenable in a continent whose wind of change had been recognized so clearly by the British Prime Minister, it was too late. France finally yielded to the fact of African independence at the sixth meeting of the Executive Council of the Community at St. Louis on December 11–12, 1959. There, the Council of the Community recognized the existence of the Federation of Mali and conceded that it could take independence and remain associated with the community.[49] De Gaulle, not caring to repeat the experience with Guinea, then journeyed to Dakar, the capital of the Mali Federation. There, before the Federal Assembly, he made his historic speech acknowledging what he preferred to call Mali's impending "accession to international sovereignty." Houphouet, meanwhile, in pique, had left for Abidjan.

The Mali Federation became independent on June 10, 1960, after protracted bargaining with France over the terms of continued aid and in particular the concession to France of the right to retain her military bases in Dakar and Thies, as well as some troops in Sudan. Independence was adopted more enthusiastically by the Sudanese than by the Senegalese, who were becoming increasingly fearful of Sudanese domination.

Perhaps the most dramatic effect of Mali's decision to become independent was that Houphouet was forced to rethink his position. In one sense he had already made this more than clear. Once the community had decided at St. Louis to transform itself into a commonwealth, he lost interest in it. So, as if to spite the Maliens, and indeed to humiliate them, on the eve of Mali independence he announced that the four members of the Conseil de l'Entente would take independence without prior accords with France, such as Mali had had to negotiate. Any accord would be negotiated after international sovereignty had been assumed. Furthermore, they would take independence outside the community. Thus the *coup de grâce* to the community was delivered by the very man who had tried so hard to make it a reality.

The belatedness of a demand for independence among French West African politicians is only too easy to explain in economic terms. French West Africa, generally poor in resources, was receiving aid in the postwar period on a scale such as no other colonial dependency received from a metropolitan country. Export crop prices were stabilized by subsidies from France at a level well above that of the world market price. A substantial part of the administrative costs of the colonies was borne by the metropolitan budget.[50] The only economically viable unit among the territories of French West Africa was Ivory Coast, which alone had long-term income prospects of the order that could support a full-scale independent government, an army, and diplomatic representation. Guinea, despite her large mineral resources, could only become economically viable by intensive short-run capital investment, particularly in the financing of the proposed Konkouré Dam.

As it was, all the French-speaking West African states had become accustomed in the postwar period to living well above their income, and this was more true of Senegal than of any other state. In such circumstances, any abrupt break with France, involving loss of aid, technical assistance, and price subsidies, was impossible to contemplate for any leader without political control over his people as firm as that of Sékou Touré, who was able to persuade his people to accept economic sacrifices for the sake of independence. The extent and intricacy of France's aid to French West Africa, both before and since independence, is brought out clearly in *AOF 1957* and in a series of Senate and National Assembly reports on "cooperation."[51] It is easy to understand the reluctance with which political leaders undertook a program of independence that they had every good reason to believe would result in the loss of French aid and possibly even the loss of the political support of their people.

France, in addition to binding her overseas territories economically to her, also made it clear that independence was not a legitimate goal for the African political leaders. Indeed, even after Guinea's independence, De Gaulle refused to accept the fact that other African states would soon be asking for independence. As we have seen, when the newly formed Federation of Mali asked for independence within the community, he refused to acknowledge its existence right up until the Sixth Meeting of the Executive Council of the Community at St. Louis in December, 1959, which marked France's final but reluctant acceptance of the political facts of life in Africa.[52]

It is difficult at this stage to assess the different effects of French and

British colonial policy on the political attitudes of the West African leaders. For Kwame Nkrumah of Ghana and Nnamdi Azikiwe of Nigeria, independence was always a legitimate, if long-term goal. The main problem was to persuade the British Government that they represented "the people" and that they were ready for self-government. Close to hand was the example of the Commonwealth, a successful organization composed of former colonies, and, even, since the war, nonwhite members—Ceylon, India, and Pakistan. The British West African territories were administered as political and economic units entirely separate from Britain so that the prospect of rupture was not the problem for them that it was for the French African states. French African leaders, however, were constantly being reminded of, and indeed themselves subscribed to, the idea of the unity and integrity of Greater France. They were acutely aware that independence was a difficult, often bloody path to choose. Close to hand were the examples of Indo-China and the Maghreb states, which anyway were only associated states and not parts of the republic one and indivisible. The ruthless suppression of the Malagasy "rebels" and the war in Algeria served as reminders of what might happen to parts of the Republic that sought to hive off. They remembered also the persecution of the RDA in its pro-Communist days, administrative interference in elections, economic blackmail, and finally the balkanization of French West Africa into small economically unviable autonomous states, whose independence it seemed could at best be only formal if ever attained. Against such a background it is hardly surprising that overt ambitions for independence were not so intense in French West Africa as in British West Africa.

But it takes more than the economic and political policies of France to explain why French West Africa remained so long isolated from the current of ideas in the colonial world, from the spirit of Bandoeng, from the example of their fellow English-speaking African leaders. After all, even if France did not consider independence a legitimate goal, the rest of the world did, and the French West African leaders, because of their participation in the debates of the National Assembly, were usually much more sophisticated in their understanding of international affairs than their English-speaking counterparts. Even the Catholic Bishops of French West Africa had recognized the "legitimacy of the aspiration to independence as well as all constructive efforts to achieve it" as far back as 1953.[53] What must not be forgotten, however, is the very deep affection and respect most of the African leaders had for France and for her universalist ideas. The concept of a French Union, of a Greater France, of a Franco-African community in which men of different races and color, drawn together by French culture, would cooperate on the basis of *liberté, égalité et fraternité*, had a very great appeal for the African leaders.[54] The speeches of leaders at the

1946 Constituent Assembly are not explicable simply in terms of economic benefit. They were, after all, made against a background of forty years of economic neglect, and in an Assembly where the forces of colonial reaction were making themselves all too apparent.

It is difficult to exaggerate the impression made on French African leaders by their participation in the French National Assembly and in the other institutions of the Republic, where they became ministers, or presidents and secretaries of important commissions. Fily Dabo Sissoko made it clear at the Second Constituent Assembly how privileged he felt to be able to participate in it.

And even after the *Loi Cadre* and the political decentralization it involved, one was more likely to meet the Vice-Presidents of the Conseil in Paris than in the territories they ruled. Paris had an enormous attraction for the leadership. They had in many cases spent student days there, and now as political leaders and members of Parliament they were treated not so much as honored guests, but rather as special members of the family. *"Je vais en metropole"* is an expression that still comes easily to the lips of the independent French-speaking African.

France was more than the metropolitan country that welcomed its leaders warmly. She was also symbol of a culture into which, as a result of her assimilation policy, most of the African leaders had been indoctrinated. If Britain exported her parliamentary and legal institutions to the colonies, France exported her culture, and if the one thing that worries the British about their former colonies is deviation from the standards of democracy and law that she established, then it is the possible rejection of French culture that concerns the French. Even the most violently politically anti-French politicians, like Doudou Guèye of Senegal, can say unashamedly: *"Nous sommes de culture française"* before a mixed audience of English- and French-speaking Africans. In Guinea, Sékou Touré has insisted that the schools teach in French from the start and not in the indigenous languages. Even those Africans who symbolically rejected the domination of French culture and substituted for it negritude are often those like Senghor and Alioune Diop of Senegal who are most at home in French culture.

This feeling that French culture belonged not only to the Metropolitan French but to all those who accepted it acted, as did participation in the political institutions of France, as an effective brake on the demand for independence, a brake that is as important as the political and economic considerations involved.

PART **II**

THE POLITICAL
SITUATION

2

The One-Party State in West Africa: Its Strengths and Weaknesses in the Nation-Building Process

J. GUS LIEBENOW

PERHAPS THE MOST striking feature of West African politics in the post-independence era has been the almost uniform tendency for a single party to dominate—if not monopolize—the political processes within each of the new states. Admittedly, the content of the party system varies from polity to polity as does the rationale that justifies eliminating competing aggregators of the public interest. The broad outlines, nevertheless, are roughly similar. There are striking parallels between states dominated by leadership having a firm commitment to radically transform the social system and states in which control rests in the hands of a patron party that has a narrower ethnic or cultural base of support and takes a more conservative view regarding the desirability of change. The pattern is roughly the same, moreover, whether it is Liberia, independent for more than a century, or one of the newer states that reckons its independence in terms of months and years rather than decades. The developments are remarkably similar, too, whether the colonial experience was British or French. And, finally, the tendency for a single party to dominate seems to exist whether the new state was launched as a federal entity, in which a delicate balance was struck among various competing ethnic and cultural groupings, or whether it was at birth endowed with a highly centralized system of government.

What are the elements in this common pattern of single-party domination? Most obvious, of course, has been the systematic exclusion from the political arena of competitors to the governing party. The means employed have included the outright banning of all opposition parties, the specific outlawing of groups that evidence significant strength, and the manipulation of the electoral machinery in order to render opposition-party activity an exercise in futility. In the last category is the device common to many French-speaking states of establishing the single national-constituency list system, with the winning party capturing all of the seats in the legislature. Even in Nigeria, where the character of the federal system has provided the means for opposition representation at both the national and regional levels, the drive toward restriction of one of the major opposition groups is clearly apparent. The Mali Federation collapsed, moreover, at the point when the Parti de la Fédération Africaine (PFA) threatened to become in fact a single party rather than a loose coalition of two distinct regional parties. Only in Sierra Leone has a governing party after independence permitted an opposition group to challenge and almost topple it from power. The results of more recent district council elections in Sierra Leone indicate that the Sierra Leone Peoples' Party (SLPP) is not likely to be caught off guard again. In the remaining countries of West Africa, changes in the composition of the national leadership have taken place by assassination, *coup d'état,* natural death, or by purges of second- and third-rank party leadership.

A second major characteristic of the single-party system in West Africa has been the blurring and blending of all political structures so that the distinction between party officials as aggregators of interests in society and governmental officials as formulators and authoritative implementors of policy is either nonexistent or only dimly perceived. The extreme formulation of this position is assumed by Sékou Touré, who states that when one speaks of the Parti Démocratique de Guinée (PDG) one is also speaking of the government, the state, and indeed society. It is obviously an Orwellian equation, however, in which the party is more equal than others, for the formal institutions of government have dramatically declined in importance since independence and remain largely as legitimizers of actions taken by the party leadership. In this sense, the party, which initially legitimized the European-created structure of government, finds itself in turn legitimized by the latter. In modified form, the remaining states in West Africa tend toward this position even though more rigorous attention may be paid to the formal distinction between the personnel and decisions of government on the one hand and the party on the other. At this stage at least, the contest between the party bureaucracy and the bureaucracy of the state is being resolved in favor of the former.

A parallel development to the one just noted is that which Gabriel Almond refers to as poor boundary maintenance between the dominant structures of the polity (in this case the political party) and other structures of society. Increasingly, the primacy of political values over economic, religious, social, and even aesthetic values within the new societies has manifested itself. Through interlocking leadership and elaborate governmental strictures regulating the activities of nonpolitical associations, trade unions, cooperative societies, religious associations, and youth groups become instruments of the dominant political party. The subordination of voluntary groups to the party applies equally to traditional as well as to modern forms of association. Again, there is a range of variation, for example, between Guinea and Ghana on the one hand and Senegal and Nigeria on the other. In Senegal and Nigeria, a fairly high degree of pluralism survives. Nonpolitical associations function independently, and the influence upon party leadership of leaders representing religious and economic groupings is frequently significant. Moreover, the younger modernized element in Senegal and Nigeria appreciates that it may achieve high social status via routes other than those provided by the political party.

A fourth characteristic of the contemporary political scene in West Africa has been the governmental (and therefore party) control over various forms of political communications. Government ownership or subsidization of the major newspapers and radio and television stations is one facet of this tendency. Of equal significance has been the use of libel, slander, and subversion laws (frequently inherited from the colonial regime) to silence domestic and foreign critics of the regime. In the long run, however, the most pertinent development is the intimate control that the party is attempting to establish over the educational system, thereby regulating the receptivity of the younger generation to various forms of political communications.

Finally, the political systems of the new states of West Africa have been marked by the emergence of charismatic leaders, who attempt to embody the aspirations of their people and who in a sense stand above both popular criticism and the very political party that brought them to power. Admittedly, not all party leaders seek the mantle of charisma, and some, like President Modibo Keita of Mali, insist upon collective leadership as the true course for guiding the new states to modernity. It has been difficult, nevertheless, for most party leaders to resist the advantages that a charismatic base of popular support provides in the establishment and survival of a new society. Consequently, efforts abound in which the cult of personality is obviously contrived and pursued at great cost to the human and other resources of economically weak states.

The characteristics of West African politics noted above are frequently cited by Western critics as indictments of the single-party system in terms of the achievement of democracy. Indeed, the sensitivity of African leaders on this point is reflected in this elaborate defense of the single party as an instrument of democratic development. Some justify the system on the basis of its essentially traditional character. Others defend it on the grounds that the "democratic experiment" under colonial rule was so brief and the crises left behind by the colonial powers so severe that African states can now ill afford the luxury of interparty competition. Increasingly, however, African leaders are insisting that the one-party system should not be regarded as an aberration from the norm of democracy but rather as the natural development of democratic institutions in a West African setting.

Any group that undertook the task of nation-building in West Africa would have found itself faced with a formidable task, for, in West Africa, there are in effect fourteen disparate states all seeking nationhood. Although one of the objectives of nationalism has been achieved—the securing of political independence—the other objectives of a nationalist movement are still lacking.

Social scientists do not agree on the precise ingredients that must go into the building of a nation. The prior possession of a common language, race, territory, set of historical experiences, and basic values regarding the nature of society is no longer regarded as the *sine qua non* for the establishment of national identity. The absence of any or all of these factors does call, however, for an extraordinary effort on the part of a nationally committed elite to compensate for the absence by the fabrication of myth, the rationalization of multilingualism, the establishment of systems of communication and interaction at various levels, and the accommodation of apparently contradictory goals and means. Although the similarity in language does not automatically guarantee a common national identification, its absence poses problems that no nationalist elite can ignore.

In West Africa, the fragmentation of loyalties within each state is severe. The precolonial condition, which found individuals identifying primarily and exclusively with others on the basis of clan, tribe, religion, or even physical characteristics, remains one of the fundamental obstacles to the creation of a system of national loyalties. Colonial rule, as Rupert Emerson so well documented in his book *From Empire to Nation,* led to the establishment of a system of interaction above the parochial tribe and provided a common system of law, administration, and language, and to a lesser extent an economic and political system, in which Africans could engage in transactions across tribal lines. Colonialism, nevertheless, provided disunity of another sort. The uneven pace and manner in which the colonial administrators carried out the modernizing revolution pitted tribe against tribe, generation against generation, urbanized Africans against their rural kinsmen, and tradition-oriented leaders against those committed to modernity. Modernization under colonial rule was undertaken with a larger polity in mind—the Empire rather than any given territory.

Colonialism, moreover, failed to encourage (where it did not positively discourage) the establishment of nationally oriented elites. The British system of indirect rule, which persisted in fact well into the postwar period, denied the modernized elite a legitimate role in politics at the local level; at the same time, the slow and deliberate development of the territorial legislative councils seemed designed to delay the formation of a nationally responsible political elite. The obstacles placed in the path of national political-party formation was characteristic of British colonial practice in other parts of the empire as well. The French, it must be said, did provide an outlet for the more modernized element in bureaucracy at the lower level and, under the Fourth Republic, actually encouraged its involvement in political-party activity. Nevertheless, the focus of the modernized African, at least until the *Loi Cadre* of 1956, was to be directed outward: to West Africa as a whole or more properly to Metropolitan France itself. (Less can be said about the manner in which the French encouraged active African participation in the governing of the Ivory Coast, Senegal, or Niger.) Similarly, the trade unions in French-speaking Africa placed a higher value on external association than on autonomy within a particular territory.

Although there are many ways of defining nation-building, I prefer to regard it as a process whereby an elite extends its control over populations within a given territory by establishing systems of communication and interaction between itself and the citizenry at large. The end product of this process will be an automatic identification of the citizen with the polity and its elite and a built-in preference on the part of the citizen to pursue his goals through this particular system of interaction. A common language, religion, race, and culture serve, of course, to reinforce this identification, but the basic criterion of nationhood seems to be contained in the process defined above.

There are many factors, obviously, that go into successful nation-building in a heterogeneous state. However, I shall attempt to deal with only three: (1) the character of the nationally committed leadership; (2) the ability of the leadership to create organizational means designed to intensify the identification of the citizenry with the objectives of the national elite; and (3) the ability of the elite to manipulate symbols leading to the strengthening of various kinds of ties throughout the polity. It is through the analysis of these three factors that the development of the single-party system in West Africa becomes more meaningful.

On the first point, the character of the elite, it must be noted that in the history of nationalist movements political parties have not been the only structures through which an elite group has attempted to accomplish national integration. The army in Egypt and the Greek Orthodox Church in Cyprus can be cited as two contemporary examples in which significant nationalist leadership has emerged from a nonpolitical source. Moreover, one cannot ignore the contribution that leaders of religious organizations, trade unions, veterans' associations, and other nonparty groupings made to the development of nationalism in West Africa itself in the early stages. Nor can we ignore the role that any of these structures may play in the future in altering the course of national development.

The prominence of party elites in West Africa is partly accounted for by the relatively minor roles that Africans were permitted to play in the armed services, the churches, the professions, or the economy under colonial rule. Obviously, we refer here to the quality rather than the quantity of participation. It is well known, for example, that many Senegalese were in the French armed services in West Africa. How many, however, were officers? Similarly, the number of Nigerians who participated in the colonial cash economy was considerable, but this number was not matched qualitatively with African control over capital and managerial skills. Europeans, Lebanese, and others dominated most of the structures that might have been instrumental in building nationalist movements in West Africa.

The political party, on the other hand, seemed to be the one modern structure that was left largely to African devices. It was a structure within which the modernized elite could achieve high status quickly and which, curiously, could also be used to preserve the high status of traditional elites against the erosion of colonial rule and the assaults of the modernized elite. It was, in the case of mass parties in particular, a modern structure with which the peasant cultivator, the pastoralist, or the urban proletariat could affiliate with a minimum of effort.

Political parties had distinct advantages over traditional associations, which were often based upon the possession of an ascribed characteristic; over religious associations, which required not only one's acceptance of a fairly elaborate system of belief but also one's renunciation of previously accepted doctrine; and over trade unions, cooperative societies, and veterans' groups, which usually required some minimum skill or experience for membership and which only succeeded in establishing a limited network of affiliation. Membership in a political party, on the other hand, provided one, potentially, at least, with a wide universe of association that cut across ethnic, regional, religious, sex, and generational lines. It was an affiliation that was attainable normally by only the vaguest commitment to follow the party leadership. Beyond this one had a considerable latitude in deciding whether to provide more significant outward and visible signs of an inner commitment—that is, whether to pay dues, to attend rallies, to vote, and in other ways to support the party and its efforts.

The superiority of the political party as a structure of affiliation, however, did not automatically produce a monolithic national leadership. If one segment of the elite could accomplish its objectives through political party activity there was nothing to prevent another segment of the elite from pursuing a different set of goals via the same avenue. The intensity of the anticolonial struggle usually led one of the parties to demand and actually secure a monopolistic position, but this was not so in every case in West Africa at the time of independence. Indeed, the comparatively mild character of the independence movement and the early capitulation of the colonial powers in a sense deprived the West African states of their nationalist revolutions. Only in Guinea, where the crisis at independence gave the leaders of the dominant party (PDG) the popular support necessary to carry out a radical transformation of society, did the leadership of a political party in a West African state early achieve a militant unity throughout the society as a whole.

Elsewhere the conflicts between modernists and traditionalists continued to divide the national leadership after independence. Moreover, even among those who were considered modernized, it was realized that modernity could be interpreted in various ways. Although one might establish ties with other modernized individuals at school, in the trade unions, or in government employment, one did not immediately sever the ties that bound one to clan or tribe. This was a form of security, and, in the game of "ethnic arithmetic" that even the Parti Démocratique de la Côte d'Ivoire and the other mass parties are forced to play, it has been advantageous to stress one's subnational ties.

Hence the conflict is not simply one of the forces of nationalism and modernism against the forces of tribalism and traditionalism. The conflict, which has caused the leadership of Ghana and other states to react so decisively against tribalism, is the realization that modernized leadership within the state may seek to restore the tribal unit as the legitimate polity.

The divisive tendency among the modernized elite is produced by centrifugal as well as centripetal forces. The attractiveness of the notions of Pan-Africanism, negritude, and the "African personality" lead some to withhold full commitment to the arbitrarily defined state in favor of loyalty to a broader idea. Admittedly, each of these concepts, as well as African socialism, is variously interpreted. It is a paradox that one of the greatest threats to Pan-African unity is Pan-Africanism itself. The longer the idea is discussed in the absence of concrete action, the greater the tendency for it to be interpreted in national, rather than universal, terms. Nevertheless, the appeal that Kwame Nkrumah and Sékou Touré have outside their own borders indicates the extent to which there is a withholding of support from national leadership in favor of a commitment to leadership that seeks a broader grouping of African peoples.

One further quality of the nationalist elite that should be noted is its full-time commitment to the pursuit of politics. In one sense this is a strength, for it secures the undivided attention of a substantial segment of the educated elite to the task of directing the construction of a nation. Yet the very attractiveness of the political party as well as the primacy of political over other roles in West African society has been a deterrent to the orderly development of the nation. A modern society obviously cannot get along without individuals trained to serve as ministers of government, party officials, and ambassadors, as the experience of Congo-Leopoldville indicates. Neither, however, can it get along without doctors, teachers, engineers, businessmen, and other nonpolitical persons. To the extent that the society fails to produce these talents from within its own ranks, it will either have to forfeit plans for modernization or be compelled to rely upon expatriate personnel, for in which case the task of nation-building is delayed and the material and psychological losses to the new state may be considerable. Real command over modernization is in danger of being surrendered to the expatriate adviser. The African leader becomes, then, like the monarch in Hans Christian Andersen's fable about the emperor and his new clothes, naked and exposed. Moreover, when the party leadership is ultimately challenged to "drive the foreigners out," the positions will likely be filled by individuals who are poorly trained and who lack the talent to advance in the party hierarchy.

With respect to major roles in economic development we find, somewhat curiously, that the leadership of both the PDG in Guinea and the True Whig Party in Liberia prefers to rely upon expatriate personnel rather than to permit an indigenous economic elite to develop independently and challenge the supremacy of the dominant party. The fact, however, that modern society is inevitably a pluralistic society cannot be avoided. As the bureaucratic, the military, the academic, and the managerial communities increase and become more efficient, each develops a corporate character and a logic of its own with regard to the pursuit of professional or other goals. The student riots in Guinea, the actions of the military in Togo, and the strikes in Nigeria are all indications of a restiveness on the part of those who reject the thesis that the party leadership always knows best.

In carrying out the task of nation-building, the mass party in West Africa is better equipped both emotionally and organizationally than the patron party. Indeed, the very *raison d'être* of a patron party in many instances is the frustration of its efforts to establish a nationalist movement. Patrons seek the preservation of political power, not the construction of a larger polity within which the parochial bases for their authority might be threatened. Only where the creation of a new unit of politics becomes a necessary step to the attainment of the former objective do patrons make common cause to control and thereby moderate a nationalist revolution. The Northern Peoples Congress in Nigeria, the True Whig Party of Liberia, and the ruling party of Mauritania represent three variations of the patron-type response to the demands for modernization and national integration.

Mass-party leadership, on the other hand, is committed to the idea of cutting through the intricate web of traditional loyalties and establishing direct contact between the masses and the national elite. In accomplishing this goal, every sector of the community is to be involved in the party apparatus with functionally organized units complementing the geographic branches of the party. In theory, membership is open to every adult citizen of the state. The objective of the elaborate organization is to establish an effective two-way communication system between the leaders and the masses, with the former formulating plans for the new society and explaining them to the masses and the latter indicating its acceptance, rejection, or modification of policies and actively participating in the implementation of party programs. The colonial administration maintained only minimal contact with important urban or mining centers or with traditional leadership in rural areas, but the mass party seeks to involve even the remotest hamlet in its nexus.

The mushrooming of party cells throughout the West African hinterland reflects the sincerity of the mass-party leadership in attempting to translate theory into practice. In many ways, however, the effort is doomed to a measure of failure. The startling contrast between the educational attainment of the elite and that of the peasant in the field does not encourage the former to take too seriously the untutored wisdom of the latter. Rejection of a program by the peasantry does not necessarily indicate the undesirable character of the program but rather signals a need for a redoubled effort on the part of the leadership to instruct the masses with respect to their own best interests.

The Platonic dialogue between the leaders and the masses will continue as long as the educational distance between the two levels remains great. The disproportionate emphasis upon mass literacy in the national budgets of West African states may in the long run be highly significant in establishing national identity and in preparing people for economic modernization. Mere literacy, however, poorly prepares the peasantry to engage in meaningful debate with the party leadership regarding economic planning, foreign policy, and other complex matters.

The party, moreover, finds itself organizationally weak at the local level. It lacks a cadre of moderately educated lieutenants who make the rural area its home and who can effectively interpret the wishes of the leaders and the masses to each other. The very attractiveness of the party, which led the university-educated to seek a career in government or the party rather than in commerce or the professions, leads the moderately educated party leader to drift from the countryside to the city—the hub of party activity. One goes where opportunities are. Inasmuch as the party desperately requires talent not only to keep the party strong but to man the machinery of government, it finds it difficult to halt the drift. Thus, the process of nation-building is an uneven one. The party is having a much stronger impact upon the urbanized communities than it is upon the rural areas. Considering where the bulk of West Africans live and the heavy reliance that the West African states will have to place for some time to come upon agricultural production if they are to achieve economic modernization, this bodes ill for the nation-building process.

The leadership of the mass parties now realizes that its earlier efforts to mobilize society swiftly and directly were not made without sacrifices, most notably in the indispensable area of rural leadership. The automatic assumption that traditional leadership was irreconcilably antinationalist led to the alienation of talent that could have been effective in implementing party policies. The recently observed deference paid the Asantahene and certain other traditional leaders in Ghana indicates some second thoughts in this regard. At a minimum it has been appreciated that the retention of traditional leadership can be an effective holding operation in the areas of the country where the ability of the party to carry out a modernizing revolution simply cannot match party promises and the expectations of the masses. If traditional political systems could be molded to serve the needs of the colonial powers under indirect rule, why could they not similarly serve the cause of African nationalists?

In the manipulation of symbols relating to nation-building, the political elites of West Africa have achieved a remarkable measure of success in getting people to identify themselves as members of national communities. The feat is all the more striking when one considers that the names of modern Ghana and Mali were absent from the map of Africa less than a decade ago and that the various West African colonial units had then as great or even greater significance for European administrators and Lebanese merchants than they did for Africans. Admittedly, the task is still far from complete. Pockets of parochialism continue to exist in those areas where the presence of the national elite today is as dimly perceived as that of the European administrator was in the past. In the international markets, moreover, and along the arbitrarily delimited boundaries, the arguments over national jurisdiction and affiliation seem relatively unimportant. To the itinerant Hausa trader as well as to the modern champion of Pan-Africanism the larger unit of economic reality or political promise has greater meaning than the national state.

The inability of the political party to capture the full loyalties of all residents of the state need not be viewed with alarm. No loyalty system can be expected to be complete. On specific issues the most complex of societies as well as the least complex find certain individuals placing a higher value upon associations that are greater or smaller than the community that claims their loyalty on most issues. Even the small-scale political system that was based upon the unilineal descent group found it necessary, under the ubiquitous custom of exogamy, to seek marriage partners outside the basic unit of loyalty. West Europeans, moreover, are today in the process of altering their traditional loyalty systems to accommodate their expanding economic and other goals.

The role that political parties—and mass parties in particular—have played in the restructuring of loyalties in West Africa has been crucial. Through rallies, elections, and referendums, the parties have managed to elicit the enthusiastic involvement of the masses in a new and exciting unit of action that promises escape from the frustrations, the boredom, and the abuses of the past. Indirectly, too, by drawing trade unions and other associations under its wing, the political party has at the same time lessened the tendency to make particularistic demands upon the new polity and has provided an additional channel through which one may identify with the party and with the purposes of the new nation.

Even more significant than the party apparatus and the involvement in party activities has been the emergence of the head of the party as a charismatic national leader. The leader provides a living symbol of the new society with which one may identify in the same personal way that one in traditional society cast his lot with his clan head or tribal chieftain. Compared to the importance of this social role in the establishment of a new nation, the economic and intellectual costs involved in the cult of personality seem negligible. What happens to nation-building at the demise of the current crop of charismatic leaders is a question that the youth and vitality of the leaders may leave unanswered for some time to come.

Beyond emphasis upon nationality and the leader as symbols of integration, the content of nationalism in West African states is in many instances intentionally vague. Party leadership has seemingly been reluctant to spell out in any great detail what the new society is to be like and precisely how one is to arrive there. Hence, one is impatiently led to ask, Where is the nation? There are vague commitments to full civic participation and modernization of society. The symbols that are presented, however, frequently apply to a unit of loyalty above the state. Negritude, African socialism, and the African personality tell us little about Senegal, Guinea, or Ghana in particular.

Even the effort to write a history of Ghana or Mali invariably produces a history of West Africa. This tendency has its weakness, for it means that a competing leadership that attempts to be explicit by providing a radical solution to the problems of tribalism, poverty, and illiteracy will find ready defectors from the ranks of the present leadership. And yet, the strength of this intentional vagueness regarding ideology lies in the constant striving of the leadership to educate itself through a constant exposure to new ideas. Far from being the closed societies that critics of African democracy insist they are, the West African states have produced leaders who are eagerly searching for new means to facilitate the political and economic modernization of their societies. Both within their own borders and through residence and travel abroad, African leaders have been receptive to workable ideas, whether their origins are capitalist or Communist, Israeli or Arab, or the product of experience in other African states. Instead of being programmatic, most political parties tend to be pragmatic in their approach to the crises they face. Even in Ghana and Guinea, where the party leadership has been quite precise about the nature of the struggle and of the new society, an increased measure of flexibility is detectable, particularly as it applies to the role of the private sector in a socialized economy.

The necessity of negative symbols of nationalism has yet to be clearly demonstrated. A recurrent feature of nationalist ideology, nevertheless, is the positing of an "enemy at the gates"—an alien force intent upon depriving the national society of its land or liberty. Former colonial powers are ready-made for this role. In the case of West Africa, however, the relatively favorable circumstances under which the colonial power departed (with the obvious exception of Guinea), and the continued reliance upon Britain and France for economic assistance, the staffing and equipping of the military forces, and higher education, have made it difficult for the party leadership to cast the former colonial regime in that role. It is for this reason, perhaps, that the United States and other powers are from time to time presented as neocolonialists by certain nationalists who are searching for a suitable surrogate for Britain or France. Even more likely candidates for the role of "enemy at the gates" are the Republic of South Africa and Portugal, which continue to permit the domination of Africans by white minorities. To the dismay of Pan-Africanists, however, the surrogate has on occasion been another African state and its leadership. During their long history of strained relations, Ghana has unquestionably served in that capacity for Togo; and, at least during the period immediately following the dissolution of the Federation, both Senegal and Mali filled the role for each other.

Political party leaders in West Africa would be the first to admit that the task of nation-building has only commenced. The victory over the forces of colonialism has given the party leadership a popular mandate that can carry them safely through many a wrong turn on the road to nationhood. But the mandate is not a blank check. There are many who have merely acquiesced in the designs of the dominant party, and still others who regard the machinations of the party leadership as a positive stumbling block to the creation of greater loyalties. The habit of thinking together as Ivoiriens or Nigerians has been developing swiftly. It is the task of the leadership to translate this habit into a habit of acting together. Surely, if the present party leadership fails in that regard, there are others who would be eager to take its place.

3

The Course of Political Violence

VICTOR T. LeVINE

THE PROLIFERATION of major instances of political violence in Africa since 1960 has been a matter of deep concern and considerable embarrassment to African leaders, a cause for quiet rejoicing on the part of those who see in that violence opportunities for extending their political and ideological war against the West, and a confirmation of the position of those who have long contended that Africans were neither "ready" for self-government nor able to manage their own affairs themselves. This chapter does not intend to offer comfort to the embarrassed, refutation to the scoffers, or arguments to meet some of the more fashionable polemics about "neo-imperialist" or "Communist" penetration of the continent. Its purpose is more modest and, hopefully, more dispassionate—i.e., to provide a meaningful typology of political violence in sub-Saharan Africa, and to suggest some generalizations about the causes of political violence and the prospects for nonviolent political change.

Four limitations of this chapter must be specified: First, it will not deal with the North African states of Morocco, Algeria, Tunisia, Libya, and the United Arab Republic, and only peripherally with the Republic of South Africa.[1] Second, the relevant data is current only up to July 1, 1964. Third, the data tends to be incomplete, inasmuch as instances of political violence on a lesser scale—below revolutions, coups, and major urban disturbances—are often poorly reported, sometimes even deliberately concealed by governments anxious to protect their public images. (For example, anyone who has followed the course of the protracted insurrection in the Cameroun cannot but be struck by the remarkable scarcity of hard data available about it.) Both French colonial governments and African governments in 'rench-speaking states, it must be added, have been extremely reluctant to ublicize information relating to public order in their territories. Fourth, 1e focus of this chapter will be on the postindependence period not because 1e pre-independence period is irrelevant or devoid of political violence but ecause it is after independence that the relationship between violence and olitical viability becomes most crucial.

Violence and the threat of violence are found in all societies.[2] Violence epresents a means by which a government can enforce its will, reinforce :s authority, and ensure present and future compliance with its wishes. imilarly, and on a broader level, the threat or the use of violence provides ndividuals and groups the means by which they can force the government o adhere to agreed-upon terms of collaboration. If government is to be ffective, therefore—that is, if it is to carry out its various functions within olerable limits—it must seek to monopolize and institutionalize the use f violence; if it cannot do this, it must seek to control violence by keeping ts use on levels that do not affect its own authority. The inability of govern- nents to control internal violence may make it impossible for them to hreaten or use force in their relations with other governments. Even more ignificantly, such failure may lead to a major or minor restructuring of 1e society, of the government, or, *in extremis,* to the collapse of the state tself. It is not an exaggeration to suggest that the increasing frequency f violence within African territories and states poses the stark question f survival for many African leaders, for their governments, for the white •ligarchies, for the residual colonial regimes, and indeed for all those lirectly or indirectly involved when violence breaks out. In fact, it may be vell to affirm from the outset that what makes violence in Africa of in- erest is not the fact of the violence itself—common enough throughout the vorld—but the increasing frequency of its occurrence. The various cases f political violence in Africa are unique only as discrete events in par- icular contexts, not as new forms or patterns.

An investigation of the patterns and functions of political violence begins vith a question that can, perhaps, only be answered by definition: When s violence *political?* There are several ways out of this thicket, all of them ınsatisfactory. One path is to assert that *all* intra- and intersocietal violence epresents attempts to restructure human relationships by force, and since ıll such attempts affect the distribution of authoritative values all are hence political. This formulation is obviously inadequate on a number of grounds, 1ot the least of which is its tautological nature. A second, perhaps more ıseful formula is to admit that all violence can *become* politically relevant, out only becomes so when it begins to impinge upon the activities of that ·omplex pattern of leadership and influence we call the political system.

Third, and even more pragmatically, since we are concerned here wit
the formal political systems of the African states and territories, th
varieties of violent conflict of interest to us are those that have actual c
potential consequences for the authority of the governments of these area
For example, violence incident to a quarrel between two families will no
become politically relevant for us until it reaches such dimensions an
involves so many people that the ability of the government to exercise i
authority in the part of the country where the quarrel originated is seriousl
called into question.

The next problem is obviously a taxonomic one, since political violenc
seems to exist in an almost endless variety of forms, and instances of
vary enormously in duration, scale, number of people involved, numbe
of casualties, goals of the participants, and so on. Cases range from th
Lysistrata-like women's revolt in the Southern Cameroons in 1957 (the sc
called *Ahnlu* demonstrations) to the 1947 revolt in Madagascar in whic
tens of thousands lost their lives. (One authority, Raymond F. Kent, es
timates that there were about 60,000 victims.[3]) In addition there are, fc
want of a better term, what can be termed "periods of unrest" that hav
gripped entire territories or parts of them and during which a high in
cidence of violence prevailed for extended periods of time. A case in poin
is Southern Rhodesia, which experienced protracted periods of unres
coupled with violence during the years 1959–62. Further, any classificatio
must take into account occurrences of actual or threatened interstate vio
lence, such as have been increasing along the periphery of the Soma
frontier.

Without going into a lengthy review of the literature on violence, severa
attempts at classifying it may be noted with profit. Samuel Huntington
discussing "insurrectionary wars" (a form of domestic violence in which
the insurrectionists aim at the total control of the state), surveys catalogue
provided by Lasswell and Kaplan, Gabriel Bonnet, W. S. Stokes, and Edwin
Lieuwen. The sum total of the categories presented by these four writer
is twenty-eight, reflecting, according to Huntington, differences seen by
these authors in the nature of the participants, their relations with one
another, and the political culture of the society in which they exist.[4] Hunt
ington himself draws a useful distinction between intergovernmental and
antigovernmental violence, arguing that while patterns of intergovernmenta
war reflect the processes and structure of international politics, antigovern
mental—insurrectionary—war reflects the processes and structure of do
mestic politics.[5] He argues further that the dominant forms of insurrection
ary violence in the underdeveloped areas during the post-World War I
period have been the revolutionary war and the *coup d'état*—forms related
to the dual problems of the struggle for independence and the modernization of the polity.

Characteristically and crucially, Huntington says, revolutionary war involves a "contest between a counter-elite and the government for the support of a communal or socioeconomic group that is imperfectly integrated into the existing political system."[6] In the African context, his definition would include the Algerian revolt, where both the French and the FLN concentrated major efforts at both intimidating and making friends of the *fellagah;* the Mau-Mau uprising, where the majority of Kikuyu occupied the intermediary position; the Cameroun insurrection of 1955–61 (where the allegiance of the Bassa and Bamiléké groups were crucial to the revolt); and the present conflicts in Portuguese Guinea and Angola, where the ability of both government and revolutionaries to win the support, or even the neutrality of the nonassimilated African majority may prove decisive in the struggle.

The coup, on the other hand, can "only be undertaken by a group that is already a participant in the existing political system and that possesses institutional bases of power within that system. In particular, the instigating group needs the support of some elements of the armed forces."[7] Huntington distinguishes three types of coups: (1) the *governmental coup,* or palace revolution," in which the leadership of the government is changed but no significant change takes place in the institutional or group structure of the political system; (2) the *revolutionary coup,* in which the leadership changes and wholesale changes in the political and socioeconomic systems are attempted or made; and (3) the *reform coup,* a compromise between the other two types, in which reforms are effected but not to a drastic degree. A characteristic of the reform coup, contends Huntington, is that the group that leads it tends to disintegrate after a few years, opening the door to further coups.

Another highly interesting approach to the problem is advanced by Thomas Hodgkin in his *African Political Parties.*[8] Hodgkin sees violence in instrumental terms. In the colonial situation, it represented one method in a spectrum or range of methods available to African parties and groups in the realization of their goals. But, in "parties in independent, or near-independent, African States, when there is no longer a colonial regime to serve as the main target of opposition," violence appears to be present in three recurrent types of context: (1) It is used by members or supporters of the dominant party against those who are regarded as "enemies of the people," former collaborators, "lackeys," or members of minority groups. Hodgkin cites the activities of the *troupes de l'éléphant* (RDA strong-arm groups) in the Ivory Coast in 1956, but his list could be extended to include the attacks of Convention People's Party members on United Party leaders and followers between 1960 and 1963, the mass slaughter of Batutsi by Bahutu in Rwanda during 1964, the mass expulsion of resident Dahomeans by Niger in December, 1963, and the attacks upon the persons

and property of Arabs during and after the January, 1964, revolt in Zanz
bar. (2) It is also used by irreconcilables who may be associated with a
opposition party, an underground party, or a minority movement withi
the dominant party: "They claim [says Hodgkin] that the revolution ha
stopped too soon, has failed to achieve its objectives, or has passed out o
the hands of patriots into the hands of politicians." This rationale wa
advanced by the dissidents for continuing their armed violence afte
Cameroun became independent in 1960, and provided some of the just
fication for the attempted coups against Leon M'ba in Gabon in 196.
and the abortive coup by Mamadou Dia against the Senghor governmer
in December, 1962. It is also likely that some of the violence in Ghana
including the several attempts to assassinate Nkrumah, derives from th
motivation of Ghanaian irreconcilables, whatever their ethnic or part
derivation. (3) And it is used in a "whole range of situations in whic
old antagonisms—the products of both the precolonial and colonial peri
ods—reassert themselves through the modern channels of party conflict.
Hodgkin cites the National Liberation Movement–Convention People'
Party conflict in Ashanti in 1954–56, the tensions between the Nationa
Union Party and the Liberal Party before and after the 1955 mutiny ii
the southern Sudan, the Kano disturbances in May, 1953, and the blood
clashes between rival parties in Brazzaville in January, 1959. To this lis
might be added the various instances of Lulua-Baluba, Bayaka-Bakongo
Lunda-Baluba conflict in the former Belgian Congo after 1959, the Arab
Fulani violence in Chad in 1957 and 1958, the clashes in French Guine
between Soussou-Malinke and Fulani during the elections of January, 1956
and the Masai-Kisii tribal violence during August, 1962, in Kenya. Thi
element clearly was present in the Bahutu-Batutsi conflicts in Rwanda ii
November, 1959, September, 1961, March, 1962, and February, 1964
and in the rebellion that broke out in the southern Sudan in October, 1963

Another fruitful approach to the classification and analysis of violence
was attempted by Harry Eckstein and several of his colleagues in *Interna
War*. Eckstein defined "internal war" as "violent conflict between partie
subject to a common authority and of such dimensions that its incidence
will affect the exercise or structure of authority in society."[9] A virtue o
the definition is that it is broad enough to include a range of manifestation
of violence from small riots to civil war, but narrow enough to exclude al
incidents of violence in society that do not affect authority, includin
sporadic individual attacks on representatives of authority in dimension
too small to alter existing institutional arrangements. Andrew Janos cite
seven techniques of internal war—strikes, demonstrations, terrorism, guer
rilla warfare, civil war, insurrection, and *coup de force*. William Kornhause
classifies cases according to the authority structures in which internal war

ise and toward which they tend (alien, insufficient, arbitrary, and ex-
usive forms of authority, or combinations of these, will call forth different
sponses).[10]

The approaches to violence of Huntington, Hodgkin, and Ekstein are
presentative of the increasing variety of classificatory schemes developed
students of violence in their attempt to find broad criteria for the analy-
s of what is surely a universal phenomenon. The very disparity of their
pproaches reflects the obvious difficulties they encountered, not the least
which is the formidable barrier posed by the broad range of the data
ith which they deal. Moreover, as Eckstein has perceptively pointed out,
his disparity is due to the fact that every writer on internal war bases
s classifications on some one element of internal war or some small com-
ination of elements that happens particularly to interest him or that,
ften for reasons not even intimated, he feels is particularly crucial—
erhaps a determinant variable in a world of dependent variables."[11] This
true of Huntington, who, dealing with what is literally a world of vio-
nce, understandably focuses on the larger aspects of the problem; it is
ue of Hodgkin, whose primary interest is the behavior of organized po-
tical groups; and it is true of the writers in the Eckstein volume. Each
pproach does, however, contain much that is valuable, and it is no way
the discredit of these writers that a satisfactory, or nearly satisfactory
lassification has yet to emerge from their or others' efforts.

Granting, then, the difficulties of emphasis and delimitation, and the
act that any classification represents an arbitrary ordering of the available
ata according to what appear to be discrete and distinguishable elements
the data, the starting point of any typology of political violence in
frica must be the data itself. An examination of the data on political vio-
nce during the period 1946–64 for the 40 states and territories surveyed
evealed that somewhere between 300 and 400 instances of political vio-
ence occurred in areas surveyed, using the broad definition of "political
iolence" suggested on pages 59–60. Although the incompleteness of the data
recludes an inclusive taxonomy of forms, it did appear that the *form*
nstances of political violence took in Africa was a function of six sets of
ariables, each of which represented a continuum of possibilities:

Variable	Possibilities
Context	Interstate–Intrastate
Salience	Nonpolitical–Political
Situation	Antigovernmental–Progovernmental
Structure	Organized–Unorganized
Position	Civil–Military
Scope	High–Low effect on political system

Context. Political violence either took place within the territorial limit of African states, or, alternatively, affected two or more states. This wa the most easily dichotomized variable, since there are only two possibilitie.

Salience. The term as I have used it refers to the range of possibilitie between completely nonpolitical violence and violence that has the highes salience, or greatest relevance for the formal political system.

Situation. I refer to the situation of the participants vis-à-vis the gov ernment. Here the range of possibilities extends from outright oppositio to direct and/or formal support. *Situation,* then, becomes crucial in man instances in defining for the participants the form violence will take, if th form is subject to their manipulation. At the progovernmental end of th continuum, violence can be initiated by government itself, or by its sup porters with or without its knowledge or approval.

Structure. Violence can range in *structure* from the purely anomic t the highly organized. In highly organized violence, the participants hav well-defined roles to play, objectives have been carefully defined, mean disposed and allocated to participants according to plan, and so on. Th difference is basically that between planned and unplanned violence, be tween running amok and fighting a modern offensive war. It can be argue that every instance of violence has some structure imposed upon it by th participants and, particularly, by the unique context in which it occurs Even granting this, what is important for us is not so much whether th violence is *patterned,* but the extent to which it was *planned* or *directed*

Position. The *position* participants in violence occupy in social, po litical, and economic strata of society will affect the forms their violence will take, if for no other reason than the fact that the means available fo expressing violence will vary according to the capabilities of the partic ipants. The significant positional continuum for Africa appears to be th civilian-military one.

Scope. By *scope* I refer to a continuum of both involvement and affect easy to envisage in the abstract but rather difficult to define in relation t the data. The idea of scope may, however, permit a rough scale of forms o violence to be constructed under the rubrics provided by the other variables. (*Involvement* refers generally to the number of people directly affected by violence, be it political, social, or economic.)

By using the first five variables as general rubrics and roughly scalin forms as they appear in the data according to scope, a schema can be devised to show both variables and forms in relation to one another. Chart 1 is a tentative attempt to do this. The forms listed, it will be seen, reflect actual types of violence noted at the most primitive level of denotation, that is, with only a nominal attempt at definition (for definitions, see the Appendix, pp. 78–9). Also, in the interest of economy, the chart does not depict all the continuums that might appear if absolute logical symmetry

(1) Interstate		Intrastate							
		(2) Nonpolitical		(3) Antigovernment				Progovernment	
				Political					
(2) Nonpolitical	Political	(4) Organized	Unorganized	(4) Organized		Unorganized			
				(5) Civil	Military	(5) Civil	Military	(5) Civil	Military
anomic private communal border incursion	subversion sabotage aid to Freedom Fighters undeclared war reprisal war	private communal banditry	anomic private communal banditry	demonstration riot strike period of unrest party conflict communal warfare assassination insurrection coup revolution	mutiny assassination insurrection coup revolution	demonstration riot period of unrest party conflict communal war assassination	mutiny assassination	demonstration riot strike party conflict communal war	police action military action

(6) *Scope* →

Key to variables:
- (1) Context
- (2) Salience
- (3) Situation
- (4) Structure
- (5) Position
- (6) Scope

were desired; only those forms that directly emerged from the data ar
listed.

With the typology as a point of departure, several descriptive generaliza
tions about the patterns of political violence may now be made:

1. Overwhelmingly, political violence during the period in question wa
an internal affair for the states and territories surveyed. There were ne
instances of *interterritorial* violence of large scope, as represented by de
clared or undeclared warfare. With the accession to independence of mos
of the states in the survey, however, breaches of border security that had
previously been the exclusive concern of colonial governments became mat
ters of crucial importance to the new African states.

Small-scale military and police actions have been fought along the Soma
border since 1959, becoming increasingly larger in scale along both th
Kenyan and Ethiopian frontiers since the Somali Republic became inde
pendent in 1960. Repeated Turkana raids from the Sudan into Kenya be
tween January, 1960, and March, 1962, embarrassed both the Sudanes
and Kenyan authorities. Relations between Rwanda and Burundi hav
worsened as a result of the violence that followed the attempted re-entry
of Batutsi into Rwanda from Burundi and other neighboring states durin
1964. Relations between Mauritania and Morocco have been strained sinc
1962, following a Moroccan attempt at internal subversion, on the basi
of shaky territorial claims to an area that included not only all of Mauri
tania, but parts of Mali, Senegal, and Algeria as well.

Incidents of interterritorial violence have recently become more frequen
in Africa, and some newly independent African states have actively en
couraged groups dedicated to the overthrow of other African regimes
"Freedom Fighters" have contributed to the violence by seeking to elim
inate the remaining colonial regimes in Africa. The examples are many; a
few will illustrate the point: The U.A.R., Ghana, and Guinea provided
a base of operations between 1957 and 1963 for exiled Union des Popula
tions du Cameroun leaders seeking the overthrow of the Ahidjo regime
in the Cameroun; Mali has long provided haven for Djibo Bakary, forme
Prime Minister of Niger, and his colleagues, all dedicated to the overthrov
of the government of Hamani Diori; Congo-Brazzaville has been the sea
of operations for the Comité National de Libération, a Lumumbist splinte
group; Ghana, Congo-Leopoldville, Guinea, Mali, Kenya, and Tanganyika
(among others) are actively engaged in helping to train and arm revolu
tionaries to fight in Angola, Portuguese Guinea, and Mozambique.[13]

2. Although the evidence is incomplete and will permit only a tentative
statement, it appears that both organized and unorganized antigovernmen
violence of lesser scope is decreasing in frequency in all areas except the
residual Portuguese colonies, Southern Rhodesia, and the Republic of Sout

frica. On the other hand, in the independent states, instances of violence
f greater scope seem to be increasing in frequency, except for insurrec-
ons, which thus far have been pre-independence phenomena. The decline
I the frequency of communal warfare, riots, demonstrations, violent
rikes, and periods of unrest has apparently followed the consolidation
f power—in particular, the multiplication of one-party states—in the
idependent states. The use of violence of lesser scope was a favored
iethod of antigovernment pressure utilized by nationalists before inde-
endence; indeed, with the means for violence of larger scope in the hands
f colonial governments, nationalists were generally restricted in the forms
f violence available to them. This situation still prevails in the European-
ontrolled parts of Africa. With independence, however, the means for
irge-scope violence became available to both opposition (particularly op-
osition elements already participating in the political arena) and the new
frican governments. Of the forms of large-scope violence, insurrections,
oups, and assassinations have had the greatest actual and potential salience
or the political systems of the African states and territories. Some pattern-
gs of these latter forms have been especially noteworthy:

a. Large-scale insurrections have occurred almost exclusively in the
olonial situation; none was successful in overthrowing the existing regimes,
iough the possibility exists that current rebellions in Angola and Portu-
uese Guinea may achieve this aim, and that the rebellions in the southern
udan and the North-Eastern Region of Kenya (the latter predates Kenyan
idependence in 1963) may achieve important political and institutional
evisions, if not the actual secessions of the areas concerned. With the ex-
eption of the UPC-inspired rebellion in the Cameroun, the 1947 Madagas-
ar revolt, and the Mau-Mau uprising in Kenya between 1953–56, anti-
olonial insurrections have been the exception rather than the rule in
frica.

b. The *coup d'état* and the attempted coup are also postcolonial phe-
omena in Africa. If one accepts Huntington's useful definition of the
oup and the distinctions between the three types he lists, it is plain to
nderstand why this must be so. Until Africans were themselves full par-
icipants in the political system, by definition impossible until independ-
nce, coups could not occur. There has, however, been no dearth of suc-
essful or attempted coups since independence. Five states have experienced
uccessful coups (Sudan, November, 1958; Togo, January, 1963; Da-
omey, October, 1963; Congo-Brazzaville, August, 1963; and Zanzibar,
anuary, 1964); coups have been attempted in six states (Gabon, Ghana,
:thiopia, Ivory Coast, Somalia, and Sudan, where no less than four at-
empts have been made to unseat General Abboud); and the governments
f eleven states have claimed that coups were attempted or plotted (Nigeria,

Cameroun, Chad, Ghana, Guinea, Ivory Coast, Burundi, Mali, Liberia
Togo, and Niger). The alleged attempts or plots were usually followed
by trials for "treason," "subversion," or the like, in which important mem
bers of the opposition were jailed or, occasionally, executed.

c. Instances of assassination or attempted assassination of heads of stat
or important political figures have been relatively few in number durin
the period in question, but what instances have occurred have taken plac
since 1959, with an upsurge after 1960, the date of independence for man
African states. The most widely publicized attempted assassinations hav
had Ghanaian President Kwame Nkrumah as their object; thus far, Nkru
mah has survived two bombs, a hand grenade, and shots from a rifl
fired at almost point-blank range. Alleged assassination plots have bee
uncovered in the Ivory Coast, Liberia, Togo, and Chad. Only two to
African leaders have thus far succumbed to assassination: Prince Loui
Rwagasore, the Prime Minister of Burundi, who was killed by a Gree
youth on October 13, 1961, and Sylvanus Olympio, President of Togc
who was apparently unintentionally shot by rebellious Togolese soldier
during the army revolt of January, 1963. This list might include Patric
Lumumba, former Prime Minister of Congo-Leopoldville, but what infor
mation is available about his death would seem to point to political murde
rather than assassination.[14] Another possible addition to the list might b
Dr. Félix Moumié, President of the exiled splinter of the Cameroun'
UPC, who died by poisoning in Geneva, Switzerland, on November 3
1960. At least one theory seeking to explain his death calls it an assassina
tion and blames the shadowy, anti-Communist "Red Hand" organizatio
for the deed.[15]

3. The participation and/or intervention of the military in antigovern
mental violence has become increasingly frequent since 1960, though, i
the countries and territories surveyed, only one military figure involved i
a successful coup actually assumed more than provisional-governmenta
power (General Abboud in the Sudan), and in only three instances di
military leaders remain for any length of time in the political apparatu
of the state after their intervention (General Abboud and his officers
Colonel Soglo, who, after the Dahomean coup in October, 1963, becam
Head of State until he resigned from politics in January, 1964; and Gen
eral Mobutu, who rose to the head of the Force Publique in 1960, led a
apparent *putsch* in 1961, and still remains one of the main participant
in the political arena defined by the extent of the effective authority of th
Congo-Leopoldville central government). The important point is that thu
far the military's role in antigovernmental violence has been mainly a
instrumental one. Except for the Sudanese coup of 1958, the army mutinie
in Kenya, Uganda, and Tanganyika in January, 1964, the Togolese cou

of January, 1963, the attempted coup in Ethiopia of December, 1960, and the revolt of the Force Publique in the Congo in July, 1960, military elements appear in supportive, rather than leading roles.

Of the exceptions noted above—all instances in which some or most of the impetus for violence came from the military elements themselves—only in the Sudanese and Congolese cases did military leaders derive much political capital from their acts of rebellion. In this connection, it is instructive to recall the dilemma of the Togolese military rebels who, after having overthrown the Olympio government and killed Sylvanus Olympio, were at a loss to run the government and had to call home from exile Meatchi and Grunitsky, neither of whom had been directly involved in the revolt itself. It will also be recalled that the failure of the army mutinies in the southern Sudan, Tanganyika, Kenya, and Uganda was probably due as much to a *lack* of connection with the nonmilitary political arena as to failures in organization, timing, and leadership. In virtually every other instance, the military acted as the weapon of a civilian opposition to the government.

That certain inducements such as higher pay and the elimination of European officers were sometimes offered by the politicians in no way changes the validity of the generalization that the military has played a role subordinate to the civilian one. The military in Dahomey, Gabon, and Congo-Brazzaville had long-standing grievances against their respective governments, but it took civilian politicians to provide the incentive—participation in a coup or attempted coup—to inspire them to rise up. The instrumental role of the military is exemplified by the relations between Justin Ahomadegbé, Sourou Mignan Apithy, and Colonel Christophe Soglo in the October, 1963, Dahomean coup; between Abeid Karume, Abdul Rahman Mohammed ("Babu"), and self-styled Field Marshal John Okello during the coup in Zanzibar in January, 1964; between Jean-Hilaire Aubame and Lieutenants Mombo and Essené during the abortive Gabonese coup in February, 1964; between Mamadou Dia, the gendarmes, and Chief of Staff General Amadou Fall during the attempted coup in Sudan on December 17, 1962; and between Modibo Keita and Colonel Abdoulaye Soumaré during the attempted coup against the Mali federal government on August 19 and 20, 1960.[16]

4. Communal violence—including such forms as tribal warfare and violence directed against members of minority ethnic or religious groups—continues to trouble many African states. Hodgkin's third "context" (situations in which old antagonisms, originating in both precolonial and colonial periods, reassert themselves through the modern channels of party conflict), falls within this generalization. Such violence appears frequently where the government is generally weak or unable to assert its authority through-

out the territory of the state; in situations of political instability in which the survival of governments are in doubt; or where governments, feeling threatened, take direct action against actual or supposed opposition groups and communities. It is hardly likely that, given a strong central Congolese government, communal violence in Congo-Leopoldville would erupt so often. The Belgian administrations in the Congo and Ruanda-Urundi apparently "sat" (at least until 1959) on ethnic tensions with sufficient strength to prevent them from becoming more than occasionally troublesome.

In the outlying areas of Kenya, Uganda, Sudan, Ethiopia, Mali, Chad, Liberia, and Upper Volta, precisely where governmental authority tends to be most tenuous, communal violence has been and continues to be relatively frequent. Excellent examples of situations that put the survival of the government in doubt can be found in Zanzibar: the Arab-African election riots in Zanzibar between June 1–6, 1961, and the wholesale slaughter of Arabs by Africans during and after the January, 1964, coup. The Batutsi-Bahutu conflicts of November, 1959, and September, 1961, occurred in such a context also. Examples of situations in which the government took direct action against actual or supposed opposition groups are the government-inspired reprisals against resident Batutsi in Rwanda during and after the three attempted invasions by banished Batutsi (November 25, December 20 and 27, 1963); the attacks by UDDIA supporters against Matsouanists in Brazzaville on June 18, 1959; the several outbreaks between Luo and Kikuyu in Kenya during August, 1962; and the attacks on Asian shopkeepers in Chiromo township (Nyasaland) by Malawi Congress youth leaders during July, 1963.

Most of the literature dealing with the political problems of contemporary Africa provides catalogues of the continent's social, economic, and political ills. There is, of course, an obvious general correspondence between political instability and violence; the causes of political instability are very likely to be same ones underlying political violence. To attempt another catalogue of "problems" is not, however, likely to add much to the discussion. Possibly a more productive approach is to suggest, as does Hodgkin, that political violence may arise within certain generally definable contexts.[17] Six such contexts can be singled out as having the greatest relevance for our discussion: (1) using an amended version of Hodgkin's formulation—situations in which old antagonisms arising in both the pre-colonial and colonial periods reassert themselves through the channels of party conflict, or outside them; (2) the transition to independence, a context that Brian Crozier has aptly named the "Morning After";[18] (3) the unresolved role of labor both in relation to the new African govern-

tents and to the process of modernization; (4) the new status conferred
y independence upon the military establishments; (5) interstate rivalries;
nd (6) the presence of residual colonialism and the continued involvement
f non-African powers—both European and non-European—in African
olitical affairs.

1. *Reassertion of old antagonisms.* Clifford Geertz has pointed out that:

onsidered as societies, the new states are abnormally susceptible to serious
isaffection based on primordial attachments. By a primordial attachment is
eant one that stems from the "givens" . . . of social existence: immediate
ontiguity and kin connection mainly, but beyond them the givenness that stems
rom being born into a particular religious community, speaking a particular
anguage, or even a dialect of a language, and following particular social
ractices.[19]

n the new states, these "primordial ties" of community, ethnicity, lan-
uage, and land often come into conflict with the newer, more diffuse
lemands for allegiance to the civil state. "It is this crystallization of a
lirect conflict between primordial and civil sentiments," maintains Geertz,
"that gives rise to the problem variously called tribalism, parochialism,
ommunalism, and so on. . . ."[20] Geertz argues that "the reduction of
orimordial sentiments to civil order is rendered more difficult . . . by the
act that political modernization tends initially not to quiet these senti-
nents, but to quicken them."[21] The reasons for this phenomenon are not
lifficult to find: Parents tend to socialize their children for participation
n the local authority systems with which they are already familiar rather
han for roles in the national system.[22] Therefore, in a situtation where
only a relatively few persons have assimilated the values of the modern
tate, political appeals by even the most sophisticated and westernized
nembers of the new elite must be tilted toward and accommodating to
ocal issues and identifications.[23] In the process, the facts of ethnicity, com-
nunity, and language become focuses of political power and thereby
valuable new political prizes.

Old antagonisms born of primordial attachments will, then, reappear
n new forms and often with a new politicized guise; they may, by virtue
of their politicization in the context of the new state, even re-emerge with
greater intensity and scope. If they were previously violently expressed,
hat violence may break out with greater ferocity; if the conflict was nonviolent in its old context, it may become violent as the participants acquire
new perspectives to sharpen their mutual antagonisms and find more effec-
ive means for expressing them.

Both of these factors are present in the current Congolese violence. In
ooth the Kwilu and Kivu provinces, for example, ineffective operations by

central government troops have failed to root out terrorist bands of youth between the ages of thirteen and eighteen organized by Pierre Mulele, wh returned in July, 1963, from China where he allegedly received guerrill training. In Kwilu, Mulele apparently recruited most of his followers from the Bapende and Babunde tribes, groups with long histories of anti-Belgia and antigovernment violence and of conflict with their neighbors, th Baboma, Bambala, and Bayauzi. In Kivu, Bafulero pygmies, Watutsi refu gees, and other tribal groups have contributed to the unrest.

The revolt in southern Sudan, noted previously, is another timely ex ample of the reappearance of old communal-ethnic antagonisms in nev political dress. There, long-standing enmity between northern Muslims an southern animists and Christians was given a new dimension by the appear ance of southern Sudanese (led by Joseph Oduho and William Deng armed with modern political and ideological weapons.[24] The rebels' politica party, the Sudan Africa National Union, claims that, since the rebellion broke out, 275 people have been killed in eastern Equatoria Provinc alone.

Confirmation of the thesis that independence may attenuate conflicts o "primordial" interest abound during the past several years. Many of th bloodier pages of recent Congolese history have been written by newl politicized tribal groups or by groups released from the restraints of Belgia rule renewing old conflicts with a violence the greater for being bottled u by the Belgian regime. Certainly the thesis finds confirmation in the cas of the Zanzibar revolt; long-simmering animosities between Arabs an Africans—which broke out in violence in 1961—finally had both focu and organization provided for them by politicians anxious to undermin the Zanzibar and Pemba People's Party (ZPPP)–Zanzibar Nationalis Party (ZNP) alliance and the island's rule by its Arab minority (only 19 per cent of the population). The January, 1964, violence far exceeded tha of previous outbreaks in scope and casualties; perhaps 500 persons wer killed and another 2,000 wounded.[25]

Between 1954 and 1958 in Ghana, two ethnic-centered parties, the National Liberation Movement (NLM) in Ashanti, and the Northerr Peoples' Party (NPP) in the Northern Territories, arose to challenge the the dominance of the Convention People's Party and to press for politica concessions for their ethnic constituencies. The NLM and NPP did not hesitate to resort to widespread violence in their bid to secure a federa system for independent Ghana, a violence that was fanned by a revival o the old animosities between the Ashanti and the coastal peoples. At one point, some 5,000 CPP supporters and non-Ashanti resident in Ashanti areas were forced to seek refuge on the coast.[26] A final example has already been briefly noted: the Brazzaville riots of February, 1959, where Bakongo supporters of the ruling party—the Union Démocratique de Défense des Intérêts Africains (UDDIA)—gave vent to old animosities by attacking M'Bochi and Vilii supporters of the opposition Mouvement Socialiste Africain (MSA).

2. *The transition to independence.* A growing literature has begun to concern itself with the problems attending the transformation of political societies in Africa from dependent to independent status.[27] Although this literature varies a great deal in emphasis and substance, certain common themes are found throughout. One recurrent concern has been the multiplication of one-party states—a response to the need for the consolidation of power in the postcolonial period. Another has been the persistence of what Wallerstein has termed "ethnic fragmentation,"[28] which constitutes a serious threat to political integration. A third has been the difficulties in establishing the central authority of the new states in the face of a general institutional fragility inherited from colonial regimes. A fourth is the problem of the interstate relations of the new African regimes. A fifth concerns the many economic adjustments that the new African states have had to make upon attaining independence. In each area, the possibility of political violence has existed and will continue to exist. It is, however, in the first and third areas that the prospects for violence are the greatest, and that an examination of causes may be most illuminating.

It can be argued with considerable persuasiveness that the incidence of violence will tend to increase as the effective control a government can exercise throughout its territory lessens. Lucian Pye, for example, makes the point for insurrections, though it applies as well to lesser forms of violence:

Within highly industrialized society it is almost impossible for political controversy to develop to the point of sustained and organized violence. The possibility of an insurrectionary movement arising and then employing organized violence depends upon the existence of sharp divisions within the society created by regional, ethnic, linguistic, class, religious, or other communal differences that may provide the necessary social and geographic basis for supporting the movement; *and a central authority that is unable to maintain uniform and consistent administrative controls over the entire country.* Such situations are most likely to arise in essentially agrarian societies or in countries where there are extreme differences between the life of the urban and industrialized segments and that of the rural elements. [Italics added].[29]

One of the unhappy legacies of the colonial period has often been an institutional and administrative structure ill adapted to the needs of independence. While such structures were operated by colonial civil servants within a context in which ultimate decision-making powers resided in the metropole rather than within the territory, the maintenance of public order was generally effective. In only the rarest instances did indigenous opponents have either the means or the organization to challenge the power of the colonial regime. As the expatriate cadres were withdrawn and colonial status terminated, these structures were often simply inadequate to the needs of the new state. Congo-Leopoldville is, of course, the best example of this situation. In the panic that followed the events of June-July, 1960, almost 8,000 of the more than 10,000 Belgian civil servants in the country left. The immediate result was to deprive large areas of the country of administrative, health, and police services. Freed from the old restrictions, and with the Congolese army unable to assert control in most parts of the territory, tribal conflicts erupted with long-pent-up fury, and separatist governments began to flourish in the provinces. It was not until the United Nations brought in both soldiers and personnel to man administrative services that even nominal order was restored.[30]

More important than the problem of reorganizing or shoring up fragile institutions, and more politically dangerous and fraught with possibilities for violence, has been the struggle for the consolidation, stabilization, and, increasingly, the totalization of power. The push for independence had the effect of broadening the bases of political participation, and with it, of increasing the range of demands and expectations of the groups that had become politicized in the process.

With independence, the anticolonial struggle, which had brought political groups together, ceased to have its former credibility due to the absence of a visible colonial presence. Moreover, independence brought a newer, less diffuse set of goals, and political goods (such as jobs, offices, land, leadership roles) that had formerly seemed unlimited in quantity, were now visibly restricted by technical and logistical considerations. The new forces and groups (e.g., army, labor unions, professional associations, educated young men) socialized to nationalist goals during the colonial period and accustomed to easy access to the political process and to having their demands satisfied—at least symbolically by the promises of their leaders—now had to learn to operate through the bureaucracy of the state, or of the leading party, or both. The net result of self-government, or independence, for these groups has been a formalization of relations between themselves and the new power holders. Independence may have had, therefore, the effect of narrowing, rather than broadening political horizons.

With the emergence of the one-party state—considered by many African leaders a necessary instrument for rapid modernization and the preservation of order—the avenues of political involvement and for making political demands have become increasingly circumscribed. Whatever the rationale for the one-party state, *it does not and cannot engage the support of most of the politically active strata;* the effect of its operation is to close political doors, not to open them. At the very least, the one-party state operates to narrow political alternatives for the participants of the system; some of these alternatives may be unacceptable to those whose demands remain unsatisfied, whose expectations remain unfulfilled, or who may not have realized the political benefits independence was to have conferred upon them. Such personal motives seem to have played a part in the mutinies in Tanganyika, Kenya, and Uganda in January, 1964 (independence brought the military neither better pay nor their own African officers), and in the complaints of the new masters against Maga in Dahomey and Youlou in Congo-Brazzaville. (The complaint was that Maga and Youlou had sought personal power at the expense of their friends and opponents, something made possible by independence, but not envisaged by those who fought for it.) Of even greater consequence was the reaction of political groups alienated in the process of the consolidation of power. Dieter Lindenlaub provides some instructive examples:

Politically, the recent putsches are seen as lifesaving attempts by groups that, in the process whereby African states have become one-party systems, have been forced into illegal status or find themselves on the road thereto. . . . In Congo/Brazzaville, Dahomey, and Gabon, characteristically, elections were the occasions for revolt. In Congo/Brazzaville, where Youlou's UDDIA rules parliament as the majority party, and in Gabon, whose parliament was simi-larly dominated by a single party after the elections of February, 1961, the op-position armed itself against a complete loss of power. The opposition in Congo/Brazzaville—organized by the labor unions—frustrated Youlou's plan to legalize the one-party state on August 15, 1963. The unsuccessful coup in Gabon was launched five days before elections (on February 23) for a new—and more restricted—parliament were to take place. In Togo (where the Comité d'Unité Togolaise was the only party since January 13, 1962) and in Dahomey (where the Parti Dahoméen de l'Unité was the single party since April 11, 1961), the opposition attempted to reverse the process whereby Presidents Olympio and M'ba had secured virtually unlimited power for themselves. In Togo, Congo/Brazzaville, and Dahomey, it appeared that the rebellions were directed not so much against the system, but more against the power-holders. . . .[31]

The list might also include the case of the UPC members in the Cameroun, who, after successive electoral defeats, after seeing the nationalism of which they were the first champions pre-empted by other parties, after being hounded by the authorities and their opponents, found in revolt a partial release of their frustrations.[32] For the UPC, the Cameroun's political doors were closed by proscription from 1955 to 1960; by mid-1962 (after independence), however, the East Cameroun had become a one-party state following the arrest, trial, and imprisonment of the leaders of the principal opposition parties.

The narrowing of political horizons that appears to have accompanied independence and the creation of the one-party state has had, then, the effect of making political deviance a much more costly affair for both government and oppositional elements, if only because the stakes (often involving the power of the state itself) are much higher now than they were previously.

3. *Workers and soldiers.* Of the groups that took shape and orientation during the colonial period few have had the impact on political life of the trade unions. In French-speaking Africa, the creation of trade unions predated the birth of organized political parties. Metropolitan trade unions were given license to set up affiliates in Afrique Noire in 1944, but it was not until 1945 that the first metropolitan political parties established *filiales* in Africa, and not until 1946 that the first significant African political parties saw the light of day. In many parts of French Africa, therefore, political demands were first voiced through trade-union organizations. One recalls the role of the Confédération Generale du Travail (CGT) in setting up the Union des Populations du Cameroun (UPC) in the Cameroun, the trade-union origins of Sékou Touré, and the complimentary role of trade unions to nationalist movements in Ghana, Nigeria, Mali, Ivory Coast, Tanganyika, Northern Rhodesia, and so forth.

In the process of such collaboration, the strike came to be used not only to achieve economic aims, but for the political ends of nationalism as well. Strike-connected violence more often than not had political overtones, and the political experience and involvement with nationalist leaders and groups made labor one of the most important groups that the governments of newly independent states had to accommodate. When such accommodations could not or were not found, it was to the peril of the new governments. In Dahomey, Hubert Maga tried in 1961 to pull the political teeth of the two principal trade unions, the Union Générale des Travailleurs d'Afrique Noire (UGTAN) and the Confédération Africaine des Travailleurs Croyants (CATC), by forcing them to merge into his Union Générale des Travailleurs Dahoméens (UGTD). The move did little to satisfy the demands of the unions or to solve the endemic unemployment in the country, and the UGTD, almost predictably, turned against Maga by helping to pull his government down in October, 1963. The general strike in Nigeria called on May 31, 1964, appeared to stem from a similar disenchantment. *West Africa* noted this in one of its articles on the strike:

During September [1963] a general feeling was apparent among workers that the coming of the Republic should mean a bonus for workers. The psychology of this was that "independence" had seen abundance for a few, while the masses had seen little difference in their condition. Would the Republic be any different? . . .[33]

The point is clear: Trade unions are among the best organized and most politicized groups in Africa; imperfectly integrated into the new African polities, they can become rallying points for social and political dissatisfaction, and thereby the sources of potential violence.

With the possible exceptions of the Sudan, Nigeria, and Congo-Leopoldville, none of the newly independent states of Africa inherited well-organized armies from their former rulers. In almost every other instance the political socialization of the military cadre—as distinguished from purely military training—began shortly before or at independence. With independence, too, came new responsibilities and, significantly, the possibility of independent political action. Without a tradition of obedience to the state, with long-standing grievances unregulated, with the continued presence of expatriate officers and foreign military personnel, the small armies became tempting fields in which political oppositions could sow the seeds of violent discord.

4. *Residual colonialism and "neocolonialism."* If only because the charge has been made so often, "neocolonialism" must be briefly examined as a possible source of political violence. "Neocolonialism," indicates Nkrumah, "acts covertly, maneuvering men and governments, free of the stigma attached to colonial rule. It creates client states, independent in name but in point of fact pawns of the very colonial power which is supposed to have given them independence."[34] It takes many forms—the attempted balkanization of African states, "subservience" to the Common Market, the conclusion of pacts that give control of foreign policy to the former colonial powers, and the presence of the Peace Corps and of foreign military personnel and bases on African soil.[35] Insofar as the neocolonialists—by definition, the former colonial powers plus the United States—attempt to prevent the full independence of African states and stand in the path of African unity, they are regarded as instigators and perpetrators of political violence.

Ghana radio alleged that during the Dahomean coup, Maga asked for and was sent Togolese paratroopers to put down the revolt.[36] Parenthetically, Grunitsky himself visited Cotonou on November 5 and denied the report. The intervention of French troops in Gabon on February 18 in support of President M'ba, and the statement on February 26 by France's Minister of Information, Alain Peyrefitte, that French troops had intervened in five African countries since 1960 at the request of their governments (Cameroun, 1960, 1961; Congo-Brazzaville, 1960; Congo-Brazzaville and Gabon, 1962; Chad, "several" times between 1960 and 1963; Chad, 1963; and Mauritania, 1961) have done little, however, to mitigate the charges of "neocolonialism" levied against France. Similarly, the admission that American civilian pilots were flying sorties in Kivu for the

Congolese Government (June 15, 1964), the presence of Belgian "advisers" in Rwanda, and the intervention—by request—of British forces to put down the mutinies in East Africa in January, 1963, have all tended to reinforce the belief that "neocolonialism" has been at least partially responsible for recent violence in Africa.

Withal, it must be pointed out that the term "neocolonialism," with its heavy normative overlay, is too insubstantial to be useful in an analysis of the causes of political violence. This is so because "neocolonialism" is *by definition* a cause of violence, and because its users have tended to obliterate any differences between the broad range of involvements so characterized.

Finally, even though it may be trite to say so, residual colonialism is a context in which violence can be expected to increase. Not only have most of the areas of residual colonialism got their own nationalist groups currently actively engaged in antigovernment violence, but the newly independent states have taken it upon themselves to assist in the violent elimination of the remaining colonial outposts, including European oligarchies that are hardly colonies at all. It is only where the colonial power is actively moving its dependencies to self-government or independence (as in the Spanish colonies and the High Commission Territories) that the transition from dependence may be accomplished without major violence.

APPENDIX

*A Typology of Forms of Political Violence
in Africa: Definitions*

I. Interstate

1. *War*

2. *Undeclared war*

3. *Reprisal*

4. *Interterritorial communal warfare*

5. *Aid to "Freedom Fighters"*

6. *Sabotage*

7. *Subversion*

The difference between *war* and *undeclared war* is that the former involves a formal, declared commitment of intention. Interterritorial *communal warfare* is violence committed by ethnic groups or communities that spill over frontiers (Turkana raids into both Kenya and Uganda). *Aid to "Freedom Fighters"* might fall into what the French term *la guerre révolutionaire,* that is, insurrectionary violence instigated and/or supported from the outside of the territory in which it is waged; here the term refers to those activities which support insurrectionary violence in other territories. *Sabotage* and *subversion* are often used synonymously; in this context they refer to violence against property *(sabotage)* and persons *(subversion)* instigated or directed by one state against persons and property in another. (During 1962, Morocco supported some Nomadic tribes in their violence against Mauritanian persons and property.)

II. Intrastate

1. *Demonstration.* Usually, a gathering to articulate some political purpose; generally, violence is incidental to, but not central to the purpose of the gathering.

2. *Riot.* The inclusive term for violent expressions of an angry crowd. The term *mob* is generally used to describe such an angry crowd. *Demonstrations* can, obviously, turn into *riots,* as can *strikes.*

3. *Strike.* The organized disaffection of workers, manifested usually by a refusal to work, and by various forms of action such as *demonstrations,* picketing, sit-downs, etc. Violence is usually incidental, not central to the purpose of a strike.

4. *Period of unrest.* Characterized by sporadic, usually noncontinuous manifestations of violence, generally of lesser scope. Might include demonstrations, strikes, riots, etc.

5. *Party warfare.* Interparty violence.

6. *Communal warfare.* Violence between groups or communities in which the primary factor of group identification is ethnicity.

7. *Mutiny.* The refusal of military or police units to obey constituted authority, either civil or military. Some sort of violence usually accompanies mutinies.

8. *Assassination.* See note 14, p. 241.

9. *Coup.* See Huntington's breakdown, pp. 60-1.

10. *Police or military action.* Violence directed by the government using police or military forces.

4

Neo-Destour Leadership and
the "Confiscated Revolution"

DOUGLAS E. ASHFORD

WHEN PHILIPPE HERREMAN of *Le Monde* spoke of Tunisia's "confiscated revolution" in 1958, he was referring to the rivalry of President Habib Bourguiba and the vigorous labor-union leader, Ahmed Ben Salah.[1] Three years later their differences were overcome and Ben Salah emerged as Minister of Planning and Finance, one of the most powerful positions in the government. The social revolution envisaged by the highly privileged and colorful labor leader in 1956 was "confiscated" in 1958 and became the cornerstone of Tunisian domestic policy in 1961. Such have been the gyrations of the one-party system in Tunisia. There is certainly nothing original in noting the capacity of a one-party government to persuade, cajole, and coerce political leadership, but Tunisia's *Grand Combattant*—i.e., President Bourguiba—is distinguished in the annals of one-party rule by having reversed himself on nearly every national issue from Nasserism to socialism.

The one-party governments of Africa are noteworthy for their resourcefulness, while using a minimum of coercion. The development of larger armies on the African continent may bring the end to the political gymnastics of Bourguiba, Touré, and others, but their extraordinary flexibility has made them the object of particular interest. In fact, there have been many earlier one-party governments in developing countries outside Africa. A "Young Tunisian" clique existed in North Africa before World War I, and Bourguiba himself was inspired by Kemalist achievements twenty years later.[2] The colonial regimes might also be thought as one-party sysems, and the lessons of their political manipulation in Africa have not been forgotten.

But the mass appeal of African one-party regimes is no panacea for Africa's political and social problems, despite the predisposing factors for one-party rule.[3] One must also remember that 1962 has been dubbed the "year of the plots," when attempts were made to overthrow one-party regimes in Tunisia, Ghana, and the Ivory Coast.[4] Since then there has been serious violence in one-party regimes in Senegal, Chad, and Burundi, and a desperate call for British troops to reinforce teetering one-party governments in Tanganyika and Kenya. The future of one-party regimes in Africa may be clearer on examining some of the leadership crises through which Tunisia, and Bourguiba, have passed under conditions that are, on the whole, more favorable than those prevailing in most of sub-Saharan Africa. The review of the Tunisian experience will also serve to illuminate how Neo-Destour solidarity has been preserved through major reversals of national policy.

Writers on Tunisia seem to agree that "Bourguibism" represents a tactic more than an ideology or even a strategy.[5] Nothing demonstrates Bourguiba's manipulative skill better than his handling of the varieties of leadership to be found in Tunisia. The Neo-Destour Party's success should not conceal that the alternatives in leadership and policy have been certainly as great, and perhaps greater, in Tunisia than in much more heterogeneous regimes, such as in Morocco. The great skill of a Bourguiba is that he never permits the alternatives to coalesce in a single major issue. By maintaining a position in the center of most controversies he makes such personal coalitions extremely difficult. The most threatening policy alternative, a form of Arab nationalism, represents a combination of Islamic fundamentalism and working-class egalitarian appeal not unlike Tory radicalism of the late nineteenth century.[6]

To appreciate Bourguiba's versatility the four focuses of political leadership and their social base must be outlined. The first of these was the Salah Ben Youssef group. Though he met a Trotsky-like end in Germany in August, 1961, Ben Youssef's sympathizers are still to be found in Tunisia among veterans (*fellagha*) of the guerrilla movement. A native of the island of Djerba, Ben Youssef had strong regional support from the south, where the resistance was active and where the tribesmen and peasants felt neglected because of the concentration of Neo-Destour strength and economic development in the coastal and northern regions. The second group is made up of the strongly laicist modernizers represented by Ben Salah, who found an organizational base in the labor movement until it was adroitly eliminated by the President. The third group is made up of the thoroughly bourgeois liberals, who share the President's faith in France but occasionally object to his arbitrary methods. The inability of this urban modern group to unite with the working class on the basis of their similar programs for development can be explained by the latter's economic nationalism and suspicion of France. An agreement between the energetic modernizers and the pro-French liberals would have been fatal to the Neo Destour. By fracturing the opposition sentiments of the two groups eager to develop the country on Western lines, Bourguiba accomplished a much more difficult feat than by discrediting the violent opposition of the pro Nasser Arabists. The fourth group is made up of the militant party leader and the core of unquestioning lieutenants needed to operate a one-party regime. Both are indissolubly welded to Bourguiba.

Political organizations in Arab countries seem to be able to tolerate only one fervent speaker.[7] Ben Youssef, a French-educated lawyer, like Bourguiba, was associated with the Neo-Destour from 1934, when it was formed in opposition to the Destour. He was a fiery speaker, using mysticism to accomplish what Bourguiba did with daring courage and supreme self-confidence. The President was discouraged by his experiences in Cairo after the war, but Ben Youssef arrived there as the North African revolutions were being planned in the early 1950's and fell under the spell of Nasser. As Secretary General of the Neo-Destour, he managed the party while Bourguiba was drumming up international support and, later, while Bourguiba was in prison. Most important, Ben Youssef was a key man in organizing the Tunisian *fellagha* for the North African uprising planned for the fall of 1954, an uprising cleverly averted at the last minute by French concessions in both Morocco and Tunisia.

The Tunisian resistance movement began on a sporadic, disorganized basis shortly after the French *ratissage* of Cap Bon.[8] Like the early terrorist cells in Casablanca, the Tunisian *fellagha* were not initially organized by the Neo-Destour, and close coordination began only in 1954 from bases in Libya, serving both Algerian and Tunisian bands. In scenes that were to be repeated in both Morocco and Algeria, Ben Youssef objected to the cease-fire agreement with the French, and remained in Cairo throughout negotiations for autonomy. Ben Youssef's threat to Neo-Destour hegemony was indicated early in 1955 with student demonstrations at Zaytuna University, the ancient center of Islamic teaching in Tunis.[9] Fundamentalist Islamic opinion shared Ben Youssef's intransigence, and provided a basis for agreement between the remnants of the conservative Destour Party and Ben Youssef. But by the time Ben Youssef returned to Tunisia in the fall of 1955. Bourguiba had won over the other Neo-Destour leaders and Ben Youssef was expelled from the party in the November, 1955 Congress.

During the spring of 1956 Ben Youssef continued to direct *fellagha* errorism in the south of the country—activity that Bourguiba sought to epress with the help of French forces. Despite three subsequent trials to emove Youssefite plotters, Bourguiba failed to assimilate and subdue the Arab extremists.[10] The evidence of his failure was assembled in the 1963 rial following the attempt on his life. The accused included several Islamic cholars, a number of discontented officers and ex-*fellagha,* and a dis-nchanted party official from Bizerte.[11] The party had bestowed substantial enefits on the guerrillas, often in the form of valuable import licenses nd transport franchises. Ben Salah's energetic efforts to reorganize the nefficient and overgrown commercial and transportation sector of the unisian economy contributed to the *fellagha's* discontent, to the creation f a more openly aggressively pan-Arab state to the east, and to the 'resident's humiliation at Bizerte.

The President made no pretense of converting the Arabist faction to Neo-Destour thinking. Within a few months after independence Zaytuna University was under strict state control, and Islamic scholars supervising he Muslim court system arrived at work one day to find the building ecurely padlocked. But the rumblings of discontent have remained, and he Neo-Destour is virtually helpless to combat Nasser's appeal, except y patching up relations with Egypt. Remnants of the Youssefist faction ave been operating in Paris, and the exiles from the coup attempt were elcomed in Algeria. Diplomatic relations improved in 1963, however, and he President's support for a more aggressive development program may eutralize the domestic appeal of the Youssefists.

Bourguiba's handling of the Ben Salah affair is perhaps more repre-entative of the leadership problems of African one-party systems. In early all the more recent one-party governments there are delicate rela-ions between workers and party. The Tunisian labor movement is no xception, and its history predates the Neo-Destour. Moreover, the as-assination of Farhat Hached in late 1952 by French terrorists was the ignal for violence across the Maghreb, violence that led to the revolu-ionary activity of the early 1950's.[12] Though Ben Salah's brilliant man-gerial skills did much to establish the Union Générale des Travailleurs unisiens (UGTT) as a major political force, his bourgeois background nd taste for middle-class pleasures hardly made him a working-class repre-entative. In addition, elements in the miners' union, justifiably considered he port and mine workers to be the backbone of the UGTT.

The second crisis of Neo-Destour leadership began as Ben Youssef errorism was being subdued. Early in 1956 Ben Salah began to champion vorking-class interests with more enthusiasm and publicity than is normal n a one-party regime. He pressed for firm policies to prevent inflation, and asked for public debate on the national budget. Over the summer, Bour guiba arranged for a series of round-table talks on the future of th Tunisian economy; at these talks, Ben Salah expressed his views that ag gressive policies should be followed to eliminate French economic influenc and monetary controls.[13] The labor leader openly criticized the country planning effort, and only supported the budget after long talks with Nec Destour ministers. The UGTT began to expand its organizational activitie among workers, and initiated a series of "Popular Education" seminar that might have easily surpassed similar activity in the Neo-Destour.

The crisis reached its full proportions in September, 1956, when th Sixth Congress of the UGTT endorsed a full-scale program for massiv development and social reform.[14] In addition, Ben Salah publicly rejecte the round-table talks as unproductive and excessively conservative. Th labor leader's proposals were essentially the same as those inspiring th Tunisian Three-Year Plan, produced almost exactly six years later. De termined that party solidarity would not be broken, Bourguiba took th daring alternative of starting a rival union organization with Habib Achou the secretary of the Sfax unions, in command. The rival group rejecte "ideological subversion based on imagination and utopian ideas" in favo of a strictly laborers' union seeking concrete benefits for the workers.' With full support from Bourguiba, a compromise figure, Tilili, became Sec retary General of the UGTT soon afterward, and the rival union wa quietly disbanded, having served its purpose. Ben Salah was consoled b becoming Secretary of State for Public Health and Social Affairs; he create a new social-security program and expanded the health program with th same vigor he displayed as a labor leader. Indeed, it was undoubtedl excellent preparation for the task he was later to perform in preparing th first national plan.

The third focus for issues and leadership in Tunisian politics has bee a group of moderates associated with Masmoudi and Ben Yahmed, th editor of *Jeune Afrique*. The subdued character of their opposition prob ably explains how they have been able to survive for so many years withou getting in the way of the Neo-Destour. This is not to imply that thei criticisms are ineffective or their reservations unheeded by the party. I anything, subtlety is a source of strength in a one-party regime. Ben Salah' flamboyancy and ambition offended many middle-class Tunisians, but th pro-French sympathies and liberal sentiments of Masmoudi are muc easier to endorse. Masmoudi, once called Bourguiba's "preferred dis ciple,"[16] has left the Neo-Destour twice. He was also the party's ke negotiator with the French during the hectic days of 1954 and 1955, whe he was ably assisted by Ben Yahmed, then a Parisian student leader.

The importance of quiet opposition is more easily judged by recallin that the Neo-Destour has always been a strongly middle-class party, depending on the merchant, small landowner, and craftsmen for support. Many could be manipulated by the party, although the wealthy, Paris-oriented factor hoped Bourguiba would move slowly in refashioning the nation. Though not openly associated with the introspective Masmoudi clique, the somewhat ponderous, unimaginative wealthy classes no doubt found sentiments they could share (or at least exploit) in the ideas of Masmoudi. Their cooperation is badly needed to achieve the goals of the plan, and their support for the regime has not been sufficiently altruistic or enthusiastic to win much confidence in the higher ranks of Neo-Destourian leadership.[17]

The first open break with the party came in the fall of 1958, when Ben Yahmed published a critical editorial on Bourguiba's proposal to try Tahar Ben Ammar for collusion with the French under the Protectorate. In addition to being a leading member of Tunisian high society, Ben Ammar had participated in several governments under the Protectorate with the full knowledge of Neo-Destour leaders. His political crimes were hardly comparable to Ben Youssef's treason, nor were his financial gains under the French greater than those of many aristocratic Tunisian families. Nevertheless, Bourguiba had the newspaper suppressed for sowing "confusion among opinions and systematically disparaging government policy."[18] Masmoudi defended the relatively mild objections made in the paper, and was removed from the party's Political Bureau. However, the President was in the midst of planning important organizational changes in the Neo-Destour, and needed unanimous support from his colleagues in the forthcoming party congress. Masmoudi was reinstated two months later, and the paper reappeared under a new name.

As Secretary of State for Information, Masmoudi was able to support more liberal press and information policies, but the trend of events in 1960 and 1961 further alarmed the liberal wing of Neo-Destour opinion. In addition, Bourguiba alarmed moderate Tunisians with his unusually aggressive handling of the Bizerte crisis in the summer of 1961. An issue of Ben Yahmed's paper placed a none-too-flattering photo of ex-King Faruk next to an editorial on *pouvoir personnel*. Noting that the police were "omnipresent" if not all powerful in a totalitarian state such as Egypt, the editorial went on to criticize the forces in Tunisia that rendered public discussion impossible by "dislocating, subjugating, or eliminating" rival forces.[19] Again Masmoudi was abruptly removed from office in the Political Bureau and the government. Though not objecting to the Neo-Destour's predominance, the group felt that the Tunisian people had sufficient "political and social conscience" to use wisely those liberties that are "the necessary cement for popular support and national solidarity."[20]

The following story is important not only for the light it sheds on Tunisian politics, but also for the implications the controversy has for one-party governments in other parts of Africa: In a series of editorials in the party paper, Bourguiba's failure to extract concessions from De Gaulle on the Bizerte issue was defended. The editorial went on to claim that the regime had not changed since the removal of the Bey in 1957, and implied that those objecting now were guilty of duplicity or hypocrisy. The paper strongly defended the view that an attack on Bourguiba constituted an attack on the Neo-Destour. In a speech shortly thereafter, Bourguiba insisted that discipline within the party must be total; he added that he personally was "revolted" by confused domestic situations. He concluded that the party would accept criticisms provided that "they do not give place to tenacious interpretations or introduce doubt in (people's) spirits."[21]

The significance of Masmoudi's subtle opposition can only be appreciated by allowing for the critical importance of unanimity among major political figures in a one-party system. Ben Youssef was in open rebellion and easy to eliminate, even though he represented a meaningful and moving alternative to Bourguiba's rule. Ben Salah's appeal was vulnerable partly because of his personal ambition, though this is hardly a rare quality among prominent politicians in any land. More important is the fact that his massive development program unavoidably took on greater importance as the magnitude of Tunisia's economic problems came to be known. Such a program can be carried out only in the framework of a government. Masmoudi represents a threat because, as Bourguiba noted when expelling him, one-party governments work better when domestic problems are simple and when top leadership presents a solid front. What the President did not add was that anything short of unanimity represents an intolerable admission of failure. Controversy among leaders destroys the popular image as well as the working relationships requisite to a one-party regime.

The Masmoudi group can be kept within tolerable limits so long as it does not form an organization, which would almost certainly have to be done at the expense of the Neo-Destour. So far, they have remained subdued critics and vigilant monitors of the one-party system, engaging in limited skirmishes. For example, they recently provoked a minor controversy over the failure of the press to report a serious miners' strike in late 1962.[22] Unless the young liberals can acquire the support of an elder Neo-Destour official, possibly a man having strong sympathy for France such as Mongi Slim, it is doubtful if they can challenge the party's organizational strength in an open contest. The result, as in most one-party regimes, is that a single discordant note echoes loudly throughout the land. Indeed, both the Ben Salah and Masmoudi groups have been able to

xercise considerably more influence on national policy and internal party
atters than a comparable group might do in a multiparty system. Where
overnment and party speak with a single voice, even whispers of divergent
pinions are heard, and may gain surprising support.

Less is known of the top militants in the Neo-Destour than of the groups
ho have criticized them. It should be understood that militancy in the
ontext of the one-party system indicates selfless, and possibly ruthless
evotion to party solidarity. Men like Masmoudi and Ben Salah may have
ntertained thoughts of curbing Neo-Destour excesses or overcoming Neo-
estour cautiousness, but it is unlikely that they imagined a Tunisia with-
ut a powerful Neo-Destour government. The present sense of "militant,"
en, includes those who have been meticulously loyal to Bourguiba, and
ho value party cohesion over any other national issue. This is not to
nply that the other leadership groups are disloyal or opportunistic. In
one-party system, militancy is constantly being tested because party
sues are regularly evaluated in relation to national issues, and the offices
f the government compete daily with party positions for prestige even
hen they have the same occupant. By tracing the role of the devoted
ilitant one learns something of the dynamics of the one-party system,
nd also gains some insight into the future of the Neo-Destour.

Because the paramount militants have never publicly challenged Bour-
uiba's judgment, they are on the whole less well known, and, until recently,
e most influential persons in government. Hedi Nouira, for example, was
ecretary of State for Finance from 1955 to 1958, when he became Director
f the Central Bank of Tunisia. He has been on the party's Political Bureau
ince 1948, and served as deputy Secretary General. He is extremely popu-
ar. His support for Bourguiba in the critical days of late 1955 must have
een most important in neutralizing Ben Youssef's party contacts. An-
ther important leader, Ahmed Mestiri, became Secretary of State for
ustice, where he was instrumental in reforming Islamic legal practices
hat effectively barred fundamentalist Muslim leaders from access to gov-
rnment. Mestiri also wrote the basic civil-service legislation, which affected
large number of Neo-Destour supporters, and reorganized the civil serv-
ce to eliminate vestiges of opposition to Bourguiba.[23]

At the core of Neo-Destour paramilitants is Bahi Ladgham, most fre-
uently seen at the President's elbow and thought to be his most trusted
dviser. Ladgham was the crucial figure in the establishment of the one-
arty state in late 1955. He has been Vice-President and Secretary of
tate for National Defense since 1956.[24] In the struggle for independence
e organized the Tunisian business community, and led the country's
United Nation's mission in the early 1950's. Closely associated with Ladg-
am is his protégé, Taib Mehiri, who has been Secretary of State for the

Interior since 1956. Mehiri, a relatively young man, was a student leader and later assisted in organizing the *fellagha*.

In the scramble for power in late 1955, Ladgham shared Ben Salah' doubts about the economic concessions, police powers, and local-repre sentation rights extracted by the French in the autonomy agreement. H was not a fervent pan-Arabist, like Ben Youssef, but he did not hav confidence in Mendès-France as did Slim and Masmoudi. Above al Ladgham hoped to maintain party unity; to this end he spent most c 1955 abroad trying to dissuade Ben Youssef from actively opposing th agreement.[25] No doubt assisted by Mehiri, he worked tirelessly in the sout to keep the *fellagha* from provoking another French invasion. He returne to Tunis in the hectic days of the November, 1955, Neo-Destour Congress where his decision to support Bourguiba was instrumental in winning ove pan-Arab feeling and in calming justifiable fears of French treachery. I a contest with urbane and popular Mongi Slim, Ladgham emerged as th successor to Ben Youssef as Neo-Destour Secretary General.

The paramilitant in a one-party system is predisposed to exercise influ ence behind doors. Indeed, it is essential to the militant's notion of Tuni sian politics that the party never make radical shifts in policy without care ful preparation, or expose itself to strong conflicting forces. Part of Bour guiba's success formula has been tackling only one center of discontent at a time, and carefully anticipating each engagement in order to isolate forces that might otherwise coalesce. The technique has had great valu in consolidating the nation and in transforming the symbolic legitimac of the independence struggle into a working, respected government. How ever, once the foundations of government are laid down, the role of part and government must be defined. Except in those states like Ghana tha have opted for a highly totalitarian regime, all one-party systems encounte the perplexing task of marking out the functions of an expanding govern ment while the party tends to lose momentum. The potential conflict ir terms of party leadership is manifest, since representatives of both view points sit in the highest councils of both party and government.

Again it should be cautioned that political relationships are too sensitive in one-party systems to assume that the leadership differences are likely to erupt into bitter personal disputes or impassioned opposition parties The Ladgham-Mehiri faction has, however, built a powerful organization within the government based on the services of the Secretary of State for the Interior and, more recently, the army. In a very real sense, the attempt to overthrow the government in late 1962 was evidence of their failure, and of the declining effectiveness of their approach in a developing coun try.[26] Under Mehiri's guidance, a governor was equal to a cabinet mem ber, a phenomenon that can be observed in many African one-party states.

The paramilitants undoubtedly favored the abolition of the Neo-Destour's regionally elected committees in 1959, and the appointment of party commissioners by the Political Bureau.[27] Within the government, the group was concerned over the future of control agencies as opposed to the expansive, decentralizing tendencies of nation-building agencies.

The paramilitants have been justifiably suspicious of Ben Salah's growing empire, partly because he defied the party in 1956 and partly because his organization for developmental purposes may easily surpass the control agencies in size and importance. The issue between Ben Salah and the paramilitants has changed with time, and Ben Salah himself is no longer the brash young man of 1956. In talks with Tunisians in late 1962, as the new plan was being implemented, the nature of the conflict was alluded to on several occasions. The most serious bottlenecks stemmed from new burdens placed on local government, and from the need for more active local support. To coordinate budgeting, planning, and finance, Ben Salah hoped to place a delegate from his ministry in each province. The delegate was to have extraordinary powers. This plan was abandoned, ostensibly because the Tunisians lacked trained personnel, and a new proposal was made to establish regional-development committees under the governors for specific projects. The first of these, a joint committee to implement regional development plans for Kairouan and Sousse provinces, was formed in late 1963.

Possibly a more significant modification was the reorganization of the party following the attempted coup. Bourguiba confessed that the highly centralized party structure and ambition of provincial party commissioners had produced a "duality of authority," detrimental to planning as well as to Neo-Destour popularity. Reportedly, some governors and commissioners clashed so severely that they were not on speaking terms. At a hastily summoned and secret meeting of the Neo-Destour National Council, a mixed body of high party officials,[28] the political commissioners were replaced with provincial "coordination committees." The new committees will group the officers of Neo-Destour cells, representatives of auxiliary party organizations, and selected technical and social advisers. The elected secretary general of the coordination committee will cooperate with the governor in development programs, and will provide better communication with grass-roots groups. The party reorganization is obviously intended to fill new developmental needs, but it is also an implicit refutation of the earlier policy to concentrate effective power in a tightly centralized party.

Though neither leadership group confined its efforts to government or party channels alone, there were additional indications throughout 1963 that the use of government as a development vehicle, essentially Ben

Salah's aim, outweighed the more cautious position of the paramilitant
Under their dominance, youth activities had suffered greatly and Tunisian
students in Paris were a constant source of political embarrassment. At the
height of the difficulty, the Parisian students elected a governing body with
Communist, Trotskyite, and pan-Arab views, completely excluding the
party. In his speeches following the attempt on his life, Bourguiba publicly
admonished the French-trained students' zeal for liberty, and insisted that
more must be done to inculcate patriotic feelings.[29] When Bourguiba's son
returned home, he took over government youth work.[30] By the end of 1963,
steps were taken to improve Neo-Destour youth organizations at the
rapidly expanding secondary educational level.

A related change has been the transfer of UGTT leadership from Tilili
to Achour. Since 1956, the UGTT Secretary General has been Tilili, also
Treasurer of the Neo-Destour. Though primarily a party man, he does not
share the paramilitary notions of the Neo-Destour hard core.[31] Indeed, his
close relation to the President was assurance against the formation of
a potentially formidable coalition of labor and Mehiri or Ben Salah. Nevertheless, the UGTT has pressed constantly for more rapid development,
and its common cause with the new development program is obvious. At
the same time, the union has also forged ahead of the government in spon-
soring workers' housing projects, consumer cooperatives, and some production cooperatives. The UGTT tried for several years to establish its own
bank, and last year was given permission to create the Banque du Peuple
to finance cooperatives, an important sector of the new plan. Throughout
this period, there were various factors among the UGTT leadership, which
in some ways corresponded to the various groups already described.

The most important of these was probably the conventional trade-union
faction, represented by Habib Achour. Achour was a close friend of Hached,
the union's working-class martyr, and had some justification in feeling
that Ben Salah's colorful leadership and political aspirations were not the
best way to achieve labor goals. In the Ninth UGTT Congress in the summer of 1963, Achour became the new Secretary General. Plans were announced to establish Neo-Destour committees for guidance purposes, but
the UGTT also achieved its goal of having workers' committees in major
enterprises.[32] Both changes sharpened the lines between party and union.
In his speech to the workers, Bourguiba defended the workers against
charges of subservience to the party and neglect of the working class.[33]
Despite indications of some labor unrest, the President's comments appear
to be more an assertion of the government's new orientation toward labor,
rather than an expression of anxiety over imminent conflict. The effect of
the changes was to cut the umbilical cord between the Neo-Destour and
the UGTT, and to install a leadership sufficiently wary of Ben Salah to
guard against a new coalition of worker and modernizer in government.

The transformation of a political revolution into a social revolution poses particularly difficult problems for the one-party state. Tunisia's peculiar brand of "Fabian nationalism" may have created obstacles that will be less formidable in other African countries, but the fundamental choice will be similar. The commitment to rapid development creates a new field of activity having specific and coordinated requirements. The success or failure of, say, an agricultural cooperative or a plant to process esparto grass can be observed much more easily by an ordinary Tunisian than, say, the struggle for the evacuation of Bizerte. Development poses radically new problems of selecting and recruiting leadership. The policies advocated, and now being rapidly effected by Ben Salah mean that many more Tunisians will have economic and social opportunities. They will inescapably develop their own talent and judgment in political life. Some of the repercussions can already be detected in Tunisian events.

In the immediate postindependence period there are few challenges to the one-party system, especially if it is built on as thorough and experienced an organization as the Neo-Destour. But the highly centralized, oligarchic party is not necessarily the best vehicle for development. The paramilitants have served a useful purpose in sheltering Tunisia against the inflammatory appeal from Cairo and in bolstering the tiny state during the Algerian war. But even in the second year of intensive planning and development, the dangers of confiscating revolutions are manifest. The student unrest, the rash of strikes, the reluctance to support marketing and agrarian coops, and the declining interest in party affairs raise important problems for the tutelary regime, which may become a refuge for the possessive professor rather than the enlightened teacher.

Leadership groups often represent major social and political alternatives in one-party systems, precisely because the society is less developed and the lines of political exchange are rudimentary. The paramilitant would like to see the Neo-Destour expand in order to dominate the more intricate pattern of political relationships of a complex society. The failure of this approach over 1962 has hopefully served to liberate the Tunisian revolution. The adjustment to youth and labor problems can already be seen. Bourguiba's conversion to "Neo-Destourian socialism" was the first step,[34] the elevation of Ben Salah another. Though Ben Salah's forthright and occasionally arbitrary action to reconstruct the country may arouse some resentment, his model of society is a very different one from that of the paramilitants, whose greatest weakness may be that they have none at all. But Ben Salah's victory will be elusive because success will be measured very differently in the society he hopes to build. The elimination of extremist leadership groups[35] has already reached a point in Tunisia where dramatic issues of national orientation are less meaningful. It remains to be seen if the Neo-Destour can adapt to its own creation.

PART **III**

THE SOCIAL AND CULTURAL SITUATION

5

Changing Cultures and
New Loyalties in North Africa

LEON CARL BROWN

ₙₒᵣₜₕ Aғʀɪᴄᴀ can be classified as part of the recently decolonized world, as an area of underdeveloped nations, or as a component in the "Third World." It is also known as "French-speaking Africa." Yet all of these classifications, useful as they can be in some contexts, are essentially superficial, for they tell us very little about North Africa itself. All too often these broad classifications stand in the way of a meaningful understanding of any single cultural area by implicitly assuming that areas of quite different traditions and backgrounds face essentially the same situation and must choose from the same limited number of responses.

Jacques Berque has commented, in a slightly different context, that there are no underdeveloped societies, merely underanalyzed societies. One infers from his distinction that only a thorough study of all factors of a society will enable one to get beyond such dichotomous rubrics as *under*-developed, *non*-Western, *de*colonized, etc. This is especially true for any discussion of the "culture" of a society or area, for to raise the question of culture or of a cultural area is to assume an entity that stands as a proper subject of study in itself. One can, and indeed must look carefully to see that he has properly isolated his cultural area. He must be especially careful to avoid once-valid but now outmoded definitions, while at the same time giving attention to new orientations just appearing but not yet tested in time. Once this determination is made, however, the major emphasis should be from within. This chapter, "Changing Cultures and New Loyalties in North Africa," is based on the belief that the subject is best served by being

95

studied as a thing-in-itself, and only very indirectly by comparison with other areas.

For this reason, however, it is important to determine whether North Africa (here defined as Algeria, Tunisia, and Morocco) is the proper area of study—i.e., whether North Africa is a culture area or at least well-defined subculture within a greater culture area. An only slightly qualified "yes" seems warranted. North Africa is and has been for over 1,200 years part of the Arabo-Islamic world. However, North Africa's Berber base and a history that since 800 A.D. has often left only the most tenuous political and cultural links with the Arab East has assured North Africa its own cultural identity. North Africa and the Arab East are now going through a process of mutual rediscovery. In view of their cultural traditions it is quite plausible that the Arab East and West may continue to move closer together. If so, at some future point in time the geographic limit for this cultural area might well be all of the Arabic-speaking world. This is not yet the case. North Africa remains a distinct cultural area, or perhaps more properly, a subculture within the Arabo-Islamic world.

The countries of North Africa in modern times have shared a particularly intensive colonial experience under the domination of a single colonizing power, France. This common experience has served as a further unifying bond among the three separate countries. It has also modified precolonial North Africa in a revolutionary fashion, but no one seriously argues that North Africa has moved or will move into the French (or European) cultural framework. Again, North Africa stands out as a properly identifiable cultural area.

North Africa has long had relations across the Sahara with her neighbors to the south. It was from North Africa that Islam reached West Africa and invasions from North Africa have changed the ethnic stock and at times overthrown existing political systems in West Africa. However, viewed from within, it is clear that North Africa itself has always directed its major attention to the east and north. The idea of common effort between North Africa and Africa south of the Sahara is quite new. As an operative ideal it has caught on among the North African elite to an extent surpassing what almost all outside observers would have thought possible a few years ago. That more links will be forged between North Africa and the rest of the continent seems almost certain, but the emergence of a common cultural identity with Africa is another matter. Even if this should happen it remains generations in the future, and it is overwhelmingly more likely that North Africa—if destined to move into a larger cultural framework—will gravitate toward the Arabs to the East.

In sum, North Africa is a distinguishable cultural area vis-à-vis the outside, but can Algeria, Tunisia, and Morocco be properly lumped together?

There are, of course, real differences among the three, more fundamental than the present differences between political leadership and programs (which are imposing enough). For example, Tunisia presents a uniformity and cohesiveness that has always been lacking in Algeria. One could go on listing imposing factors of geography, language, natural resources, and historical experience that present radical differences among the three. These many differences cannot be brushed aside. They have a real impact on day-to-day orientations in North Africa. However, to adopt the helpful distinction between the "great" and the "little" traditions or between the universal and the provincial,[1] it is apparent that those many things that divide North Africans are on the "provincial" or "little traditions" side of the ledger while the uniting factors derive from that "great tradition" that might best be labeled "Western Islam." North Africans are united on the universal level of religion, language (Berber, however tenacious its hold, does not rival Arabic as a language of culture), and common history. Their golden age is the time of the Almohades who combined the three countries and Muslim Spain into a single empire. Their future dreams explicitly call for North African unity.

"What do the people of Kairouan talk about?" asked a ninth-century traveler returning from the East. He was told that the inhabitants of medieval Tunisia's capital talked of the "names and attributes of God."[2] A visitor to Tunisia or any part of North Africa today would find the discussion centering on much more worldly subjects—politics, economic development, education, nation-building, and the emancipation of women. He would also note a certain intensity and enthusiasm always associated with intellectual ferment and social change.

There are various ways of attempting to explain the pattern of this change in North Africa. It can be attributed to the impact of the West. Or, it can be viewed as the move from the static, assured medieval Islamic synthesis to the dynamic but also tension-laden framework of modern, technical society. It can be described as a move from a theocentric to an anthropocentric world-view, what Jacques Berque has labeled the move "from the sacral to the historic."

On a less philosophical and theological (but perhaps more demonstrable) level, what is happening in North Africa can be seen as a major change in the relation of man to state and society. Today in North Africa, as never before, the state is viewed as the legitimate and proper institutionalized political expression of the total society. Even where there is appreciable opposition to existing government, as is the case in both Morocco and Algeria, there is no important opposition to this idea of the expanded—one might almost say total—role of the state.[3]

This is not to suggest that the change has been from tribalized society and/or small local political units to the modern state. On the contrary, North Africa has a longer history of sharing in an ecumenical political and cultural system than Western Europe. In fact, North Africa (just as the Arab East) has never really shaken off the "ecumenical" ideal of polity. As the political expression of Western European ecumenicalism (the Holy Roman Empire) atrophied, nation-states—small units capable of playing an all-embracing role within their boundaries—emerged to fill the gap At that time, there was no such development in North Africa either in practice or in ideology. The closest parallel was the Sharifian system in Morocco, but it remained right down to modern times more nearly an imperial system in microcosm.

In North Africa (as in most of medieval Islam), the state was peripheral to the loyalty system. There was attachment at the level of primary relations to the extended family, the guild, the religious brotherhood, the tribe (in rural areas), or the quarter (in urban). At the top, there was an overriding feeling of identity with the Islamic totality, the *dar al Islam* The "state" was an outside body to be tolerated where necessary, avoided if possible. The sense of need for the state did not transcend the pessimistic concept that any government, even tyrannical, was preferable to anarchy— a very understandable result in a society whose few urban and settled areas lived constantly under the threat of hinterland nomadic and mountain folk.

In contrast to medieval Christendom, with its separation of Church and state, there was in North Africa (as in medieval Islam generally) separation of state and society. Such a structure clearly tilted the balance on the side of political weakness, a weakness that became relatively greater vis-à-vis a Europe waxing strong within the framework of unified nation states. Out of this situation eventually came European domination, a phenomenon that Algeria's Malek Bennabi has perceptively indicated "does not begin by colonization but by the colonizability which provokes it.' This was the beginning of the dialectical process in which the colonizing power provoked—in fact, forced—a reaction and reformulation on the part of the colonized society.[5]

North Africa has been seized with this challenge of colonization and "colonizability" for a long time. French rule in Algeria began as early as 1830, a full half-century before the great imperialist scramble that divided up Africa. From that time Tunisian society was keenly aware of the threat and there were attempts at reform from within linked with the names of Ahmad Bey and Khayr al Din Pasha. Morocco, spared until 1912, chose in large measure to turn its back on the outside world during its period of respite, which partially explains some of the unevenness of development and change in that country to this day.

This long period of colonialism (threat and actuality) has had its results. Several generations of North Africans have lived with these new problems, and with each generation a larger percentage of the society has been drawn into active participation in this dialectical process. North Africa today is a far cry from the turn of the century when a mere handful of French-educated "Young Tunisians" and "Young Algerians" stood in a rather uncertain position between their own native societies and that of the French.

The Moroccan Rif leader, Abd al Krim, who fought the Spanish and French in the 1920's, now appears in historical time closer to Algeria's Abd al Qadir of the 1830's and 1840's than to the present-day Morocco of Hasan II, Ahmad Reda Guedira, Mahjoub Ben Siddiq, and Mehdi Ben Barka. In short, this new cultural orientation in North Africa is no longer the preserve of a small elite. It is a mass phenomenon, and a whole rash of new ideas that only a few decades ago were privately discussed and occasionally openly advocated by the small coteries of western-trained North Africans have been—or are well on the way to being—effectively "naturalized."

The late Ali Belhaouane, a leading Tunisian nationalist, could write in 1954 that the Neo-Destour had fought a two-front war, one against French repression, but also:

a more difficult and trying battle against passiveness, submission, outdated mentalities, disunity and illusions which overwhelmed a large proportion of the population in order to arouse the spirit, stimulate the mind, abolish superstition, destroy outdated customs, tribal particularism and odious fanaticism, and to create a revolution in the depths of the souls. As a result the people today are not what they were in the past.[6]

In a more traumatic way (and in a shorter period of time), the Algerian war accelerated on a mass scale fundamental changes in basic attitudes toward women, the family, and the utility of group action. Morocco, also, although still revealing large areas where the older traditions are more nearly intact, has with its mass political parties, trade-union organization, and increased schooling moved to the stage where the confrontation with and absorption of the new ideas approach a mass phenomenon.

In a word, there has been enough change and readjustment in North Africa for one to talk beyond a new elite and discuss what is becoming discernible, in part at least—a new society. As suggested earlier, this new set of cultural values might best be explained within the framework of the radically changed idea of the state. A brief listing of some of the major social changes should show how many changes that appear quite disparate and unrelated actually fit neatly into the new will of the group to act as an effective unit under leadership of a centralized political control—the state:

1. *The decline of the religious brotherhoods.* The *sufi* religious fraternities—well known in all parts of the Islamic world—had always played an especially important role in North Africa. Several generations of Western scholars, observing the blind obedience of the brotherhood followers to their *shaykh,* felt justified in concluding that these brotherhoods were especially adapted to pre-Islamic Berber practices and beliefs, including the alleged Berber tendency toward anthropolatry. Yet, in the last two generations, this pervasive network of brotherhoods has experienced a rapid decline which, from the 1930's onward, became a complete rout. Today, in North Africa, to ask "But what about the brotherhoods?" is a sure way to court the condescending smile reserved in any age for the Rip Van Winkle.

The brotherhoods, it is usually argued, declined because they introduced heretical practices into orthodox Islam, because most of the leadership collaborated with the French, and because of the very effective campaign waged against them by the Muslim reformist movements, such as the Algerian Association of Ulama. All of this is true, but it is equally important to realize that the brotherhoods filled a real need when the state penetrated only superficially into daily life in urban areas and hardly at all outside the cities. With the establishment of a foreign-dominated centralized state, the brotherhoods became a political anachronism, and with the growth of a nationalist movement (in this context, a desire to run their *own* centralized state), they became a despised anachronism.

2. *The decline of the* ulama *class.* In 1907 a French scholar with many years of experience in Tunisia could write:

The force of centuries-old traditions is such that the representatives of Quranic doctrine are always the guides of public opinion, the counsellors listened to both by the ignorant mass and the rich and educated bourgeoisie.[7]

Today, the Zitouna Mosque-University (the Al Azhar of the Muslim West) has been relegated to the role of a mere *faculté* in the new University of Tunis. The surviving leaders of the Algerian Association of Ulama, which played such an important (and often overlooked) role in preparing the ideological foundation upon which the FLN could create a revolutionary force, are consigned now to unimportant posts in the Ministry of Habous. Even Morocco's Allal al Fassi, who had earlier shown considerable skill in combining other elements with the religious base of his leadership, seem threatened with the possibility of appearing *dépassé.*

Why should the *ulama* class be in eclipse? Certainly, the reasons are not so obvious as is the case of the brotherhood leaders. Except in Tunisia most of the *ulama* played an active role in the nationalist movements. In fact, as implied above, it might well be argued that the members of the Algerian Association of Ulama (founded by Shaykh Abd al Hamid bin adis in 1931) were the protonationalists of Algeria. By the same token, w would deny that in more general terms the successful nationalist reac- on in all three countries grew out of an Islamic matrix, and if certain bservers and even some North African spokesmen are inclined to write ff Islam as a vital force today, this is definitely not the feeling of the vast ajority.[8]

Of course, in large measure the decline of the *ulama* class is the logical utgrowth of the colonial situation, giving the graduate of the western-type chool better career possibilities than his compatriot who had stayed in e traditional educational structure. Symbolic of this change has been e tendency of long-standing *ulama* families in all three countries to send ome (or at times all) of their sons to the western-type schools.[9]

Declining opportunities for those trained as *ulama* lead in turn to de- ining level of competence for those entering the traditional schools—this icious circle is sufficient to explain the fate of the *ulama* class. Yet, at- empts to reform the traditional religious educational structure go back o the nineteenth century—even before the Protectorate in Tunisia, for xample. This present state of affairs did not slip up on the blind side of he *ulama* class, and it seems reasonable to conclude that they would not, erhaps could not "reform." The centuries-old tradition of the *ulama* was ut of line with an ever-growing move toward a strong, unified society led y a strong state. The *ulama* (often almost unconsciously in these latter ecades, it would seem) represented separation of society from state. They tood for a private school system independent of the state and in no way eared to the needs of the state. One of the natural careers of the graduate f Zitouna or of Qarawiyin was that of judge in the Shari'a courts—that last emnant of the religious law to escape state control. Equally, the *ulama* ad a vested interest in the Islamic pious foundations (the *habous*), a sys- em that in the eyes of the modern, centralized state was an unacceptable evice for removing real property from state control.

Even assuming that the best possible talent had continued to be recruited, he *ulama* tradition was ambiguous vis-à-vis the states. On the one hand, he state was to be supported because any government was better than narchy. On the other hand, the hero of *ulama* literature had been for cen- uries the brave religious leader who stood up to the "unjust" ruler. Echoes f this ambivalence can still be seen among the present *ulama*. As long s the presently accepted ideology prevails, the *ulama* will be either pushed side or given subordinate positions in the state apparatus.

3. *The educational revolution.* An adequate treatment of the role of ducation in modern North Africa could be rendered only by giving a omplete history of the nationalist movements. One need only recall the "Young Tunisians" and "Young Algerians," whose major mark of distinc-

tion was their Western orientation gained through French education, (the generation of naturalist leaders that includes Belafrej, Bourguiba, an Abbas—all profoundly shaped by a French higher education—or the ro of such pivotal institutions as Sadiqi College in Tunis, or, finally, the can paign for additional schools—the modern Quranic or Free Schools—in a three countries, a campaign intimately linked with the early growth of a effective nationalism in each of the three countries.

Today, independent Morocco, Algeria, and Tunisia devote between 1 per cent and 20 per cent of their budgets to education. All aspire to attain ing universal and compulsory primary education, and they have made not worthy progress in this direction. In the school year 1962–63, 43 per ce of primary-school-age children in Algeria and Morocco and 55 per cent i Tunisia were actually in school.[10] These simple statistics bear witness t a revolutionary development. North Africa, for the first time in its lon history, is on the threshold of an egalitarian-oriented mass culture base on mass literacy.

Since this parallels the American ideal, there is the danger of our applau ing this development rather smugly without realizing some of the implic: tions. Indeed, why should North Africans place such emphasis on ma: education? Why are the leaders of all three countries so devoted to unifor national systems of education? Why are these newly independent cour tries—who had struggled to preserve their own Arabo-Islamic identity— willing to accept that much of their education should indefinitely remai French rather than risk the prospect of declining standards by switchin to Arabic?

These decisions can be explained in part by inertia (the new holde of power must often rely on previous plans and procedures or risk admir istrative chaos) and emulation of the more powerful nations. Howeve, it would be a grave error to underestimate the amount of deliberation th: went into the establishment of educational policies in North Africa. Th North African leaderships believe that the educational structure is th major implement for creating a strong, unified society. Education toda is seen as national; it is an essential element in that major aim—a stron state.

Probably every North African knows from personal experience how th existence of different school systems—traditional, Franco-Arab, and Frenc —can create different mentalities. And different mentalities add to divisio and weakness. As early as 1947, the present Tunisian Minister of Educa tion, Mahmud Messadi, could argue as a "sacred principle . . . the necessit of safeguarding the cultural unity of a country. . . . Education is socia integration."[11] A unified education is seen as a means of breaking dow division that can weaken the nation, divisions such as that between th abyles and the Arabs in Algeria, between the Berber mountaineers and e plainsmen in Morocco, and between the urban Tunisian and the rural unisian (the *'Afaqi,* those from "beyond the horizon").[12]

Education, then, must be unified but it must also turn its back on tradional forms, for the strong society needs not only unity but efficacy. This quires a modern technical training. A recent FLN statement announced terse Marxist style, "Algerian culture will be national, revolutionary d scientific."[13] In a more tangible way, Bourguiba has spelled out what accepted as an article of faith by almost all the ruling elite and the new neration:

the place of syntax, morphology, literature, *fiqh* [religious law], grammatical rms and *mu'allaqat* of poetry one must teach people to undertake useful ork for their country. A professional training is needed. . . . We are in the rocess of forming young men to use machines, get accustomed to central ating, electricity, etc. . . .[14]

4. *Female emancipation.* As with education, female emancipation is inparable from the whole story of national development in North Africa. 1 another sense, the two subjects—education and female emancipation— rve as guidelines in the process of social change, for the new concept f education was one of the first major changes to gain acceptance while male emancipation raised and still raises the greatest resistance. Almost ll Moroccan women remain veiled, and in spite of the provocative thesis f Frantz Fanon[15] about the revolutionary change in the idea of the veil Algeria as a result of the war, it is not yet clear that Algeria suddenly imped several generations in its thinking about the opposite sex during e war years. Still, increased school attendance by girls in all three coun- ies indicates clearly which way future developments will go, and if the ast history of Tunisia is a guide, there will likely be a major breakthrough ollowed by rapid change. In the late 1920's, Bourguiba himself was in vor of keeping the veil, and in 1930 Tahir al Haddad was relieved of is teaching position at Zitouna Mosque-University for his book advocating male emancipation. Today Tunisian women enjoy legal equality, and ere are several dynamic women's organizations.

A recent poll of Tunisian students indicates the extent of change. Three ategories of Tunisian male students—those from Tunis, those from the rovinces studying in Tunis, and those from the provinces studying in he provinces—were asked, "Would you accept the fact that your sisters reely go out with young men?" The findings are shown in Table 1.[16] What significant, surely, is not that almost 30 per cent answered no, but rather hat such a question would be seriously considered and in fact receive omewhat over 50 per cent acceptance (total conditional and uncondi-

TABLE 1

	Total in Sample	No	Great Hesitation	Conditional Acceptance	Complete Acceptanc
Tunis students	59	22%	14%	47%	17%
Provincial students in Tunis	114	32%	15%	35%	18%
Provincial students in the provinces	60	30%	18%	29%	23%
Average		29%	15.5%	36.5%	19%

tional). That the difference between Tunis and provincial students wa not more marked is also an interesting index of the extent to which the ide of unity (and in a sense uniformity) is striking roots.

The drive for female emancipation stems from many sources, includin liberal and moral considerations and—as with education—emulation o more powerful nations, but the question of social efficacy and state powe is definitely engaged. A quarter-century ago, Tahir al Haddad, in a poen answering critics of his stand on female emancipation, made this point quit clear:

> They [i.e., the *ulama*] say to Islam,
> "We want Sovereignty"
>   While their actions push back this aim
> With false words they play the coquette with Reform.
>   But they actually block development.
> How can Muslims be masters of their own lands
>   When they are ignorant of the ways and means?[17]

Today, even more clearly than in Tahir al Haddad's time, those who woul change their society realize that each generation must start afresh unles the mothers can also be changed. Bourguiba was able to make the poin by use of a very simple, but striking example:

There are countries which initiate the child from his earliest youth in manua work. Instead of an intact toy he is given an unassembled railroad or a dol in pieces in order to accustom him to put the objects back together, to arrange cut, sew, repair, in a word, teaching him to tinker, to use his hands. With us and especially among the mothers, there is an ignorance of the value of tinker ing and of manual labor for children. In her ignorance, the mother spanks th children when she sees him playing with pieces of wood or of cloth. She take them from him and throws them away, saying "Go learn your lessons."[18]

5. *The growth of new social organizations.* North Africa today teem with mass political parties, trade unions, women's societies, organization

of students or youth, and the ubiquitous sports clubs, to name only the most prominent categories. In several respects, these new, and largely Western-inspired organizations differ from older social forms: (a) They are based on the principle of voluntary rather than ascriptive membership. One joins these organizations. He is not born into them. (b) They are centralized, most of them being organized on the national level. (c) They transcend the old primary-group basis of most earlier North African social groups. They are more impersonal, deriving their *raison d'être* from certain principles or interests rather than from personalities. (d) Unlike the older guilds or religious brotherhoods, these new organizations do not exist outside of the state, fulfilling certain functions in lieu of the state. Rather, they are intimately related to the state. The present state, in contrast to its medieval predecessor, is very concerned with these forms of social organization, works through them, and usually seeks to dominate them.

It is perhaps most accurate to view these new forms of social organization as the necessary complement to the prevailing new idea of the state. They are both cause and effect, having themselves grown up with the new nationalism. A strong state existing at the apex of many extensive, impersonal social organizations can be seen as the natural consequence of the move away from the older idea of a separation of state and society, from emphasis on the primary group relationship—extended family, guild, brotherhood, and tribe.

This new dedication to unified group action—the new idea of the state —has been suggested here as the most important single framework for understanding the changing culture in North Africa today. Admittedly, this approach is not completely satisfactory. It does not face directly the question of how Arab, how Muslim, in short, how rooted to its own traditions, North Africa will remain. Yet this very limitation is perhaps its chief virtue. The new idea of the state is nourished by modern Western concepts of the nation and also by the old sense of identity with and loyalty to the *umma*. North Africans can reject major institutions of an older Islam without abandoning Islam. The problem of identity (the intrusive "outside," French language, Western techniques, etc., versus the traditional, native, Arabic, Muslim) is now less acute with independence, and, in any case, after the long colonial experience, many of these "outside" forces have been effectively naturalized.

Almost a century ago the desire to unite state and society began to take root in North Africa. The slow move of this idea from isolated individuals to small groups to mass organizations was—in several senses of the word— a matter of generations. There is now something approaching consensus, which—as always—creates a powerful human force. North Africa has entered a stage in which rapid social change is feasible. Whether this change will be for good or ill is not for the outsider to predict, or perhaps even to judge. He can—and freely does—offer his interest, sympathy, and genuine best wishes.

6

Tribalism and
Social Change in North Africa

ERNEST GELLNER

A VARIETY of notions attach to the idea of a "tribe." A tribe can be thought of as a social unit that is an island unto itself, even conceptually: Its members conceive of themselves as the totality of humankind and the tribal ancestor as the ancestor of all men. In less extreme form, a tribe can be thought of as a society that is morally, though not conceptually self-sufficient: All moral obligation is exhausted within the community, and no rights or obligations exist without it. The second of these criteria is often used by anthropologists. In these senses, there are *no* tribes in North Africa, and there have been none throughout that past that concerns us.

The term "tribe" is also often used for linguistic-cultural groupings too small, too archaic, or too lacking in self-consciousness to fall into the category of "nation." For these groups the French employ the useful term *ethnie,* but this term does not apply to North African tribalism. Throughout North Africa there are, it is true, two ethnic groups, Arabs and Berbers: but it would be absurd to refer to all North African Arabs as one tribe, or to all North African Berbers as another tribe, in *any* sense of the word. Both Arabs and Berbers display a linguistic continuity (though not identity), and indeed they share a cultural continuity. There are no sharp cultural boundaries between them, no breaks in communication.

In what sense, then, is North Africa a tribal region?

Two concepts, at least, are required to answer this question. North African tribal groupings are *segmentary,* and they are *marginal.* The notion of "segmentary" social organization is in common use among anthropologists. The idea of "marginal" tribalism, though perhaps often implicit in the treatment of Muslim societies, needs to be elucidated.

Segmentary tribalism. Professor E. E. Evans-Pritchard says the following of the Bedouin of Cyrenaica:

> The tribal system, typical of segmentary structures everywhere, is a system of balanced opposition . . . and there cannot therefore be any single authority in a tribe. Authority is distributed at every point of the tribal structure and political leadership is limited to situations in which a tribe or segment acts corporately. . . . There cannot, obviously, be any absolute authority vested in a single Shaikh of a tribe when the fundamental principle or tribal structure is opposition between its segments. . . .[1]

The manner in which segmentary tribes are organized—and all North African tribes are segmentary—is well summed up in this passage, though possibly in a manner too condensed and cryptic for a nonanthropologist. I shall endeavor to make the ideas involved more explicit.

Segmentary organization dispenses to a considerable extent with the concentration of power or authority in individual centers; it dispenses also with specialized law-and-order-maintaining agencies. In brief, it minimizes political specialization. Instead, order is mantained—to the extent to which it is maintained at all—by the balance of power between reasonably well-matched groups. An Arab saying sums up this attitude; "I against my brothers; my brothers and I against our cousins; my cousins and brothers and I against the world." The principle of social cohesion implied by the saying does not require ranking and authority: "Brothers are united not by the authority of some senior branch of the family but by a fear of the threatening outside world. The external enemy, not the authoritative internal leader, is the agent of cohesion.

To make the saying a more exact account of segmentary organization, it would need to be expanded: "I against my brothers; my brothers and I against our cousins; my cousins and brothers and I against distant cousins; my cousins and distant cousins against the rival clan in the village; the whole village against the neighboring village; a group of villages (say, "canton") against the neighboring canton; and so forth. Loyalty and group membership is relative to the conflict in question, to the size of the groups involved. A division of a house may separate brothers, the inheritance of field cousins, the use of an irrigation ditch between fields intravillage clans, the use of a pasture villages.

The individual is thus encapsulated in a series of concentric circles. Although these circles are of differing sizes, they never cut across each other: family, wider family, intravillage clan, village, clan-of-villages, and so on. A diagram of the society as a whole resembles a tree, the trunk being the total society, the major branches being the larger clans, the minor branches the subclans, and so on.

Each group is fairly symmetrical: There is further subdivision into similar, symmetrical subgroups and segments, but there are no specialized agencies or political leaders to ensure the cohesion of the groups. The cohesion is only activated by threats and dangers from similar "opposed, balancing" groups.

To what extent does this political organization, which minimizes leadership and specialization, actually fit North African rural life? The answer is, very closely. It fits Berber tribes more closely than it does Arab tribes, for Berber tribes frequently do without hereditary leadership, electing and rotating chieftains instead: Power is diffused. Arab tribes, like the ones mentioned by Evans-Pritchard in the passage quoted, do have shaikhly families, and to that extent approximate a segmentary type of symmetry and diffusion of power.

Two mistakes, or rather exaggerations, are current in some of the literature on North Africa. One is that this segmentation is always conceived genealogically; the other that the principal agent of maintenance of order is the *moiety,* the famous *"leffs"* and *"soffs."*

The simplest way to conceptualize a segmentary organization is through unilineal descent. If descent is reckoned in males or females only, and if every individual knows a fair number of his (real or supposed) ancestors, the result is inevitably a tree-like structure, such as is required by a segmentary society. And, or course, all North African societies are patrilineal (unless we count the Saharan Tuareg as being in North Africa). But segmentary organization can also be expressed territorially, and sometimes is.[2]

Robert Montagne's brilliant and fundamental study of Berber society popularized the notion that order is maintained in anarchaic Berber lands by the coexistence of two permanent leagues or parties arranged characteristically like the squares on a chessboard.[3] This dualistic organization may hold for some areas, but it is not general.[4] Tribal groupings *sometimes* segment in a binary way, but more often they divide into a larger number of segments.

But a more important criticism is this: Even if the chessboard-pattern moieties *were* universal in the Berber tribal world, this would not constitute an adequate explanation of the order-maintaining mechanisms of these societies. Suppose that each "square" on this chessboard represents a "canton," a valley, or a group of villages. What is to keep order if a dispute breaks out (as, it will) within this group, or within subgroups of it? There are, after all, no specialized political institutions within each unit on the board, any more than there are any between them. Either there is another chessboard system of moieties within each unit of the larger system, which would lead to a social structure of unmanageable complexity (and in any case, there is no evidence for this, and no one has claimed to find any), or the question remains unanswered.

French research into the political life of the Berbers was badly hampered by the lack of a notion of a "segmentary" tribal structure. The *leffs,* moieties, may provide part of the answer as to how order is maintained, in those areas where they effectively exist, but they only provide the answer with respect to conflicts occurring between units of certain size (i.e., those units that happen to operate at the level of *leff* alliances); they cannot provide the answer with respect to units of other sizes. In fact, however, segmentary societies such as those of the Berbers do (and must) possess units of all sizes, and conflicts occur all along the line. Thus we must go beyond the notion of moieties, to that of segmentariness, to characterize and explain North African tribal life.

Marginal tribalism. North African tribal units were tribal in the past in that they tended to run their own political affairs: Order was not maintained from above and outside by some kind of state machinery. But they were not islands unto themselves conceptually and morally. They were part of a wider Islamic civilization, and they identified enthusiastically and firmly with Islam. They were on the *margin* of a wider society, universalistic and nontribal.

Hence, if tribal groups opted out of the wider political system, and refused to accept orders or officials from a central authority, they were dissidents, opters-out, and they knew it. The same was true if they opted out morally, at least to the extent of observing a tribal custom known to differ from the Holy Law of Islam. Clearly, there is a difference between a tribalism that is self-sufficient and a tribalism that shares the concepts and beliefs of a wider society and that, where it differs from them, defines itself in opposition (brazen or shamefaced, as the case may be) to that society. North African tribalism is of the latter kind.

Traditionally, North African tribes were segmentary and marginal. They were organized into groups of different sizes, the larger embracing the smaller; at each level, group cooperation was generally only activated by an outside threat. They were marginal to a wider civilization whose faith and ideas they shared, but from whose political order—and, to a lesser degree, moral order—they had opted out.

One should add that the "segmentary" principles of organization were complemented by some others. Of these, the most important were expressed in religious terms: a reverence for a local shrine or holy lineage, or an affiliation to a religious "order" in and across the boundaries of the segmentary groupings. This was by far the most important modification of the segmentary system. These local (and questionably orthodox) forms of

Islam are not merely modifications of the tribal order that make it work better, they are also essentially connected with the "marginality" of the tribes: They were the means by which passionate identification with Islam is made compatible with the partial opting out.

The connection between tribalism and contemporary social change—the drive, deliberate or otherwise, toward modernization—is generally seen as a negative one: Tribal organization, loyalty, and ethos are thought of as obstacles to social change. But tribalism and social change are also connected in traditional society: There, tribes appear as agents of change, rather than as brakes on it.

It is relatively easy to schematize the structure of the traditional North African Islamic state. A dynasty is based upon towns, which are garrisons and centers of trade and Muslim learning. The dynasty is supported by privileged, tax-exempt tribes (which, in the case of medieval Moroccan dynasties, for instance, tend to be the tribes of origin of the dynasty itself). Outside the inner circle of protected towns and privileged tribes, there is a middle circle of tribes subjected to the dynasty and administered by local notables, who are dependent on local support, rather than transferable administrators appointed from the center. Finally, there is the outer circle of dissident or semidissident tribes who successfully defy central authority. We have, then, those who extract taxes, those who have taxes extracted, and those who do not allow taxes to be extracted from them, a paradigm of the human condition.

Both the structure and the dynamics of this type of society were laid bare by Ibn Khaldun in the Middle Ages, and fundamentally his analysis continued to be valid until the intrusion of the modern European world. (Some modifications might be required to allow for the Turkish dynasties in Algiers and Tunis and for the fact that postmedieval Moroccan dynasties emerged from holy, "sharifian" lineages rather than from tribal groupings in the full sense.)

The essence of the dynamics of Ibn Khaldun's account is a kind of doctrine of the circulation of elites, where the circulating units are neither individuals nor classes, but tribes. Dissident tribes, welded into cohesion by the anarchic conditions in which they have to survive, periodically destroy the town-based dynasty, and replace it—only to be replaced in turn some generations later.

Why do not the tribes from the outer shadow of dissidence erupt permanently into the civilized world of the towns? After all, they try hard enough. Two reasons can be given to explain why they do not always succeed. First, when the dynasty at the center is still young, the tribe supporting it still retains the cohesion and vigor formed in the desert, and thus is capable of defending itself effectively. Second, the wolves beyond the pale neutralize each other in internal strife. They are—though Ibn Khaldun lacked this concept—segmentary.

This social change is of course cyclical. It leads to no fundamental transformation—unlike that social change that preoccupies us in the twentieth century. It merely rotates the personnel within a fundamentally stable structure. It also transforms the personnel itself: It turns socially cohesive and hence militarily formidable tribes into conquerors, conquerors into city-dwellers, and, ultimately, city-dwellers into uncohesive and militarily feeble groups. The fundamental proposition of Ibn Khaldun's sociology is, in effect, the antithesis of cohesion and civilization. Only tribes produce cohesion.[5] Only towns produce civilizations. Neither towns nor tribes can dispense with the other: Ibn Khaldun considers that tribes need towns economically (in contrast to a modern and questionable stereotype of tribes as autarchic), while towns need tribes for their protection. Each side needs the other, and each is also the fatality of the other. There is no breaking out of the circle.

This account, of course, does not hold true of all societies, even if Ibn Khaldun supposed it did. It held of the society he was concerned with. Notoriously, it does not apply to Europe. In the eighteenth century, when Gibbon was studying the decline and fall of the Roman Empire and wondering whether it could happen again, he noted with surprise that barbarians beyond the *limes* were no longer a danger: Civilization and cohesion were no longer incompatible, and the civilized were more formidable than the tribesmen, such as were left. But this never happened in traditional North Africa. Even in the twentieth century, tribesmen were liable to appear under the very walls of civilization.

It is tempting to try to use North Africa to illuminate social change that failed to occur there and that did occur in Europe. (Perhaps the absence of fundamental change calls for no special explanation, and only the European miracle does.) But if one does look for an explanation of why there was no break-out from the fatality described by Ibn Khaldun, one is bound to look first at the relative weakness of the towns. But the towns, because they required protection from the ever-menacing tribes, were unlikely to challenge the central authority.[6] The urban middle classes were weak not only militarily but even economically, it seems. In the fascinating passage in which Ibn Khaldun foreshadows Keynes and the doctrine of the need for governmental spending in order to keep the economy primed—in which he describes, in other words, the "multiplier" effect and the unfortunate consequences of governmental economizing in times of depression—it is interesting to note the point on which he differs from Keynes: The villain whose underspending causes depression is not he trading middle class, but government itself. It seems it was the rulers, he court, not the urban middle class, whose use or failure to use their purchasing power had the effect of pushing the economy up or down.

The modern period. The modern period consists of two stages: the colonial period and independence. But both the colonial and the independent regimes have in common a total change, in contrast to traditional society, in the balance of power between central government and the peripheral social groupings. Henceforth, the countryside, including mountains and desert, can be governed as effectively as towns—indeed, as the experience of the French Protectorate in Morocco showed, more so. The great new anonymous slums can go into dissidence, become ungovernable, more easily than can tribes in mountain or desert fastnesses.) This factor is common throughout: the incomparably greater effectiveness of government in rural areas. Henceforth, central government is no longer a peripatetic court and army, represented by local notables with local support (where represented at all); it is, instead, an administrative bureaucracy at the center of an effective network of communication, represented locally by bureaucrats, paid from the center, and transferable.

What effect has this on tribal structures? Plainly, it erodes tribal cohesion. Tribes, and in particular segmentary tribes, are kept together by external threats. But an effective administration, by definition, does not tolerate threats emanating from other groupings, and it does not tolerate resistance to its own demands. Hence, tribal cohesion is eroded both by governmental pressure and by the removal of other forms of pressure. The traditional society was in the grip of a certain kind of circle (vicious or beneficent, according to whether one deplores, or romantically regrets, the passing of traditional society): Weak government necessitated strong tribes, strong tribes ensured weak government. Now, this circle has been broken.

But this erosion does not operate equally and symmetrically in all contexts. In some places it is complete; in others it is partial and may even have produced countereffects—i.e., of strengthening some aspects of the social structure. The difference in effect depends on a number of variables: (1) the date of the colonial conquest; (2) the type of colonial administration and policy; (3) the geographical milieu of the tribal groupings—whether open plain, or mountainous country; (4) the type of social organization and general tradition of the tribal groupings; and (5) the extent of the economic implantation—both in the form of activity and of actual settlement of population—by the colonizing power. There may perhaps be other factors, but these are the ones that manifestly did operate.

Some tentative generalizations may be put forward about the manner of operation of each of these factors:

(1) The length of time for which a superimposed administration has

had to work on the tribal society clearly has an effect on the degree of erosion. Algeria has had the longest colonial period, as well as the longest and most disruptive period of national struggle. Present researchers into the social structure of Algeria report that, in most places, it is impossible to find anything that would be describable in the concepts of classic tribal ethnography.[7] But this factor of time does not operate alone and should not be exaggerated, for there is no simple correlation between length of occupation and erosion.

Algeria was occupied longest, but it also had an administration which, after a time, tended not to take a close interest in rural communities, partly no doubt as a result of a considerable lack of interest—administrative, ethnographic, or romantic—in the backwoods population, partly as a consequence of the fiction that Algeria was French. By contrast, French administration in Morocco had a quite different ideology, indeed, it had a mystique: Moroccan traditional institutions were supposed to be protected or maintained by the "protecting power." Rural administration was fairly thick on the ground and effective, in striking contrast to the situation in Algeria,[8] and it found romantic fulfillment in the implementation of an ideology which, in the British Empire, went by the name of "indirect rule."[9] The effect may have been the opposite of the one intended. Tribesmen left alone on the theory that they were in a part of France may have been incorporated into the modern world more quickly than those who were closely administered by officers or officials concerned with not unduly disturbing the tribal structure (or what they conceived the tribal structure to be). Thus factor (2) could counteract factor (1).

In this connection, it is worth noting that the colonial system in Morocco brought about, for the last time perhaps, one of those rotations, circulation of elites, that was the life of the traditional society: Once the wolves of the dissident outer lands were subdued, they became the sheepdogs of the central government. Tribal levies, raised by chieftains such as the Glawi, or by the French directly, were used to maintain order. But this time, the wolves were not allowed to found a new dynasty.

Factors (3), (4), and (5) tended, on the whole, to operate together, in the same direction; consequently, it is difficult to disentangle their relative importance. It was in the plains that modern economic activity and European settlement were important; it was also, on the whole, the plains that had been occupied by Arab tribes, with their more permanent and marked leadership. The mountains, on the other hand, were predominately Berber, with tribal groupings organized in an egalitarian, more purely segmentary form, and hence, I think, less vulnerable. Further, the mountains were unsuitable for modern agriculture or economic enterprise. And, of course, it is in the mountains that cohesive groups are still to be found. In the plains, they are disappearing rapidly, even in areas where the impact of the modern world is relatively recent.[10] In the lowlands of Algeria, they have in the main disappeared.

One general point can be made, however, about those areas where tribal groupings have *not* disappeared (i.e., in the main, in Berber-speaking mountain areas). Under an effective administration, it is the largest groupings, the more abstract loyalties, that disappear, even if the more specific, village-scale tribal organization survives. The larger groupings were kept together by larger conflicts, and these a modern administration cannot tolerate. Conflicts over, let us say, large summer pastures, involving tribal groupings numbered in the tens of thousands, cannot be carried on "underground," as it were. Since they must be carried on overtly, they can, therefore, be controlled by the administration.

In Morocco, these larger groupings still survive in memory, in name, in custom, perhaps in sentiment, and not surprisingly so, for in certain regions they functioned in full vitality until 1933 and retained some measure of reality under the French administration until 1955–56. The very large tribe of the Ait Atta, for instance, still has certain collective pasture rights across the main Atlas watershed, and every summer brawls take place between the shepherds and the trans-watershed inhabitants over these rights. Government gendarmes (*mokhaznis*) are usually called in to settle the disputes. But this is, I believe, an exception. Where tribal organization remains vigorous, it is the smaller groupings on the segmentary scale, the units of about village size and smaller, that survive.

It is interesting to note, however, that the smaller groupings may actually acquire a greater cohesion in these circumstances than before. In the traditional society, a village-sized grouping, Ait X (let us say), was part of a larger grouping, Ait Y, and shared its customary law and some institutions with the other villages comprising Ait Y. Under modern conditions, those wider institutions will disappear. For instance, there will no longer be a reversed intervillage saint, an *agurram,* whose arbitration could be sought and shared by a whole region.[11] Hence the village-sized units become doubly inward-turned, opting out of the administrative-legal system imposed by the official administration, but lacking, at the same time, a wider tribal context into which to fit. Without having any real field-work knowledge of the region, I suspect something of this kind must have been true of Kabylia.

The evaporation of the larger-scale tribal unit is not contradicted by another phenomenon, a certain kind of regional sentiment that appears to exist in areas such as the Rif, Kabylia, and the Middle Atlas. Local risings have occurred in both the Rif and in Kabylia since the independence of Morocco and Algeria. The local sentiment, which, in part, was at the root of these risings, is different from the old tribal feelings. During one of the troubles in Kabylia, it was not unusual to read journalists referring to the Kabyles as a "tribe"—which, of course, they are not. In part, these risings are more in the nature of an exercise of pressure on the central government by one faction, which happens to be well organized in the region, but which is not really a regional movement at all. (In Morocco, the political leader Ahardane, later Minister of War, and apparently a loyal royalist, claimed to me to have been connected with the Rif rising, without actually having taken part in it. He claimed that he was coresponsible for its termination by negotiation with the then government on terms that included the official recognition of his own political party, semiclandestine up till then. The demand for such a recognition was, he claimed, part of the motive of the rising.) I have argued this at greater length elsewhere.[12]

In part, these movements seem to resemble something like a modern nationalism, a sense of cultural separateness. Prophecy is a dangerous business, but it seems to me most unlikely that they will mature into an effective nationalism. Berbers are not quite as nonself-identifying as is sometimes claimed,[13] but it seems to me that they lack the precondition of an effective modern nationalism: a middle class and an intelligentsia. Berbers who become either of these things generally thereby also cease to be Berbers.

A Berber nationalist movement would have to do more than "go to the people" and galvanize rustics into a national self-consciousness: It would also have to create those classes that, elsewhere, have led nationalist movements. Hitherto, there have been only Moroccan, or perhaps pan-Maghrebi nationalists, but hardly Berber ones. This fact, reflected (or perhaps caused by) the lack of a written Berber language, or even a dominant dialect, and connected, of course, with the absence of Berber urban life, is most crucial —more than the geographical discontinuity of Berber-speaking regions— in militating against the emergence of a real Berber nationalism. But regional discontent is possible, and can lead to the giving of support to leaders with local appeal.

But even this phenomenon is more a matter of following a leader who has built up a local network of patronage than of a sentiment born of a shared cultural background. Patronage is necessary, both ways: The leaders need rural followers, whose support, possibly votes, they need to invoke. The rural followers need patrons near the center of government. Thus networks are built up. These networks may be unevenly distributed, but their basis is not local feeling: It is rather the need for protection, partly perhaps against central government (or some of its agencies), but partly also in local conflicts. Success is liable to snowball, and a successful leader might end with the loyalty, at least temporary, of a whole region. On

ie whole, however, it is more important to remember the principles of
segmentary organization than to credit the tribesmen with some overwhelming tribal sentiment.

In Algeria, the conflict of leaders supported by local patronage groups
as to be played out within the assumption of a one-party system, for
rival parties have failed to secure recognition, at least as yet. In Morocco
on the other hand—with its entrenched multiparty system—the game is
played out between a number of parties.

This, then, seems to be the role of the tribes, or what remains of them,
in the political conflict of the North African states and the political transformation they are undergoing. The tribes are not likely to reappear as
bearers of new dynasties (even presidential ones) or as fighters of rear-
guard actions on behalf of local traditions.[14] Rather, they appear as local
support groups, as regional redoubts for parties and leaders in a conflict
which easily become violent and in which it is consequently valuable to
have regional redoubts.

The economic aspect. In economics, as in politics, one is wise to beware
of stereotypes inspired by parts of the world other than North Africa.
Students of, say, India or West Africa, have habituated us to the picture
of tribalism, or the extended family, as an obstacle to economic growth.
The picture of the potentially enterprising individual who must share all
he gains with an extended network of kin, and whose incentive is thus
destroyed, does not seem to me to apply to North African tribesmen. A
recent American book on North Africa observes of the Berbers: "A collective mode of life is common, with the sharing of crops. . . ."[15] This is in-
correct. There is no sharing of crops. There are certain collectivist elements.
The tribes tax themselves, in order to give joint donations to the holy men,
in order to supply collective festivals, and so on. They do, as the author
observes, store the crops "in a joint, usually fortified granary." But note:
Inside the joint granary, each family has its own cubicle to which it alone
has access. There is individualism within the collectivism, and the collectivism is only kept in being by shared external dangers. It is not much
deeper than that.

In a certain sense, tribes do, it is true, hold lands in common. First of
all, pastures are owned jointly. Fields are not, or only in the sense that
tribal customary law makes it difficult to sell a field to a nonmember. (On
the other hand, the same customary law makes it relatively easy for a
foreigner to gain tribal "naturalization," so the two rules cancel out in some
measure.) This rule tends to fall into disuse in modern conditions; in any
case, in the mountains where the tribes survive, large-scale agriculture is
impracticable, so that this law does not greatly affect such avenues toward
agricultural improvement as exist.

The important point is that the spirit of economic enterprise does exist and is not damped down, as far as I can see, by a dead weight of kin obligations. Of course, in the days of anarchy, the tribesman needs his kinsmen for security, which is a more important consideration than enrichment. But give him safety from above, and the principle of fission, which co-exists with that of fusion in every segmentary society, becomes much more powerful.[16] The effective social units among which wealth must be shared are small—or become so in conditions of security. The clan does not stand between the tribesman and economic enterprise—whether it be enterprise as a petty trader or the pursuit of employment as a laborer.

Moreover, there are certain cases of interesting tribal adaptations to a modern economy: The Ibadi religious minority sends out grocers from Djerba to the rest of Tunisia, and traders from Mzab travel to the rest of Algeria. Southern Morocco has produced tribes of grocers—families keeping alive by sending their menfolk in rotation to be grocers in the towns—without the aid of any Weber-type religious psychology. And, of course, the manner in which the Kabylia lives from remittances of Algerian workers in France is well known.

One should add that a money economy is nothing new for the tribesmen: Their familiarity with it long antedates their incorporation into stable government. And most tribes were not, contrary to stereotype, autarchic. Traditional markets were places where members often met, as has been pointed out, explosively.

Just what these facts entail for economic development, whether in its Algerian socialist variant or in its more laissez-faire Moroccan form, I am not sure. In the economic, as much as in the political sphere, it does not seem to me that North African tribalism constitutes an insurmountable or even very terrifying obstacle to progress. No doubt there are others—but this one does not seem to me to predominate.

7

Sub-Saharan Education
and Rural Development

DAVID HAPGOOD

EDUCATION, in the broad sense, is the means by which a society hands on its culture from generation to generation. Social conformity is imposed on children through education. In order for education to successfully integrate children into society, the society must itself have reached agreement on the values it wishes to convey. However, the values taught by schooling are usually invisible: They do not appear in the curriculum. The course of study does not necessarily state, for example, whether it is preferable to teach children cooperation or competition, and it is easy to study school systems without observing what values they are actually imparting. The emphasis, then, is likely to be on the schools' secondary role: the teaching of skills useful to the society.

Africa, it is commonly observed, is a continent whose people are divided between two profoundly different cultures. One culture is typically called "traditional-native-primitive," the other "European-modernizing-civilized." These terms are, of course, heavy with connotations that reflect the varying degree of ethnocentrism or self-admiration of those who use them, all of whom are members of the second culture.

Little contact exists between the two cultures of present-day Africa. They are hostile and incommunicado. When we turn to education, then, we find what we might logically expect: two totally separate systems that are as hostile to and as uncommunicative with each other as the cultures whose agents they are. We shall call the two systems "traditional" and "European."

"Traditional" education takes two main forms in French-speaking Afric: tribal and Islamic. (Tribal education is designed for, and restricted to relatively small community.) Despite important differences, tribal an Islamic education are often found in combination. They share a gener: hostility to European culture.

Tribal education varies with the hundreds of cultures found in Frencl speaking Africa. Some generalizations will apply, however, to the exten that most African cultures share some common values. In tribal educa tion, children are taught rigid conformity to the community's values an its methods of living, primarily the growing or gathering of food. The poo soils and unfavorable climates that prevail in most of French-speakin Africa do not allow man much margin for error, so a community that ha discovered viable means of survival (means that include culture as we as technology) must impose those means on its members to ensure it continued existence. In the small and relatively egalitarian world of th village community, the individual is taught that his primary responsibilit is to the groups to which he belongs: extended family, clan, age-grade He exists primarily as a member of the community; that is the lesson o tribal education. Cooperation is therefore valued over competition, an harmony with the group over initiative. (The forms and degree of coopera tion vary greatly, and their relevance to development is the subject of mucl debate. The main point stressed here is simply that tribal culture is les individualistic than Western culture.) A man with no position in the com munity, which includes the dead and the unborn as well as the living, i almost literally an "unperson"; he has virtually no identity. The implie threat of denial and exile assures the individual's conformity with th values and decisions of the group; in return his survival is ensured, sinc all members of the group are required to help each other. Thus, triba education is typically highly conformist, group-oriented, and relevant t the community's immediate needs; it discourages innovation.

Islamic education, on the other hand, is based on the Koran. Boys mem orize large sections of the Koran under the guidance of a Muslim teacher known as a *marabout* in much of West Africa. In theory, the boy thu: absorbs the system of social values set forth by the Koran. In fact, he doe: not. The Koranic text is in Arabic, but only a tiny percentage of th Muslims in French-speaking Africa below the Sahara are familiar with th language whose phrases they are memorizing. Generally the *marabout* doe: not know Arabic either, so he could not explain the text even if he felt s inclined. This does not mean the student of the Koran learns nothing A cultural message often is conveyed. The boy who memorizes meaning less phrases in a strange language, and is whipped for failure to inton those phrases properly, is learning an important social value: Success lie:

in unreasoning obedience to the will of authority embodied in the *marabout*. The meaning of the lesson lies not in the Koran but in the act of memorization itself. The content is irrelevant in such cases to an interpretation of Koranic education. Indeed, the *maraboutic* system itself is in contradiction to the proscriptions of the Koran.

"European" education consists, of course, of the school system introduced by France during the colonial period. The structure of the French system transplanted to Africa is too familiar to warrant description here. In its major aspects, it remains the "European" system of French-speaking Africa today. The European system is characterized by an extremely high drop-out rate. Only a minority of those entering primary school receive the *Certificat d'Etudes Primaires* (CEP) and only a minority of those who enter secondary school receive a degree (*baccalauréat, certificat,* or *brevet*). The figures for Senegal cited by the Lebret team in 1960 are fairly representative of French-speaking Africa as a whole.[1] Of 1,000 children entering the first year (*cours d'initiation*), 320 received the CEP. Of these 320, a "minimum" of 80 per cent received no further degree. Of 198 entering classical secondary schools, 45 received the full *baccalauréat,* and 4 received teaching degrees. Of 14 entering normal schools, 9 received a degree after 4 years. Of 51 entering technical schools, 18 finished 3- or 4-year courses and received a degree (*certificat* or *brevet*). With the exception of the normal school 4-year course, the drop-out rate in each cycle exceeds 50 per cent. Since 1960, primary education has expanded much more rapidly than secondary education, so that a decreasing proportion of CEP graduates are able to continue their schooling.

Despite the great expansion of school facilities since independence, "European" education still reaches only a minority of the school-age population of French-speaking Africa. (One may note in passing what an odd misnomer the term "French-speaking Africa" is, since it is accurate only for a small minority of the people to whom it is applied.) About 16 per cent of the school-age population is in school. The rate is much lower in secondary schools. It is higher in primary schools and has exceeded 50 per cent in many major urban centers. Here we shall be mainly concerned with the primary-school graduate (the *certifié*) who does not get a further degree.

The influence of "European" education is far greater than these figures would suggest. With rare exceptions like the *marabouts* of Senegal, the decision-makers and holders of political power are graduates of the European system. Virtually the entire bureaucracy of French-speaking Africa, above the lowest levels, went at least through primary school. Since there is no present reason to suppose that this connection between education and political power will change, it must be assumed that the next generation of the governing elite will also be products of the European system. (This does not assume that power will be proportional to amount of education i.e., that "today's university students are tomorrow's ministers," but simpl that the elite will have had at least a primary-school education. That mor education makes one more qualified for political leadership seems to b assumed by many Americans, though it would be difficult to find a prece dent for this principle in the history of their own nation.)

The governing elite is united by common exposure to European educa tion more than by any other factor. It has been described variously as a "cultural (as opposed to economic) bourgeoisie" and a "diploma elite." The values taught by European schools are therefore of crucial importanc in determining the behavior of both present and future governing elites Those values have changed little since independence. Admirers of the French system often believed that Africans (at least the minority who wen to school) were being offered "exactly the same education" as French children. However, school will not have the same effect on children from different cultures. An accurate picture of French education in Africa must include the purposes for which the schools were designed and the cultural messages they conveyed.

The main function of the schools was to provide lower-level employees for the colonial administration. Decisions continued to be made by French men, but the use of Africans as clerks reduced the cost of administering the empire. To be a useful employee, an African had to be literate in French and know some arithmetic. Since his duties were routine, he did not need to be imaginative; in fact, a spirit of innovation was probably more of a handicap in the colonial than in most bureaucracies. Another quality was essential: loyalty to France rather than to Africa, to French rather than traditional African culture and values (at least in any case where the two came in conflict). In the process of acquiring this quality, the African alienated himself from his own culture and customs. Many Africans have described the pain caused by this alienation; it is the common theme in the literature of contemporary French-speaking Africa.

School was an instrument of that alienation. Education was a weapon of social division rather than integration, and it still serves that purpose today. The African child suffers a major culture shock on the first day at the *cours d'initiation,* when he is confronted by the rigid rule that only French may be spoken in the classroom. From then on, he is not allowed to speak his maternal language—the language in which he communicates to his family and his playmates. Children are taught—in lessons and in the very atmosphere of the school—that they must discard their maternal values in favor of the European culture represented by the school. In colonial times this was embodied in the famous textbook line memorized by African pupils, *"Nos ancêtres les gaulois . . . ,"* which was a direct contradiction of he African parents' veneration for their "First Ancestor," who, though perhaps mythical, was surely no Gaul. The African pupil was put in an impossible position. Though he might wish to "assimilate" completely and adopt Gallic ancestors, this conflicted with his family's values; in any case he was made aware that his French patrons did not really consider him a full-fledged Gaul.

Language continues to be of great importance in the teaching of values. It symbolizes the break between cultures, and it serves a cultural purpose illustrated in the following episode. In 1963, a French psychologist, Dr. Anne Colot, made a study of the *cours d'initiation* of Dakar.[2] She observed the teaching of *morale* (roughly, "citizenship"). The children in one class recited this lesson: *"Avant de traverser la rue je regarde bien si une voiture ne vient pas."* ("Before crossing the street I look carefully to see if a car is coming.") Fifteen children recited the lesson in French without error. Then Dr. Colot asked each of these children, in Wolof, their maternal language, the meaning of two simple and key words in the lesson: *avant* (before) and *si* (if). Of the fifteen pupils, none knew the meaning of *avant* and just one knew the meaning of *si*.

Without those two words the lesson had no ostensible meaning to the children who had so accurately committed it to memory. They did not learn the techniques of crossing a street in the heavy traffic of Dakar. But they learned something else, that to be successful in school one must memorize a string of words in French. The words may be totally meaningless, but even if they are understood, they are not likely to have much meaning in the Wolof life the child leads outside the classroom. As in Islamic education, memorizing empty phrases in a foreign language is the key to pleasing those in authority. (In secondary schools, French teachers often complain that their students are excellent at memorization but seem to show little interest in the content of their studies.)

As in colonial times, school is the means of entrée into the privileged class of government employees. Power, status, and reward are all to be found mainly in government employment; the private sector is limited and of relatively low status. Education is seen as the way in which one achieves a privileged position by passing an examination, not as a means of learning productive or innovative skills. This is in fact an accurate assessment of the present system of education.

The *fonction publique* is the goal even of those who hold only the CEP. For graduates of rural primary schools, the corollary is urbanization, since the city is the locus both of government jobs and of the new "European" culture. The *certifié* cannot stay in his village without suffering a major personal defeat, for school has taught contempt for traditional culture and for agriculture as a way of life. (Economic motives are of course important, but there is considerable evidence that cultural motives are also vital in the rural exodus to the cities.)

Nowhere perhaps is the "message" of the school to the rural pupil better illustrated than in a poster that was still to be seen in some West African schools in 1961–62. The poster shows two African families, one evidently "modern" and the other "primitive." The "modern" family is wearing European dress. They are sitting at a table and eating with implements from individual dishes; behind them is a European-style home. The "primitive" family wears African dress and sits on the ground eating by hand from the traditional calabash; behind them is a thatched hut. What is remarkable about the poster is that there is no evidence in its picture that the "modern" family is more sanitary, eats a better diet, or is more productive than the "primitive" family. The poster's message is limited to the most superficial symbols of "Europe."

The *Certificat d'Etudes Primaires* is the approximate dividing line between those who stay in the village and its culture, and those who leave. Most primary-school drop-outs are likely to stay, but virtually every *certifié* will get out of the village if he possibly can. This observation, common in French-speaking Africa, was documented in the case of Senegal by the Lebret study.[3] The Lebret team found that of 1,000 rural Senegalese who received the CEP in 1954, only 2 per cent were farmers 5 years later; and 75 per cent were living in cities.

The young migrants are motivated by two sets of goals. They are going to the city, and they are fleeing from the village. The *certifié* who has accepted the modern-primitive dichotomy laid down by the European school is seeking his place in the "modern" life of the city. If he is lucky, he will become a privileged member of the *fonction publique*. But it is better to remain unemployed in the city, hovering on the margins of the elite, than to go back to the village and accept the constraints of traditional culture and the boredom of village life, for the young migrants are also fleeing the rigid conformity of a culture that typically subjects the young to the will of the old.

Roads and transistor radios, as well as schools, are forces that promote rural exodus, and illiterates as well as *certifiés* go to the city. Yet the holder of the CEP is the surest candidate for migration. With the rapid increase in primary education, there is a corresponding increase in the tide of migrant *certifiés*. The *certifié* migrates with meager equipment for urban life. He has some French and a little arithmetic, and very little else. Virtually nothing he has learned is relevant to the needs of his society, either in urban or rural life. The attitudes he has acquired—an elitist orientation and a distaste for manual occupations—are worse than irrelevant; they are counterproductive.

The rural exodus is perhaps Africa's most disturbing social problem. The capitals of French-speaking Africa are growing in population at rates close to 10 per cent annually. The major cities have growing pools of unemployed young men. In Cotonou, it was said in 1962 that about half of the urban males between 15 and 19 were idle, neither working nor in school.

No African economy shows any sign of growing enough to meet the demand for jobs for the young migrants. As long as schools increase their output, while the economies remain relatively stagnant, the numbers of the semieducated jobless can only grow. As early as 1962, the Planning Commission of Madagascar estimated that 30,000 new jobs a year were needed for new graduates, but that the Malagasy economy was not likely to produce more than 2,000–3,000 jobs annually for the next 5 years.[4]

Migration to the cities is of course a phenomenon familiar in Western nations. In the West, however, rural exodus was accompanied and motivated by an expansion of industrial and other urban employment, and by rising per capita productivity in agriculture. Neither of these factors exists in Africa today, and it is unrealistic to hope that urban employment can absorb the products of the schools in the foreseeable future. Africa will enter the industrial age at a time when industrial technology is increasingly capital-intensive; the prospects for labor-intensive industry at present are bleak.

The increasing number of unemployed *certifiés* in the cities is a burden and a potential threat to the elite now in power. Urban bureaucrats are forced by family obligations—the well-known *parasitisme familiale*—to take in and support their young relatives arriving from the village. The bureaucrat is impelled toward corruption to support his numerous dependents, or toward nepotism to place those relatives on the state's payroll. (This is true even though having a group of retainers around the house may be politically useful to the bureaucrat.) The net result is to increase the cost of running the state, and therefore to divert potential resources from development, which might have produced jobs for the migrants.

Already most government payrolls cannot take on more than a few of the new *certifiés*. Governments are already overstaffed at the lower levels for which the migrants are qualified, and most budgets are in deficit. Many of the migrants appear in time to become unemployable. They have suffered a severe psychological shock in their leap from one culture to another. Withdrawal and autistic isolation were cited by one study as common reactions to the shock of migration.[5] With more migrants and no more jobs, the chances of each individual decrease. The accumulation of hopeless young men in the cities is a potential threat to the incumbent governments. Pierre Biarnes, editor of *Le Moniteur Africain du Commerce et de l'Industrie,* put the issue in these terms: "How to dam the flood of new generations of 'intellectuals' without jobs or holding jobs they consider inferior? . . . All these guests invited to a party at which there are not enough seats?"[6]

The effect of the exodus on rural development seems to be less widely recognized than the problems it poses in the cities. Both directly and indirectly, rural exodus acts as a barrier to the increase of agricultural production and productivity. The unemployed migrants are not producing food; instead, they contribute to the growing food imports of most nations in French-speaking Africa. Many nations are farther today from the goal of feeding themselves than they were before independence. Though cash-crop production has not in general fallen, the production of food crops is not keeping pace with the population.

Indirectly, the exodus inhibits agriculture because the young migrants are those who might have been the village leaders in technological innovation. To increase productivity per capita, as well as total production, African agriculture needs farmers who are willing to experiment with new methods. Those bound in traditional culture are likely to find innovation distasteful. The young *certifiés* are freed from those bonds, but the schooling that freed them has also made agriculture itself distasteful to them. Thus the village is deprived of its potential leadership. Once agricultural progress began, or was perceived as possible, young men might find economic motives for staying in the villages. As it is, a stagnant agriculture offers them no hope, and they flee. The European schools encourage rather than discourage this trend. "The existing school holds back agricultural progress," the agronomist René Dumont concluded.[7] The Lebret study of Senegal reached a similar conclusion: "The direct effect of primary schooling on the economic progress of rural society is nil; as to its sociological effects, they are negative because schooling in the long run deprives the village of its elite and has no positive effect in the transformation of the mentality of the group."[8]

Yet schools of this sort are still being built, on the theory of "education for development"—the theory that somehow more schools will make the nation richer. In its simplest form, this theory rests on the observed correlation between levels of income and education: Nations with a more educated population have a higher per capita income.[9] Yet the causal relationship is not proved; it is simply assumed that one factor (education) leads to the other (development), though it can be persuasively argued that development generally has preceded rather than followed mass education.

In an industrialized society with social values that encourage innovation, more education seems likely to produce more skilled innovators. But there is no evidence that the "European" schools of French-speaking Africa have

,erved this function. Innovation is not a value encouraged in the "European" school, any more than it is in tribal education. The performance of he governing elites produced by the European school does not indicate any great spirit of innovation, particularly in the crucial sector of agriculure. Such African Presidents as Léopold Senghor of Senegal and Sékou Touré of Guinea are unsparing in their attacks on the educated elite for ts failure to act as a force for development. Foreign observers of the bureaucracies of French-speaking Africa often find them formalistic, adherng to routine, fearful of change.

When the Lebret team analyzed positive and negative factors in the developmental potential of Senegal, it found both the schools and the bureaucracy they produced to be negative factors. The influence of the bureaucracy was described as "very generally negative, sometimes neutral, rarely very positive."[10] Yet it is this bureaucracy that is now counted on to provide the leadership for development in French-speaking Africa.

African governments have made superficial attempts to stem the rural exodus. Togo and Dahomey have experimented with land-resettlement schemes designed to convert jobless youths into farmers. Despite strong financial and technical support, these schemes have failed, or at best have proved far too costly to be generalized. The direct cost of the schemes is prohibitive; yet it is far less than the true cost, for the calculation of the direct cost does not include the expense of educating the jobless *certifiés*. Young *certifiés* strongly resist being made into farmers, for reasons that seem to be primarily cultural. For many of them, the state settlement scheme offers their only real chance for a steady income. Yet they typically reject it, because farming to them means a drop in status from "intellectual" to "primitive." Their reaction to resettlement, and the refusal of the urban jobless to return to their villages, support the view that rural exodus cannot be explained (or dealt with) in purely economic terms.

Rural-training schemes have been set up with the aim of producing better farmers. Examples are the *service civique* of Mali and the *chantier-école* of Senegal. Mali's is a two-year paramilitary training program. Supposedly, the young graduates will return to their villages as more productive farmers or artisans. Supposedly, also, they will be able to read and write. However, Malian officials reported in late 1962 that almost half of the first group of volunteers wanted to stay on in the secure if austere barracks of the *service civique* after their time was up. Many others, the officials feared, would drift back into the cities. The Senegalese *chantier-école* is somewhat similar, though under civilian rather than military management. It is a camp for illiterate rural boys. In theory, the boys build their housing and live on the produce of the land they farm; they are expected to take the innovations they learn at the *chantier* back to their villages. In May, 1964, the three *chantiers-école* were close to collapse, and the enthusiasm of th Senegalese Government had clearly waned. When I visited the *chantier école* at Noto, I found that, because of poor management and ill-considere innovations, the boys were producing smaller crops at much greater cos than nearby farmers using traditional methods. They were in fact learnin, nothing useful. Accounts of the other *chantiers* painted similar pictures Thus, neither the Senegalese nor the Malian program provides an economi cally and culturally viable answer to rural exodus.

Though they often express concern about rural exodus, the government of French-speaking Africa have been reluctant to grasp the nettle of pro found educational reform. The connection between school and exodus i: not widely admitted. In November, 1962, youth and labor delegation met in Cotonou for a week-long seminar on rural exodus. At the end o the seminar, the delegates produced a resolution containing thirty-two points.[11] Not one of these thirty-two points advocated school reform. Th emphasis, rather, was on providing facilities for the urban jobless and o making minor improvements in rural living conditions.

Some changes have been made in the schools since independence. Nev texts have been written, and *"nos ancêtres les gaulois"* have been prune from the African family tree. The new texts are geared more to Africa, less to France—although schoolchildren in Dahomey are said to be stil reciting *"Je suis triste parce qu'il neige"* ("I am sad because it is snowing"), one cause for sorrow with which their country is not plagued. Guinea has tried to decentralize education by building new secondary schools outside the capital city of Conakry. Most governments in French-speaking Africa have tried to shift the emphasis in secondary education away from classical and toward technical schooling. However, technical schools still command relatively low prestige, and stagnant economies do not provide jobs for their graduates, beyond replacing the few remaining Europeans.

More radical plans have been left on the ministry shelf. The French, having created the present system, have offered plans for its revision in several countries. The plan for Dahomey projected the creation of self-supporting rural schools that would combine basic education with coopera-tive farming.[12] In January, 1963, the impression in Cotonou was that there was virtually no possibility that the plan would be executed. In Senegal, opposition from the elite, especially exteachers, has blocked any major reform. Teachers raised in and practicing the present system are a formida-ble barrier to any profound reform, for the reform would have to be carried out by the teachers themselves. (The difficulties of getting any significant reform adopted might give pause to those Americans who see a role for the United States in African education. If French interests, with their much greater leverage, have failed to achieve reform, it is questionable whether

Americans can do it. Nor is it certain that American pedagogical innovations are adapted to African needs.)

Yet educational reform is crucial to rural development, which in turn is necessary for general economic development.[13] The nations of French-speaking Africa cannot for long afford systems of education that, at great expense to the state, depress the rural sector and produce a surplus of non-innovating would-be bureaucrats. It is doubtful that a school system that makes its primary goal the learning of a foreign language is relevant to Africa's current needs. But curriculum reform, necessary though it is, will not be enough in itself. Teaching agriculture in rural schools will be of relatively little use as long as agriculture remains both profitless and despised as an occupation, and as long as the schools' graduates are motivated by their education to flee the village community. Rural life needs to be given new status as well as new economic opportunities. For education to perform this function there must be a profound change in the cultural values conveyed by the European schools. This in turn requires an equally profound change in the values of the governing elite, for, no matter what the curriculum contains, it is the values of the elite that will be handed down in the schools. Thus the implications of educational reform are revolutionary in scope.

8

Comparisons in the Evolution of Pre-Independence Elites in French-Speaking West Africa and the Congo

HERBERT F. WEISS

A COMPARISON of political elites in the Congo and West Africa sheds li
on the following questions: Who were the political elites? What was t
setting in which they operated? How did differences in the rhythm
political evolution affect them? What was their relationship to their f
lowers? Since the situation prevailing in French-speaking West Africa l
been given a great deal of attention, while that in the Congo has receiv
virtually none, the comparisons made will tend to employ the former a
reference point.

In both areas, the prerequisite for eligibility was a modern educatic
Ruth Schachter Morgenthau has pointed out that French rule "has p
duced the striking by-product that Africans have chosen practically all th
political leaders from among those educated in the schools installed
the colonisers."[1]

In the Congo, very much the same situation prevailed. Out of a sampli
of 122 of the 137 members of the first Chamber of Representatives o
14 may have lacked a modern education, judging from their occupatio
It is also interesting that only 3 members are identified as customary (i.
traditional) chiefs.[2]

The reason for the pre-eminence of the modern elite among politi
leaders was also similar in both areas. Morgenthau notes that "Africa
(in French West Africa) reasoned that to be effective their representativ

d to be equipped to deal with the Europeans, their language and their
stitutions."[3]

In the Congo, one of the organizational mottoes of the Parti Solidaire
fricain (PSA) claims that "The intellectuals conceive, the aged support,
d the youth executes."[4] No doubt is left as to the primacy of the intellec-
als, a term that was employed interchangeably with "évolué" or "élite."
uring my own field research in the Congo, I was told that, at the local
vel, party leadership was sometimes divided according to the linguistic-
nctional needs of the situation. The elite dealt with everything that
quired a knowledge of French; the cooperative traditional leaders were
ven responsibilities where a knowledge of the local dialect and some
estige were required.[5] Although modern education was a common pre-
quisite for political leadership, the degree and type of education received
as appreciably different.

As is well known, France pursued an essentially elitist education policy.
teracy was not widespread, but the most gifted students were permitted
climb very high on the educational ladder. Although prior to World
ar II this did not extend to university education, except for a very few,
ter 1946 a growing number of Africans had access to universities in
rance and later in French West Africa. The Belgian policy, on the other
and, stressed primary education and allowed only a few Africans to pur-
e academic secondary-school courses.[6] University education was not
fered until the middle 1950's with the result that, at the moment of inde-
endence in 1960, the Congo could claim only about thirty university
aduates.

The importance of the "intelligentsia gap" in the Congo, has, however,
equently been exaggerated. In the first place, the often-cited "only sixteen
iversity graduates" gives an erroneously low impression of the education
ceived by the Congo's modern elite. The "sixteen," in effect, held gradu-
e degrees.[7] A large number of the modern elite in the Congo had received
education that was either the equivalent or a near equivalent of a uni-
rsity course. There were about 500 Congolese priests as well as a large
mber of persons who had attended seminaries but had not taken their
nal vows. Since studying for the priesthood was the only means by which
Congolese could continue his education, many attended who in the end
ropped out or were eliminated for nonacademic reasons. It is difficult
know precisely how many such persons existed just before independence,
t the total number of former seminary students has been estimated at
out 3,000. In addition, those Congolese who attended postsecondary
chnical schools must also be included in this calculation. These included
edical assistants, agricultural technicians, administrative specialists, and
cial workers, and numbered in excess of 400.[8]

Paradoxically, neither in French-speaking West Africa nor in the Con͏ has the university-educated intellectual reservoir been fully employed in t͏ selection of political leaders. Morgenthau points out that:

Only in the last few years have any significant numbers of graduates return from their universities. Since they had been abroad while their countrym were passing successfully through the energetic first phase of the struggle ͏ political power, they found that the most important political posts—gover mental or involuntary organizations—were already filled. Although, it w generally admitted by the electorate that the leaders should be literate, it w certainly not admitted that the highest degree was a pass to the high͏ post. . . . The locally educated Africans who are now in top-level positio are on the whole products of the pre-war educational system, which had train a small elite to occupy subordinate positions in the administration.[9]

Almost the same statement could be made for the Congo. The universi͏ students and graduates did not play a significant part in the independen͏ struggle. The graduates did not all become ministers in the first cabin (only two of them were included), and thus it appears to be somewhat le important how many of them were available for public positions.

Of course, one may argue that the number of university graduates in t͏ Congo was so small that they were prevented from playing a significa leadership role. However, here it is interesting to note that, much like the French West African counterparts, even the university *students*—of who͏ there were several hundred during the crucial years of the independen͏ struggle—played a very insignificant part in political affairs. Indeed, ev͏ the limited role played by the Etudiants du RDA and the Fédération d Etudiants d'Afrique Noire en France[10] was absent in the Congo, ev͏ though the vast majority of the Congolese students had the advantage attending universities in the Congo and were thus present in the count during the preindependence period.

There appear to be several reasons for this: First, university studen͏ and even graduates were all in the first generation of a new "class." Ev͏ though youth is clearly no handicap in African politics, the indigenous s͏ cieties apparently were not willing to hand over political leadership to group that had no accepted previous role or function—a group that w͏ without a doubt alienated from the life and concerns of the ordina͏ African. This reluctance is surprising, since, up to the university leve͏ modern education *was* the most common prerequisite for prestige a͏ leadership. It stopped short of university training, partly because by the tim university students existed in any appreciable numbers the older but le͏ well-educated elite had been able to wrest some concessions from t͏ colonizer. At that juncture, prestige was no longer granted to the be͏ educated but to the more successful champions of African demands.

In the Congo, this shunting aside of university students and graduates was, to some degree, the product of their own attitudes. Having matured under a system in which modern education was the source of overwhelming respect and prestige, they tended to see themselves virtually as elder statesmen. Frequently disdainful of the capacities of existing political leaders, they were willing to advise—either the whole society or specific leaders—but hardly ever willing to participate in the less "dignified" aspects of political action, since to do so would have placed them under "lesser men." One gains the impression that in French-speaking West Africa these attitudes also played a role, but were masked by differences between students, who tended to follow rigid ideological positions, and the more pragmatic leaders.

Of special political importance were the members of the teaching profession in the French West African setting:

The data for the occupations of the Legislative Assembly members in the eight territories of the former French West Africa immediately after the 1957 elections . . . [show that] 22 per cent of the total were teachers, rising to as high a proportion as 33 per cent in Senegal and Dahomey.[11]

This situation is not repeated in the Congo. Of the sampling of 122 out of 137 members of the Chamber of Representatives, only 10 were teachers.[12] A possible reason for this difference will be mentioned below.

On the other hand, the protopolitical organizational backgrounds of the elites in the two areas are very similar. Basically, these organizations fall into two types: those that were exclusively elitist, and those that had more universal memberships, especially in the urban centers, but were led by the elite. Examples of the latter type were ethnic and mutual-help associations and labor unions. Elite associations include alumni groups, "cultural" circles, and ideologically oriented discussion groups.[13] In this structural sense there are hardly any differences worth noting between French West Africa and the Congo. However, the ideologically oriented discussion groups were radically different in terms of the European political philosophies that their European patrons introduced into the African environment. In French West Africa, according to Hodgkin and Morgenthau,

Initially such political education as [the elite] received came from contact with liberal-minded Catholic missionaries, or with Frenchmen of the Left—Socialists or Communists—who came to West Africa, mainly as teachers, from 1936 on. Later, in 1943 the organization known as the Groupes d'Etudes Communistes (GEC's) established itself in Dakar, Conakry, Abidjan, Bamako, and Bobo-Dioulasso. In these groups the younger members of the elite discussed the application of Marxist ideas, interpreted by French Communists, to the problems of contemporary Africa.[14]

In the Congo, much as in French West Africa, the "study groups" reflected the political divisions of the Metropole, but this meant that the entire political spectrum was appreciably further to the right. Catholic, liberal, and socialist study groups were set up, but no Communist ones. It is also interesting to note that in French West Africa the European "leftist" was often a teacher; in the Congo, the virtual monopoly by the missions of the educational system meant that the Europeans in education were on the whole very conservative and paternalistic. This, perhaps, is the reason why African teachers were so important in the nationalist movements in French-speaking West Africa, whereas they played an essentially unimportant role in the Congo. A Congolese teacher with early and avid political interests was unlikely to last very long in the mission school, whereas the opposite was presumably the case in French-speaking West Africa. It should also be noted that significant Communist influence was felt in the French Administration during the Popular Front in the 1930's and in the immediate post-World War II period. No parallel for this existed in the Belgian Administration, and again this difference appears to have had an impact on the modern elite.

Although there are important differences in the backgrounds of the political elites of French-speaking West Africa and the Congo, they were fundamentally similar. The second question must now be asked: What was the setting in which they operated?

In the most general terms, the colonial system that Belgium evolved in the Congo was marked by two rare characteristics: first, the refusal to give any African elite, be it traditional or assimilated, even theoretical or symbolic equality with the colonizer; and, second, the important role played by the Catholic Church and especially the Congolese clergy. The argument has been made that Belgium did not want to make "Belgians" out of the Congolese and therefore did not allow an assimilated elite to emerge. But whatever their intention, the system led to assimilation. True, this assimilation was not directed toward the metropolitan "culture," as was the case in French areas. Rather, it stressed Christianization, monogamy, and the adoption of an essentially Western way of life. This pressure, applied at all levels, was one of the reasons why the traditional leadership was so profoundly weakened in the Congo. Traditional leaders were, until very late, seen as the main carriers of precolonial African values.[15] Only with respect to language at the primary-school level was there a practical result from the formal rejection of assimilation as a colonial policy by Belgium. Unlike French areas, in the Congo children were first taught in African languages or in lingua franca such as Lingala.

When one goes about destroying a people's traditional leaders, religious beliefs, and economic and social life, it is manifestly absurd to claim that

ιe desires this people to remain true to its own culture. Precisely because
ιe impact of Belgian rule was compartively great it was probably in-
ιvertently the most assimilationist of all colonial rules.

Under such a system the modern elite holds an especially important posi-
ιn. Jean-Paul Sartre, in his introduction to *La pensée politique de Patrice
ιmumba,* points to this when he states that "Les masses indigènes sont
ιres de leurs 'évolués', qui font la preuve *pour tous* qu'un Noir, pourvu
ι'on lui en offre l'occasion, peut égaler ou surpasser un Blanc!"[16] ("The in-
ιgenous masses are proud of their elite, who are the proof *for everyone* that
ι Negro, given that he is offered the opportunity, can equal or surpass a
ιhite man!")

In other words, it is suggested that the average African identifies with
ιe modern elite because the latter has the possibility, or is closest to having
ιe possibility of establishing the inherent worth of the African under
ιlonial rule.[17] But, unlike the African under French rule, the Congolese
ιd a firm limit set on how far he could be assimilated. He was *not* given
ιe opportunity to prove that he could "equal or surpass a white." This
ιndition was further accentuated by the exclusively white nature of
ιelgian rule. The schism between colonizer and colonized was total not
ιnly in the political sphere, it was total in the racial sphere as well. Under
ιrench rule this was not quite the case; men like Léopold Sédar Senghor
ιnerged, and Negroes and mulattoes from the Caribbean and from the four
ιommunes in Senegal were given virtual equality, and even shared in po-
ιtical power.

The one exception to this pattern in the Congo was the evolution of the
ιfrican clergy. The first Congolese priest was ordained in 1917; the first
ιniversity student was graduated in 1956. Even in the 1930's the Church
ιready aimed at maintaining racial equality within the Church: *"Ils
ιrêtres indigènes] y sont mis sur le même pied que les missionnaires euro-
ιéens, suivent le même reglement, exercent le même ministère; sont loges
ι nourris comme ceux-ci et ils y prendront place d'après leur anciennete
ιordination."*[18] ("They (indigenous priests) are placed on the same footing
ι the European missionaries, they exercise the same ministry; they are
ιoused and fed alike, and they are placed in the order of the seniority of
ιeir ordination.")

In other words, assimilation all the way to the top was possible. The
ιongolese priest and bishop could and did in Sartre's words prove that the
ιfrican can *"égaler ou surpasser un Blanc."* And the Church was not un-
ιware of the psychological value of such equality:

*ιomment? Nos prêtres, nos frères de sang, dit-il, [l'indigène] sont traités sur
ι même pied que les prêtres européens: leurs relations réciproques sont fra-*

*ternelles et respectueuses; ils exercent les mêmes fonctions, ils sont honorés a
la visite de leur évêque! Mais c'est là un signe de la vraie religion. . . .*
Le noir est fier de son prêtre.[19] *. . .*

(How? Our priests, our blood brothers, are treated on the same footing as th
European priests; their reciprocal relations are fraternal and respectful; the
exercise the same functions; they are honored by visits from their bishops! Her
is a sign of the true religion. . . .
The African is proud of his priest. . . .)

The Church was, in effect, the only modern structure in the Congo tha
was progressively Africanized. It is important to take note of this, since i
probably explains why the Church was the only national structure to sur
vive the collapse of 1960. But, it is also important to note that not onl
did the Church-controlled education system *not* produce secular equivalen
to the Congolese clergy, but the clergy was never allowed to exercise leader
ship functions outside the narrow confines of Church activities. On the con
trary, the Congolese priest was instructed to cooperate with the colonia
administration, sometimes even in a humiliating fashion. For instance, her
are some excerpts of instructions for priests from Equatorial Province:[20]

*Après avoir salué un Blanc et avoir repondu aimablement à ses question, s
retirer. S'il invite à rester, ne pas rester trop longtemps, pour ne pas gener. . .*
*S'interdire toute critique, surtout d'une autorité quelconque, et éviter d'avoi
l'air d'approuver une critique qu'on entend. . . . (p. 58)*

On ne peut exercer aucune fonction publique.
On ne se melera pas à la vie politique du pays.
(Ne rien faire, dire ou écrire contre les autorités établies.) (p. 60)

(After having greeted a white man and having answered his questions in
pleasant fashion, withdraw. If he invites you to stay, don't stay too long, i
order not to disturb him.
Forbid yourself every criticism especially of any authority, and avoid givin
the appearance of approving a criticism which you hear. . . . (p. 58)

One may not exercise any public function.
One cannot get mixed up in the political life of the country. . . .
(Do not do, say, or write anything against the established authorities
(p. 60)

Msgr. Huys goes on to explain:

*Ce clergé indigène, rattaché à Rome, qui a été formé dans un esprit de loya
isme envers le Gouvernement de la Colonie, rendre nécessairement de grand
services à l'Etat, en affermissant par son influence morale la population in
digène dans son loyalisme envers la Belgique.*[21]

This indigenous clergy, attached to Rome, which was educated in a spirit f loyalty toward the Government of the Colony, will necessarily render great ervice to the State, in that it will affirm, through its moral influence on the 1digenous population, its loyalty toward Belgium.)

Admittedly, these instructions were given in 1936. Church policy changed fter World War II, and the Church's relationship to the Administration ecame markedly cooler, indeed, after 1954, sometimes antagonistic. Also, ome members of the clergy did play marginal roles in the nationalist truggle. Nonetheless, the African clergy was probably the most prestigious lite group in the Congo until shortly before independence; its function gave t exceptionally close access to the urban and rural populace. No secular lite of this stature existed, and yet it was almost completely segregated out f political affairs. Obviously, this was in sharp contrast to the situation in ?rench-speaking West Africa, where Africanization to the top *was* possible, ind increasingly realized in the secular field, which also meant that this lite did not have the constraints of Church discipline upon it.

The next comparison to be made is how differences in the rhythm of olitical evolution affected the two areas. Time has rarely been considered is an independent variable in analyzing a given political development. Yet, n the Congo, the period between the earliest manifestations of the in-lependence struggle and the achievement of independence was so short that he tempo of political change becomes an important factor. The first aspect f this question concerns time to gain experience. Leaders in French-speak-ng West Africa had at least twelve years (from the Constituante in 1946 o the Constitution of the Fifth Republic in 1958) in which to adjust to, ind to manipulate, a variety of different political situations.[22] A realistic, :quivalent period in the Congo would begin with the Communal elections in December, 1957, and end in June, 1960. Even this is too generous, since olitical parties did not really start until the middle of 1958; the rough :quivalent of the Bamako RDA Conference in 1946 was the Luluabourg Congress of Political Parties in April, 1959. In other words, the period of 1ationalist agitation leading up to independence lasted only a year or two n the Congo.

Furthermore, there were no parliamentary or even quasi-parliamentary bodies of any significance in which Congolese participated. The only elec-tions held prior to those in May, 1960, detracted from, rather than helped, a rationalization of the political evolution. The Communal elections in 1957 and 1958 initiated a number of fierce political rivalries based on the ethnic balances existing in several of the largest urabn centers. Later it became evident that with the extension of the suffrage to the rural population these conflicts were utterly artificial.[23] The December, 1959, elections were held for territorial and communal councils. The best-organized parties boycotted them, and the others found little to interest them in local elections that bound their potential supporters together. The result was that three-fifths of the votes cast went to purely local or individual lists and, of the remainder, about one-fifth of the electorate refused to vote. The frequent elections in French West Africa between 1946 and 1956 "gave voters training in electoral procedures and party militants experience in mobilizing mass support,"[24] but they had no equivalent in the Congo. It should also be noted that the leaders of French West Africa profited not only from the parliamentary experience gained at the Territorial and inter-Territorial levels, but also, and perhaps more importantly, from full participation in the French Parliament in Paris.

The difference between the two areas was, of course, even greater in regard to executive experience. The lack of Africanization in government prevented individual members of the Congolese modern elite from gaining such experience. The lack of any extended interim period in which some executive authority was given to political leaders meant that here too no experience could be gained. The only exception to this was the establishment of the national and provincial "executive colleges" in March, 1960. But this came during the electoral campaign and only three months before independence. It was clearly too late to do very much good.

It would be possible to go on and on in this vein, listing the variety of experiences that the political elite in French-speaking West Africa gained in the twelve years preceding independence or Community membership, but that the short two years the Congo had did not afford. On the assumption that additional elaborations are unnecessary, I shall go on to point to a different area in which the lack of time affected the Congolese political elite. Congolese nationalism had embarked upon a path that involved political parties, mass participation, very militant protest, parallel government structures, and elections; lack of time, however, frequently prevented even a minimum rationalization of the many forces at work. Nationalism can occur without mass parties, but if such organizations do evolve—especially under the circumstances prevailing in the Congo—then certain functional requirements become apparent. If they are not met, or there is not time to meet them, the body politic faces extremely grave problems. For instance, the founders of parties were never confirmed in their positions by lower echelons. Party constitutions did include clauses calling for annual congresses at which the leadership would be elected, but no party congresses found time to fill this function. Since founders were usually urban residents and their followers predominantly rural, a great deal of friction developed between urban and rural groups, but, in most cases, no structured way existed for them to come to realistic compromises. There were no legislative elections in which the rural "boss" could prove his value to the party by etting out the vote, and there were no party elections in which he could ise to "national" leadership.

In French-speaking West Africa most major parties had the time to institutionalize methods for resolving internal conflicts. "Elections were fairly regular; officers gave some account of their stewardship to the members; discipline was given serious attention; a predetermined procedure was followed when important decisions were to be made."[25] Even the parties that had recourse to largely personal leadership had the time to establish patterns that took the local situations into account, and were accepted by local leaders and members.

In the Congo, an attempt was made to use both of these methods, and institutionalized methods of conflict resolution in the highest councils of the parties frequently emerged, but such methods were largely absent between the lower and upper echelons of party leadership.

A further problem was posed by the electoral system devised for the May, 1960, elections—in effect the only election that was of real political significance. This system involved proportional representation *between* party lists, optional preferential ballots within party lists, and simultaneous elections for the provincial assemblies and the national parliament with candidates being able to run for both assemblies, but, if elected, having to choose between one or the other. The net impact of this system varied widely from party to party, but it did, for the first time, give lower echelons the opportunity to choose the party's top leadership by exercising their preferential ballot option. Obviously the system tended to increase divisions within parties, and indeed most of the larger ones split before, or soon after, independence.

Another problem that can be attributed, at least in part, to the time factor is the concentration of energies of most Congolese party leaders in provincial political arenas. True, in dealing with the Belgians, it was usual to speak in the name of the Congolese people, but, even as late as April, 1960, interparty conflicts were largely acted out at the provincial level. The only major exception to this generalization was Patrice Lumumba, who more or less developed a national electoral strategy.

In French West Africa, a long-established interterritorial political tradition existed, but the setting in which it operated was so conditioned by both African and Metropolitan forces that the choice was one between federated and separate states; ultimately, completely independent sovereign units resulted. In the Congo, the interprovincial political tradition was hardly more than nominal and yet the practical alternative immediately before independence was between a unitary or a federal state. The decision arrived at favored the former. But the political elite that inherited this unitary state, unlike the political elite in French-speaking West Africa, still thought largely in provincial terms. This is not to argue that creating a single state out of the Congo was impractical. Indeed, the most severe political and ethnic conflicts that occurred before independence were *within* the provincial arenas, not between them. Even the subsequent breakdown of the Congo's unity was in part the result of intraprovincial conflicts.[26] Thus, following the French West African pattern and creating six states would not necessarily have solved anything. The point is that, for the leaders, one or two years was simply too short a time in which to make the jump from urban to provincial to national political arenas in a calculated and satisfactory fashion.

The last matter that this chapter will seek to examine is the type of support that the political elites of the two areas received from their followers. In a sense, this is an attempt to approach the subject of "political elites" from a different perspective, responding to what might be a very legitimate criticism of the comparisons made up to now—namely, that it is not who they were that matters, but how they were followed.

In approaching this question, it will be useful first to make certain comparisons between political parties and the roles they performed in French-speaking West Africa and in the Congo. The distinction made by Morgenthau between "mass" and "patron" parties can be applied to the Congo.[27] The patron parties filled a much less important role in the Congo than they did in West Africa. This may be attributable to the paucity of elections in the Congo. The December, 1959, elections did, however, engender some of the characteristics ascribed to patron parties in West Africa. Most such parties merged into the Parti National du Progrès (PNP), and typically relied on "notables" at the local level.

Mass parties in the Congo also had many of the characteristics of their counterparts in West Africa. They "wanted to enroll each man, woman, and even child."[28] Their activities extended to the creation of elaborate satellite organizations—youth, labor, and cooperative. As in West Africa, "They published newspapers, set up central and regional headquarters, hired permanent staffs, distributed membership cards, charged dues. . . ."[29]

One important distinction, however, is that in the Congo these parties never came to dominate the entire national arena. Indeed, in all but one province, they did not even dominate the provincial arenas. But, they did in almost all cases completely dominate a fief, which might be the size of two districts with a population close to a million, as in the case of the Bakongo Political Party (ABAKO), or it might be much smaller.

Congolese mass parties must also be divided into ethnic and regional parties. The ABAKO received exclusively Bakongo support, while the MNC (Lumumba) and the PSA received support from a multitude of ethnic groups. Obviously, ethnicity played an important part even in the latter case, resulting in a sort of ethnic "balancing," again similar to the West African patterns.[30]

Party activities, after the division of the Congo into numerous party fiefs, proliferated to a point where they paralleled government structures. Indeed, it would appear that the extent of this development in the Congo went beyond the West African examples. For instance, not only did many parties set up rough judicial systems and even perform police functions, but in most cases party militia were organized and some parties even had their own prisons. Thus, from the point of view of the villager, the function of the mass party in the Congo and in French-speaking West Africa was very much alike.

Despite all these basic similarities between the mass parties in the two areas, there was a fundamental difference between them. The leaders of key Congolese parties established their organizations upon a base of pre-existing and largely spontaneous protest. In other words, they did not "invent" protest against the colonizer, they merely structured it. This phenomenon was especially pronounced in Leopoldville Province, which, being the principal arena, colored the nationalist movement in the rest of the country. Apart from elite declarations that did not carry much weight, the struggle against the colonizer in the Congo really began with the Leopoldville riots of January, 1959. Here an urban mass without leadership rose up against the colonizer. Within months this rebellious mood spread to the rural areas surrounding the city, notably the Lower Congo and Kwango and Kwilu provinces with their combined population of about 3 million. This occurred at a time when the top leaders of the relevant parties were either in jail or still in the process of organizing their founding committees. Nonetheless, the net result of this largely spontaneous protest was the virtually complete collapse of the Belgian Administration in these regions.

The parties did fill the vacuum that resulted from the boycott of Administrative structures—spontaneously begun but soon urged on the populations by leaders—but the amount of discipline involved was probably far lower than in West Africa. So long as the leaders urged increased militancy they were obeyed, but when they tried, just before independence, to persuade their followers to pay their taxes they found total noncompliance.

It would of course be interesting to deal with the causes for this type of spontaneous protest and especially the rural radicalism that resulted. Was it the fact that there was greater dissatisfaction with life under colonial rule in the Congo than elsewhere? Or was it the ineffectual Belgian response to the earliest manifestations of protest? Or were both factors involved? This is not the place to answer these questions, but they must at least be asked, because they raise the possibility that the nature of the anticolonial protest in the Congo was fundamentally different from that in French-speaking West Africa, and that, even given experience and time, the elite would still have been faced with problems of discipline that would have been very difficult to deal with.

PART IV

THE ECONOMIC SITUATION

9

The Legacy of
French Economic Policy in Africa

MARK KARP

"FRENCH-SPEAKING AFRICA" is a label currently used to distinguish former French dependencies from other African countries, particularly former colonies of European powers other than France. It is an informal, but convenient label; it has the advantage of brevity; and it has gained wide acceptance within the last few years. Yet it is by no means accurate. Taken literally, it would include several countries that never had close ties with France. Language alone, therefore, cannot serve as a distinguishing element in this case. The Jeanneney Commission, which the French Government set up in 1963 to examine questions of aid to developing countries, apparently recognized this fact, and in its report suggested as an alternative a criterion based on two features: French culture as the predominant form of Western influence, and affiliation with France's monetary system.[1] The difficulty with the Commission's criterion is that it may not suit some purposes because its application results in the exclusion of Guinea, which left the franc zone in 1960.

All in all, it is to be doubted that the problem of definition can ever be solved satisfactorily. As it is now used, the term "French-speaking Africa" is nothing more than a vague reference to a group of African countries that share a unique fund of experience as the result of long and intimate association with France. It is a short-hand expression, useful as a reminder of the peculiarities of a situation created in those countries by a complex historical process.

In shaping that process, the colonial economic policy of France played

145

a role of supreme importance. The purpose of this chapter is to discuss its origin and evolution, but more especially the basic principles that governed it. In doing so, it is hoped that an erroneous notion fostered by a voluminous historical literature on the subject will be dispelled. This is the notion that the so-called Colonial Pact (Pacte Coloniale) represented the central principle of France's colonial economic policy. Most writers, it seems, were so fascinated by the policy's more obvious political implications that they lost sight of other aspects of the matter. The conclusion reached by them takes no account of, and is utterly incompatible with, some of the most fundamental propositions of economic theory. The Colonial Pact is a myth, but a myth that has been given wide circulation, whereas those ideas that actually served as guidelines for economic action have for the most part remained buried in the relative obscurtiy of technical documents and treatises.

Historians are generally agreed that the colonial economic policy of France had its origin in the activities of Jean-Baptiste Colbert, who served as minister of finance during the reign of Louis XIV in the latter half of the seventeenth century. It is worth noting here what a distinguished economist, Professor J. A. Schumpeter, thought of him. In his last and monumental work, *History of Economic Analysis,* Schumpeter gives us this brief but thought-provoking appraisal of Colbert:

He was an honest, able, and energetic administrator who knew how to raise money, intimidate creditors, improve administrative and accounting methods, stimulate industry, build palaces and harbors, develop the navy, and so on, though he was distinctly unlucky in the execution of his larger plans, e.g. colonial enterprise, the history of which shows that the wastes of public planning may easily surpass anything that, on the score of wastefulness, can be charged to private enterprise.[2]

Colbert's interest in "colonial enterprise" was not motivated by dreams of glory and imperial aggrandizement. He did not fear population pressure at home and saw no need to establish large French settlements in remote parts of the world. His interest in colonies stemmed from a desire to bolster France's fiscal and balance-of-payments position. This fact was clearly seen by Montesquieu, who tells us that in building France's first colonial empire "the design of the settlement was the extension of commerce, not the foundation of a city or of a new empire."[3] Colonies were to serve merely as trading posts. Foreigners were not allowed to trade with them and commerce with France was organized on a barter basis, so as to avoid any outflow of specie. It was Colbert's hope that the barter terms of colonial trade would move in favor of France, thereby relieving fiscal pressures at home and improving the chances of achieving a favorable trade balance with other countries. Hence colonies were forbidden to produce goods that might compete with those produced in France. Colbert was particularly interested in establishing trading posts in tropical areas, for tropical products were unlikely to pose a competitive threat and had the added advantage of enabling the French people to enjoy a higher standard of living. To carry out his colonial schemes, he relied heavily on chartered companies. He played a key role in organizing some of them and used his influence to obtain much of the initial capital they required. But, as Schumpeter caustically points out, his colonial ventures met with a dismal lack of financial success.

In theory, Colbertism was merely a French version of British mercantilism. It rested on three premises: (1) trade with the colonies should be monopolized by the mother country; (2) the colonies should specialize in the production of primary products; and (3) all shipping with the colonies should be under the French flag. In practice, there were certain differences. In the execution of policy, for example, the French relied much more heavily upon bureaucratic methods than did the British. Another important difference was that, while in England mercantilist ideas were eventually discarded, in France Colbertism continued to dominate colonial affairs long after it had ceased to influence domestic economic policy.

In the changed context of the nineteenth century and later periods, however, the colonial doctrine of Colbertism could not be applied in its original form. It required interpretation. The point to be stressed here is that Colbertist doctrine, when applied to modern times, can be interpreted in two different ways. If attention is focused upon its second premise, its central policy appears to be to prevent colonies from industrializing. If, however, primary consideration is given to the first and third premises, the basic principle that emerges is that of insulation from world market forces. The existing literature on French colonial policy emphasizes the former interpretation; analysis of practical conduct, especially in the field of commercial policy, shows that in reality the latter was adopted.

It may be noted parenthetically that from a purely logical standpoint the two principles—nonindustrialization and insulation—are not mutually exclusive. The simultaneous application of both is conceivable; it is not, however, essential. Colonies may be prevented from industrializing and yet be allowed to carry on unrestricted trade with countries other than the metropole; on the other hand, colonial industrialization may be permitted while contacts with third countries are kept to a bare minimium. Adherence to one principle, therefore, does not necessarily involve adoption of the other.

The principle of nonindustrialization of the colonies is commonly referred to by the French as the Colonial Pact. The expression is intended to suggest a policy that can be imagined as the result of a contractual arrangement whereby the colonies had agreed to exchange their primary products for French manufactures. It carries the further implication that trade on this basis was invariably disadvantageous for the colonies. Indeed the point is often plainly made that the fictitious contract should be thought of as one to which the colonies had submitted under duress. Stephen H Roberts, author of a classic work on the history of French colonial policy puts it quite tersely: "Reduced to fundamentals, the French system is simply subordination."[4] And French writers underscore this view by repeatedly citing a slogan coined by the eighteenth-century Encyclopedists: "The colonies have been created for the metropole and by the metropole."[5]

The main body of evidence offered by French and other writers in support of their belief that the Colonial Pact served as the basic principle of colonial economic policy consists of various public statements issued at one time or another by a number of prominent French political figures. In point of fact, the evidence cited does not support the thesis advanced by these writers; that they should have thought that it did can only be explained as the result of a failure to distinguish between statements calculated to evoke political support for certain actions and those designed to make explicit the aim of economic policy.

Much, for example, is made of the fact that Jules Ferry, the man generally regarded as the chief architect of France's second colonial empire, frequently sought to justify colonial expansion with the argument that France needed outlets for her industrial products. He appeared to be much impressed by the evolution of the American and German industrial systems on a protectionist basis. He repeatedly warned his countrymen that France had either to follow suit or face the distasteful prospect of economic and political decline. If France were to build an industrial machine, its successful operation would require a market large enough to absorb all the products it would be capable of producing; in a world in which the popularity of the free-trade system was beginning to fade, his argument went on, the only way for France to make certain that such a market would always exist was to build up a vast colonial empire overseas. His views on this subject were summed up in a famous slogan: "The colonial policy of the Third Republic is the offspring of her industrial policy."[6] It is necessary to point out, however, that the success of the overseas ventures contemplated by Ferry depended in an important measure upon his ability to overcome the opposition of large segments of French public opinion that were strongly imbued with anticolonial sentiments, which, incidentally, were shared by nearly all of the leading French economists of his time.

If Ferry gave the impression of being obsessed with the need for outlets ne of his closest and best-known political followers, Eugéne Etienne, also vinced some interest in colonies as sources of raw materials. In 1894, Etienne issued a statement before the Chamber of Deputies that may be egarded as a classic formulation of the Colonial Pact. "We have created," he declared, "and we intend to preserve, by developing it, a colonial empire hat will assure the future of our country on the new continents by providing outlets for our goods and raw materials for our industries."[7]

But concern with colonies as sources of raw materials did not become widespread in France until after World War I. By then many Frenchmen had become impressed with the useful role that colonies could play in this respect, especially under emergency conditions. Certain external events urther stimulated public interest in the question of raw materials.

In the early 1920's, Professor Corrado Gini completed a study of raw materials under League of Nations auspices. Its publication in 1922 impelled Italian Prime Minister Tittoni to launch a violent diatribe that marked the beginning of a bitter international controversy over the question of access by European states to raw materials overseas. The controversy raged throughout the interwar period, pitting the so-called have-not nations—principally Italy, Germany, and Poland—against the so-called have nations—chiefly France, Great Britain, and Holland. Concern with raw materials was so intense that as late as 1944 a former French Minister of Colonies, Jacques Stern, could write: "The economic goal is to bring he raw materials buried for centuries in the African or Asiatic soil and complementary to those of European France to the outside world, by an association profitable to all the partners, for the well-being of the French of the white race and the French of all the colored races."[8]

It is thus fairly evident that the notion of the Colonial Pact played an important part in shaping French attitudes toward the colonies. Above all, it served as a political rallying cry, meeting different purposes as circumstances changed. But it did not, and could not, serve as a guide to economic policy. The colonies, it is true, did produce primary products and import manufactures, but this was not due to French policy. It was due to the existence of relative differences in the endowment of productive agents between the colonies and Europe; because of these differences, specialization along different lines would have been unquestionably less advantageous for all parties. The theoretical proof of this proposition could be easily given, though it would be lengthy. Here it may be sufficient to point out that in Africa not only did the French colonies exhibit this trade pattern, but so also did the colonies of other European states, as well as countries (e.g., Ethiopia) that had not been subjected to colonial domination for any significant period. There existed, in short, no practical alternative to the external trade pattern that had shaped up in the French colonies and hence no logical basis for making this pattern the object of policy.

The only additional evidence cited in support of the view that the Colonial Pact served as a principle of economic policy is the fierce and highly vocal opposition of certain firms in France to the establishment of competitive processing industries in the overseas dependencies.[9] On this point, the following should be noted: (1) metropolitan firms were equally vehement in opposing colonial primary production in any lines in which their interests might be injured by competition; (2) these firms were not always successful in their efforts to block the rise of processing industries overseas; (3) their behavior is in any event better explained as a by-product of a policy of economic insulation, a policy that France did pursue and that, among other things, helped to limit competition and concentrate production in the hands of a few firms.

One of the most notable features of France's policy of insulating its colonies from world-market forces is the consistency with which it was applied ever since the days of Colbert. French policy-makers showed themselves extraordinarily adept at elaborating specific measures to fit changing circumstances and problems, without ever deviating from the basic principle. The only apparent deviation was a tariff law passed in 1861, at a time when France had no important colonial possessions. The law contained provisions that allowed the colonies to buy and sell abroad all classes of merchandise and to use foreign ships to transport their products, even to France. Though the law thus suggested a big step in the direction of trade liberalization, it was riddled with so many exceptions that it was hard to tell which system, free trade or Colbertism, was really intended to prevail.[10]

In 1892, even the illusion of trade liberalization was swept away. A law was passed in that year designed to bring the overseas dependencies into a sort of customs union with France. For tariff purposes, it distinguished between two groups of territories, assimilated and nonassimilated. French merchandise, and foreign merchandise so classed by passage through French customs, was admitted free into assimilated territories if shipped direct. Nearly all imports into these territories from foreign countries paid the same duties as into France, while exports were subject to differential levies, with preference being accorded to goods sent to the metropole. Nonassimiliated territories (the West African possessions, the Indian posts, Tahiti, and Morocco) were exempted from this customs regime either because their geographic location would have made its application too difficult or because international obligations had been incurred that expressly forbade it. Countries in this group applied duties on imports from France, while their exports to France were subject only to the minimum metropolitan tariff. At the same time, several measures, including direct subsidies, were taken to ensure a preferential position for French shipping serving the colonies.[11]

Another important tariff law was passed in 1928. Its net effect was to weaken the distinction between assimilated and nonassimilated territories. Nearly all goods from those nonassimilated territories that accorded preferential treatment to French imports were from that time on allowed to enter France duty-free.[12]

A new and radically different situation arose during the 1930's, when the Depression eventually reached the franc zone. To meet it, an Imperial Conference was summoned in 1934. The Conference engaged in lengthy deliberations and did not conclude its work until a year later. The measures it finally recommended were numerous and varied. In general, it looked with disfavor upon the previous practice of relying mainly on tariff duties to promote the ends of French commercial policy in the colonies; it preferred measures, such as priorities and quotas, that could provide a stronger element of rigidity in sheltering the French colonial empire from external economic influences. It sought to establish, as one writer puts it, "an ordered and coherent structure of imperial economy independent as far as might be of the vicissitudes of international commerce."[13]

The situation changed again after World War II. Like most other countries in Western Europe, France had to contend in the immediate postwar period with a severe disequilibrium in her balance of payments. The "dollar shortage" compelled her to institute foreign-exchange control and to discourage imports from hard-currency zones. It also induced her to stimulate imports from the overseas dependencies, since purchases from the latter did not necessitate payment in foreign currencies. As a consequence, striking shifts took place in the structure of French imports. In the interwar period, for example, France, had normally purchased about 70 per cent of its coffee requirements from countries outside the franc zone, the remainder being obtained from the colonies. Within a few years after the end of World War II, these proportions were nearly reversed. However, despite the highly favorable conditions created in France by foreign-exchange restrictions and the stimulus provided by a rising flow of metropolitan grants, output in the overseas dependencies could not, for a variety of reasons, respond quickly enough to the new conditions of French demand. With only relatively small quantities being shipped in, prices of colonial goods in France soared to levels far above those that prevailed on the world market.

By 1954, the dollar shortage had eased considerably and France began to move toward liberalization of its foreign trade and payments regime.

It could then be foreseen that, in the absence of special measures, th combined pressures of international competition and rising output in th dependent territories would soon force French import prices down. Stron fears were felt in this regard, apparently because it was believed that highe sales volumes would not compensate overseas producers for revenu losses due to lower prices. As a result, an intricate system was devise to prevent prices of goods imported from the dependencies from fallin too rapidly.[14]

Despite a general policy of import trade liberalization, tariff duties wer therefore imposed in France on certain goods originating from countrie outside the franc zone. The duties were designed to protect franc-zon suppliers whose costs of production were higher than those of producer outside the zone. Thus, for example, coffee imports from nonfranc coun tries were subjected in March, 1955, to a duty of 10 per cent; a fev months later it was found that the duty was too low for protectionist pu poses and was quickly raised to 20 per cent.

Where tariffs could not provide the required degree of protection quantitive restrictions were imposed. Imports of certain high-grade Arabic coffees from Central America and Ethiopia used in France for blendin, were limited to about 10,000 metric tons per year. Similarly, banana imported from nonfranc countries were limited to 4,000 metric tons i 1954 and again in 1955.

Goods that franc-zone producers could supply in quantities too sma to meet the requirements of the French market were protected from foreign price competition by linked-purchase regulations. This meant tha licenses for the importation of such commodities from countries outsid the franc zone would be granted in France only upon submission of proo that certain quantities had already been purchased from franc-zon sources, in accordance with specified ratios. A case in point is that o grated cocoa. Imports from nonfranc countries were permitted, but only in amounts equal to those purchased from the overseas dependencies.

The dependencies were able to produce certain goods—such as, peanuts for example—in relatively large but still insufficient quantities to mee metropolitan demand. In such instances price protection was afforded through market guarantees. For peanuts and other oilseeds guarantee were provided through a special organ, the Société Inter-professionnelle de Oléagineux Fluides Alimentaires (SIOFA). If the market price in Franc fell below the guaranteed price, SIOFA was authorized to buy from Franc zone sources; if it rose above the guaranteed price, SIOFA was empowered to buy from nonfranc countries. The price guarantee was applied to a predetermined quantity, the purchase of which was thus also guaranteed. I covered the c.i.f. price in France, as well as the producer price at the por of embarkation.

The steady increase in the production of Robusta coffee in the Ivory Coast, Madagascar, and other franc-zone countries made it increasingly difficult to market the entire output in France at prevailing price levels. To maintain French prices, measures were taken to market the surplus abroad. The most important of these measures was the adoption of linked-sale regulations. Firms in Africa were required to sell certain quantities outside the franc-zone before receiving authorization to export to the metropole. In the Ivory Coast, for instance, the ratio was set at 1:7 to 6:7 in June, 1955, and at 1:4 in December of the same year.

Since coffee exporters could be expected to claim that by being forced to sell a part of their stocks at the lower world-market price they were incurring losses, compensation was provided through export bounties. Exporters obtained reimbursements amounting to 6 per cent of the f.o.b. value of coffee shipped to nonfranc countries until April, 1955, and to 12 per cent thereafter, 2 per cent of which was contributed by the overseas territory and the remainder by France.

In addition, stabilization funds were set up for all major tropical exports beginning in 1955. They performed various functions, but were particularly useful in helping to administer and coordinate the complicated system of price supports that France had seen fit to establish for the benefit of producers in the overseas dependencies.

Thus, as time went on, French policy became increasingly complex, yet it clung all along to an ancient principle. Its full effects are difficult to assess. It is obvious that the dependencies derived many benefits from it; but there were also debilitating effects. Since they were economically underdeveloped, the dependencies suffered from certain inherent rigidities, and the French policy of insulation further reduced their capacity for rapid adaptation to changing economic conditions.

Today, as a result of France's entry into the European Economic Community and the acquisition of sovereignty by nearly all of the French dependencies in Africa, the policy of economic insulation is in the process of being abandoned, though some of its effects will inevitably linger on for a while. Because of the aforementioned rigidities that French policy helped to reinforce, any sudden and drastic changes are bound to cause serious economic dislocations in French-speaking Africa. Fortunately, both France and her former African dependencies appear to be conscious of the need for gradual adjustment to the new conditions that have arisen. To this end, some measures have already been taken; others will surely follow. What these additional measures should be is clearly up to the parties directly concerned. All that outsiders can do to be helpful is to show sympathy and understanding patience.

10

External Tensions:
Resulting Development

WILLIAM J. MAZZOCCO

WHEN INDEPENDENCE came to Africa the inevitable drive for economic maturity was not far behind. Africans knew that political independence would not automatically bring economic modernization in its train, and French-speaking Africans, who had been among the very last to attain sovereign status, were particularly aware of the need for modernizing their economies. They had much more "catching up" to do, economically speaking, if the blessings of liberty were to be meaningful. It is no wonder, then, that to most African peoples economic development is tantamount to economic "emancipation." They see in the satisfaction of their economic aspirations their liberation from the inhuman enslavement of poverty.

Local efforts were mobilized, concurrently with the advent of independence, for the attainment of certain economic objectives. In addition, great reliance was placed on international economic mechanisms to accelerate the process of economic growth. Through greater participation in international trade, Africans hoped to escape the strictures of the limited home markets; through access to the international financial markets, they looked for sources of development capital to compensate for their inadequacies in domestic savings and export earnings; and through widened associations with international aid donors, they saw opportunities to obtain vital resources for economic development not normally available through the conventional trade and financial mechanisms.

In the few short years since independence, there has indeed been a general growth in Africa's trade, in its foreign financial transactions, and in its arrangements for receipts of foreign aid. There has also been considerable economic modernization. The casual visitor returning to French-speaking Africa for the first time since 1960 is struck by the sight of new and modern hotels in Dakar, Ouagadougou, Abidjan, and elsewhere; the jet ports in Cotonou, Brazzaville, and Niamey; the increase in the use of communications media, including television; the modern housing developments; the new port facilities being built in Lome and Cotonou; and the vastly improved conditions of the urban and rural road systems. The returning student of African affairs also sees the beginnings of campaigns to extend education, literacy, and health services. One might well conclude that African economic aspirations are on the road to attainment, and that economic and social welfare will in time be the property of the latest newcomers to the family of free men.

Economic progress, however, has been a mixed blessing for Africa, for it has been accompanied by a disturbing rise of social disaffection. In all too many instances, ruptures of the social peace have assumed the form of societal warfare, otherwise known as insurrection or insurgency.

These turbulent events have pained not only Africans but their friends around the world as well. And for good cause, for no one in this day and age can be at ease when his brothers must take up arms to free themselves from poverty and despair. President Sékou Touré once said, "If a finger of Africa is cut, the whole body of Africa suffers." This organic quality of African solidarity is equally present within the whole family of man today. When the body of Africa is wounded, the security of the whole family of man is threatened.

Prescriptions for stabilizing the process of economic development in French-speaking Africa have not been lacking. However, there is less than general agreement among Africanists regarding the causes of and cures for social tensions. Indeed, one school of thought counsels against zealous programs for attenuating such tensions, contending that they are useful fever signals indicating the emergence of imbalances inescapably induced by progress. They are the inevitable cost of economic development.

Nevertheless, there appears to be good reason to subject these feverish developments to careful scrutiny. Will they be acceptable costs of African nation-building? Or will they tend to become contagious, infecting not only the African continent but also the international community? Which of the undesirable costs of progress are avoidable? What measures can be formulated to filter such unacceptable social and political costs out of the modernization process?

Africans and others have sought to determine why social unrest has marked the process of African economic development. They have generally concluded that the economic aspirations of the African peoples have been inadequately satisfied. Many of these observers have ascribed much of the blame for this state of affairs to the workings of international economic mechanisms. The manner in which international trade is conducted, the ways in which the international financial markets operate, and the presumed deficiencies of foreign economic and technical cooperation arrangements are all called into question. In short, we are told, these mechanisms have not been adapted to the objective requirements of the new world environment, and are therefore ineffective as instruments of African economic development. Because of their ineffectiveness, vital economic aspirations go unsatisfied. This is presumed to be in large measure the cause of social tensions in Africa.

The prescription offered by these critics for redressing this situation can be simply stated: International mechanisms must be reformed. They must be revised to secure for the less-developed countries opportunities, within the international economic environment, with which to speed up the tempo of their economic development. Precedence must be accorded to this objective until the developing countries can participate responsibly and benefit equitably from international economic activity. Otherwise the emancipation of the African peoples from the insecurities associated with the functioning of the world economy will not be possible. The African peoples would be doomed to a meaningless political independence marred by mounting social tensions and human suffering. Social tensions will only disappear when international economic mechanisms become effective instruments for the economic development of the less-privileged societies.

I do not intend to make a detailed investigation of the grievances respecting the international mechanisms or to appraise the economic efficacy of the prescriptions offered. Rather, I propose to direct my inquiry to an appraisal of the legitimacy of the notion that better international economic tools are all that is needed to counter the tendency for social tensions to emerge as economic growth proceeds.

It is not my contention that the international mechanisms do not require review. Indeed, no responsible authority denies that improvement is desirable. I am simply proposing here that the reformation of these mechanisms to make them more effective as instruments of economic development will not *automatically* remove the primary causes of social tensions. If this be a correct premise, then obviously more than their reform is required.

For the moment let us briefly examine the nature of the grievances. Why are the international tools said to be inadequate to satisfy economic aspirations? First, the proponents of this view say, because history has not been charitable toward the developing countries. History has contrived that the trade and financial rules, which govern the workings of the world economy, were formulated when the new societies were not yet members of the family of nations. Consequently, the rules could only have been devised to serve the interests of the few nations whose presence dominated the international scene. These nations have become affluent and prosperous, partly because it was in their power to see to it that international economic arrangements were not organized at their economic expense. Now, however, there are eighty or more new nations seeking the assistance of international economic mechanisms to satisfy the vital economic aspirations of their peoples. But the rules are still very much those that served the interests of a handful of already developed societies. The new countries of French-speaking Africa are even more disadvantaged than others, for they have only recently joined in the game of international economics, the rules of which are even less relevant to their economic development needs.

History's perversity is multidimensional. History waited until spectacular scientific and technological progress had occurred before according sovereignty to African peoples. Not having had the opportunity to participate as equals in international life in the past, these peoples have not been able to organize their societies so that they, too, could share more fully in the benefits accruing from the scientific progress of the present. The advanced countries, on the other hand, are technologically qualified to benefit in large measure.

As a consequence, the so-called rules of world trade and international finance are designed to serve the interests of equals. Furthermore, rapid technological advances are tending more and more to pass the unprepared societies by. Accordingly, French-speaking African nations see themselves at the end of a receiving line that grows progressively longer. They fear that a new and modern form of enslavement awaits them, unless the adversities of rules designed for equals can be effectively countered. Otherwise, economic progress will only yield increasing frustration, bitterness, resentment, and eventually violence. The proponents of this theory conclude that nothing less than a reorganization of the international economy will repair these trends and deter the spread of social tensions.

And what do they propose in the way of reforms to make the international economic mechanisms capable of adequately satisfying African economic aspirations? Briefly, they propose the establishment of preferential and privileged arrangements favoring the emerging nations in international transactions. They seek the creation of opportunities that will permit developing countries to benefit more from world trade, finance, and aid. They also seek to build security into the international system over a long term to ensure the availability of these privileged opportunities for as long as they may be necessary. They advocate increases in the levels of foreign aid and qualitative revisions designed to have that aid serve primarily, if not exclusively, the objective of economic development.

In the field of international trade, they prescribe preferential access to the markets of the developed societies, including commodity agreements, special incentives for industrialization, one-way preferential tariffs (particularly the abolition of tariffs on imports of tropical products), and the attenuation of internal taxes and other devices that act as deterrents to African exports The insistence on preferential devices to speed up industrialization is strongly put forward. Africans feel that economic modernization cannot proceed fast enough via improvements in agriculture, and they wish to see evidence that the advanced nations will not deter the rise of (presumably potentially competitive) industries in Africa. They seek assurances of long-term access on a privileged basis to the world's great markets for programmed industrial production, as well as capital borrowings or extremely liberal terms.

To those who would prefer to effect reforms in the trade rules without discarding the principles of nondiscrimination and reciprocity the Africans have ready answers. Trade discrimination in favor of developing countries for the mutually desirable objective of speeding up economic development has its precedents; the European countries were permitted to discriminate against imports of extra-European origin as a basis for assuring European economic reconstruction during the Marshall Plan era. As for those who support concessions of equal value in trade negotiations, the African replies that equal treatment of unequals is tantamount to inequality.

The advanced nations and certain international organizations are engaged in studying means for improving the trade rules and for innovating special trade arrangements for economic development purposes. But we are concerned here with social and societal effects, rather than with the economic impact of such measures.

The French-speaking African nations point out that historical factors have treated the developed countries generously in matters regarding international finance, as well as in matters of international trade. Opportunities were open to them to develop nontrade sources of foreign-exchange earnings during the modernization period. For example, the affluent societies benefit greatly from the commodity portion of international intercourse as well as deriving the "invisibles" benefits. When an African commodity moves in world trade, it usually moves on a carrier bearing the flag of a developed country; the cost of its movement is usually borne by a fiancial house of an advanced nation; and the insurance involved is usually written by a Northern Hemisphere underwriter. In the case of French-speaking African countries, African items entering overseas commerce from inland Africa will generally move over African roads and railways, and through African ports built largely by foreign capital, perforce requiring that part or all of the invisibles receipts make their way to foreign treasuries. Accordingly, even with huge increases in foreign trade, under present circumstances African nations cannot expect to derive foreign exchange and invisibles receipts therefrom in anything like the proportion receivable by the advanced nations.

Furthermore, the manner in which the world has developed has provided the advanced countries with other handsome sources of invisibles earnings. Remittances from tourism, emigrants, and private foreign capital loom large in payments balances of some developed countries. They are generally hard to come by in French-speaking Africa.

Consequently, many observers feel they have a case when they suggest that, if the advanced world is seriously interested in African economic development, then it must make international financial resources preferentially available to Africa to compensate for her limited earning capabilities.

The grievances respecting the wide variety of foreign-aid arrangements are numerous. Even though there are today approximately twenty countries providing economic and technical assistance, plus the many international organizations, the increase in donors has been matched by an increase in dissatisfaction with this unconventional mechanism.

Basically, the common African complaint is centered around the proposition that much of the aid employed today is dissipated by the deficiencies of the international trade and financial mechanisms. In fact, one observer has remarked that if present trade and aid trends continue, in 1970 the aid level will be inferior to the exchange losses that would occur as a result of regressive export-earning capacities of the developing countries. Accordingly, Africans propose that foreign aid's effectiveness as a developmental tool requires, first, the reformation of international trade and financial instruments, and, second, a revision of the aid arrangements themselves. Among other things they feel that foreign aid must (1) be made available at higher levels for an assured long period of time; (2) be harmonized so that the plurality of sources will not engender confusion; (3) be available at liberal, unburdensome terms from all sources; and (4) shed its seeming association with unilateral commercial or other policy objectives of the donor country. Many Africans, believing that African development and viability are significantly impeded by the mass unpreparedness of their populations, particularly seek expanded technical-cooperation arrangements.

As with the other mechanisms, the Africans want foreign aid to serve primarily the *economic* developmental needs of their countries, and only incidentally, if at all, as an auxiliary tool of commercial policy or export promotion of donor nations.

This chapter will not evaluate the economic aspects of the grievances and the prescriptions for their redress. We will assume that reforms, satisfactory to Africans, are accepted and immediately put into practice; that these reforms will indeed quicken the pace of economic development in the continent; and that desired increases in gross national product, per capital income, and other indicators symbolizing economic progress are achieved. In short, that *economic* aspirations are being adequately served. Those who contended that the international mechanisms were faulty can now expect tensions to disappear as a result of stepped-up economic development. But will the reformation of the international economic instruments be sufficient to ensure social peace? My answer is No.

I rest my case on observations of instances in which economic development, avidly sought and reasonably attained, has seemingly begotten societal turbulence. The primacy often accorded to *economic* objectives may have been unfortunate, for, in the rush to create new economic opportunities, the *social* need to ensure their equitable distribution has been frequently ignored. Many years ago, this maldistribution of new opportunities may have had limited social effect. But in the world of today this no longer holds true. Economic opportunities are becoming more and more the indispensable means for the satisfaction of man's principal aspirations—his social and human fulfillment. The denial or lack of economic opportunities is becoming more and more tantamount to the denial of the means to participate in the modern world, and to benefit from its progress.

Just as history has seemingly favored some societies over others, so does progress inherently tend to benefit certain individuals more than others. This natural tendency is present in the process of economic growth. Economic progress also creates opportunities for favored groups to establish conditions that become barriers to an equitable distribution of economic opportunities. When these natural and unnatural barriers are deliberately and successfully countered by public policy, economic progress can be accompanied by social peace. When they are not, economic progress will more likely beget social tensions.

Drawing on the lessons of history, let us now try to perceive, conceptually, how economic development, accelerated by improved international mechanisms, might under some circumstances proceed without reducing social unrest. Let us assume that Country X has, as a result of these reforms, enjoyed an unprecedented economic advance. Trade has increased; prices and marketings of primary commodities have been satisfactorily stabilized; international loans have become easily and liberally accessible; industrialization has expanded; and foreign aid is greater than ever, and has contributed much to breaking down the barriers to literacy and higher education. The prevailing view is that under such conditions Country X should not only be satisfying its economic aspirations but it should also be enjoying a large measure of social peace. But we need only recall the instances in which this was not so to suspect a flaw in the theory. All countries, rich or poor, have found that economic development alone is not enough. Historically, the *social* outcome of even astounding economic growth has rarely been a peaceful one. How do social tensions arise in societies that are creating new economic opportunities? What does a glance at history suggest? What about Country X?

This mythical country was once a traditional society. Its economy was generally static. New economic opportunities were not being generated. A few people enjoyed a favored position, benefiting most from the few opportunities that existed for material gain. No one seemed to mind much. This society was at peace with itself, although it might from time to time war with a neighboring society. There was no inequitable distribution of new economic opportunities.

But Country X is now no longer a traditional society. It is in transition, seeking to modernize its economy. Economic development has increased opportunities for economic gain. With the expansion of foreign trade, abetted by international economic reforms, new economic opportunities have emerged in the commercial sector. Some of newly educated young people see in this development the economic means to the achievement of their *social* aspirations, a dignified pursuit of the blessings of liberty. But what occurs if these young men find entry into the economic field difficult or impossible? What happens if they begin to feel that they are being unfairly deprived of these new opportunities? How will they react to inequality of opportunity? Will they rejoice in the increase in economic activity of Country X, or will they be more inclined to protest against the manner in which progress is shared?

It is conceivable that new opportunities in the import-export field may be legitimately limited even though trade has increased. However, the young people who have been educated may still seize on other aspects of distributive justice. Let us assume that the personal gains resulting from expanded trade are, as they should be, rising. However, the taxation mechanism may still be that which it was before development. The lag in fiscal reforms inhibits the absorption by society of a reasonable portion of the income increments and their utilization for the advancement of the social interest. With the modernization of Country X, more and more people have become capable of making these observations. If they judge economic progress to be occurring at the expense of the social interest, they may well have reason to feel alien to and not cohesive with the society.

We have also assumed that commodity agreements have contributed to the economic objectives of Country X. This development has also opened new opportunities. The new opportunities may take several forms:

sharing, even in a minor way, in the ownership of land upon which th
exportable commodities can be produced; participating in the marketin
thereof; sharing in job opportunities created; and sharing in the productivit
gains resulting from the price and market security of the commodity agree
ments. But if the *opportunity-sharing* machinery of the society has not bee
modernized to match its economic modernization, many people in Countr
X may have the uncomfortable feeling of being shut out of the process (
growth. Farmers, laborers, youth, and others may well fear that the
social aspirations will be unrequited while progress seemingly inequitabl
favors a relative few.

New industries have made their appearance in Country X as a result (
international reforms. As is usually the case in a young country, th
modern factories are concentrated in the only major city in the country. I
come from industrial activity is now a significant component of th
national income. Jobs have been created and there are workers to fill then
However, on the social side of Country X's balance sheet all is not wel
Rents continue to rise as the city's population grows. The workers for
trade unions. They listen to labor leaders and to educated youth who ta
about economic problems. Productivity increases, they hear, are not bein
equitably shared between management and labor; inflation dissipates part (
their new incomes; social insurance against job and income insecurities
inadequate because of wide-ranging tax avoidance and evasion. They ar
told that vital social needs go unrequited while favored groups improv
their positions. If the management of industries is of foreign origin, th
charge becomes "economic imperialism." The emergence of labor, yout
and student groups is inevitable in a modernizing society such as Country)
The judgments such new groups make about the justice of progress w
have much to do with the presence or absence of social tensions.

Our mythical Country X has tasted a bit of history. It has made th
satisfaction of *economic* aspirations a primary goal of its society. It ha
drawn on the international economic mechanisms to expand trade, obta
financial resources, industrialize its economy, and attack illiteracy and po
health. In order to speed up the transition from poverty to modern stat
hood, Country X requested reforms in the international economy in th
light of the disparate conditions between developed and developing nation
It would be difficult to be critical of Country X for seeking all means f
speeding up its economic development.

While Country X was deeply involved in economic matters, it apparent
assumed that social needs would somehow automatically be satisfied on
economic development was rapidly under way. But, because history ar
the inherent nature of progress are a bit perverse, this could not be the cas
A society in transition needs economic modernization; but it needs no le

a modernization of its social structure if economic objectives are to satisfy social aspirations. When the structures are left unchanged, the verdict of history is that economic progress will beget social tensions.

The foregoing is not an argument against economic development or progress. It is not an argument against making international economic mechanisms more efficacious for the task of national development. It is, however, history's powerful argument for specifically seeking social progress and development, for making deliberate efforts to serve the social as well as the economic interests of a society. Economic progress should be the means, not the end, of a nation's activity. Economic progress should be the means to legitimate social ends, the means by which man's liberty and dignity are protected and strengthened.

This suggests that in addition to international reforms, there must be adequate internal reforms. Only internal reforms can determine the shape of the structure through which new opportunities are distributed to its members. As vital as international economic reforms may be, they will help ensure a society's peace with itself only when the society's social structure is such that economic resources are consciously and satisfactorily made to serve the social interest. The opportunity-creating mechanism of a society admittedly needs to be developed. The establishment of an opportunity-sharing mechanism is no less important.

Not too long ago, one African leader wrote: "We know that we must rebuild Africa. To win and proclaim a nation's independence but keep its old structures is to plow a field but not to sow it with grain for harvest." An African proverb says: "It is no use to look skyward for help until you have tilled your own field." Both comments are evidence that the wisdom or attuning African efforts to African social and human aspirations exists in that great continent. Indeed, the more one learns about Africa the more one realizes that the African struggle for emancipation is more social than economic. It is not so much the lack of material things that afflicts the African, even though his material lot is abysmally low. It is freedom from the lack of opportunities for human betterment that is at the center of his drive for emancipation.

The war on the poverty of opportunities is singularly African but is not limited to that part of the world. It is being fought in every corner of the world today, in every nation, rich or poor. Victory in this war cannot be limited to any one region, since in this shrinking world avoidable human suffering in one society is cause for pain in all others.

In this war, international economic mechanisms have their role. They must be continuously examined and revised, when necessary, to become effective instruments in the service of the family of man. But I would submit that their service will be most useful not so much when they become

better instruments of economic development, but when they become bett
instruments of social and human progress. Since their effectiveness for th
purpose depends mightily on the structure of the developing society, it
obvious that man can be better served by a harmonization of internation
and national mechanisms for social development.

Fortunately, many international organizations with considerable expei
ence with the world's economy already exist and are already enlisted
this war. Fortunately also, most of the French-speaking African nations a
members of these organizations. Their contribution to the cooperati
efforts to bring a harmonized unity out of this endeavor cannot be in doub
Their role in bringing unity out of the vast diversity of the great Afric
continent in the few short years since independence is sufficient eviden
of that fact. Working together, the family of nations can avoid the rise
social tensions that marred the economic development of Country ?
Working together, the family of man can develop the societal tools that w
inhibit the inherent tendency of the modernization process to build di
criminatory barriers to a social sharing of the fruits of progress.

In our scientific age, international mechanisms are essential if developii
societies are to emancipate themselves from the structures of the past. B
our age has also made it mandatory that all societies protect the rights
their citizens against the avoidable opportunity-denying features of tl
modernization process. Man must claim these rights, if for no other reasc
than as a mark of his dignity.

Social tensions in part derive from our modern age's new forms of soci
insecurity: the adverse impact progress can have on the sharing of ec
nomic opportunities. The whole family of man must be concerned with th
challenge, for to fail in our age to emancipate man from this form
tyranny is to invite the inevitable question: "Can the family of man su
vive for long half slave and half free?"

The need to make international economic mechanisms more effecti
as instruments for the modernization of the French-speaking nations
Africa is not being questioned. But economic modernization must not pr
ceed at the expense of the vital social and human aspirations of the Afric
people. Consequently, efforts are needed to ensure that the process t
which the modernization occurs facilitates the use of international econom
mechanisms in the social as well as the economic interest. The harmoniz
tion of international with national instruments for this purpose appears
offer an attractive meeting ground for international cooperation. The a
tenuation of preventable social insecurity is a concern of all nations, ri
and poor. The progressive strengthening of economic measures to mal
them effective instruments of social progress is today more than ever
universal imperative. In the French-speaking nations of Africa, such mea

ures can act as a powerful deterrent to societal warfare. In developed coun-tries, they are essential for waging the war on poverty of opportunities.

Admittedly, the urge for economic modernization in all emerging coun-ries is fairly overpowering. Understandably, there could be some concern that an equally powerful pursuit of social progress would inevitably incur great economic costs. In some instances, in French-speaking Africa as well as elsewhere, these presumed economic costs of social progress might be considered unacceptable. An equitable sharing of a meager national income might easily incite as much social tension as an unfair distribution of a larger product.

Apart from the validity of such a proposition, there is ample scope for challenging the notion that the attainment of social achievements ines-capably requires a sacrifice of economic progress. Obviously, there must be a balanced pursuit of these twin aspirations. A process that redresses a social inequity by overcorrecting or by inequitably redistributing economic opportunities will not serve the over-all social or economic interest of the society. However, a process of economic modernization that is tempered by social measures to promote equality of opportunity and equitable income distribution and by countermeasures for deterring the opportunity-denying tendencies inherent in progress is in the long run probably the best way to promote self-sustaining economic growth. A fuller utilization of the society's population and an ever-increasing aggregate demand, which would flow from such a program, facilitates productivity increases along with eco-nomic expansion.

The unremitting search for measures to make economic and social progress compatible and mutually reinforcing is a vital requirement for reducing the incidence of tensions associated with economic development. The reformation of both international and national economic instruments must take this fact into account.

11

Selected Cultural Barriers
to the Modernization of Labor

GEORGE R. HORNER

IN ORDER TO CONSTRUCT a dam at Edéa, Cameroun, in the early 1950's
the French Government imported 500 skilled and semiskilled laborers from
Italy. At the completion of the project the workers returned home. They
had remained in the Cameroun for approximately two years. The rationale
for "importing" a foreign labor force was not that there was a scarcity of
Camerounian labor, but that the Camerounians refused to perform manual
labor, considering it undignified. This chapter will investigate some of the
social beliefs and patterns of economic behavior that relate to problems of
labor development.

The family. The Western idea of "family" usually means members of the
same home: father, mother, and children. The African idea of family usually means members of the same lineage and/or clan. Blood relationship
is the key factor in both the lineage and the clan concepts. The extended
family functions in about the same way as an American business corporation functions: It is an "incorporated" group, bound by reciprocal duties,
obligations, responsibilities, and loyalties. Members of the same lineage and
clan are bound by the same social umbilical cord.

The good of the individual is subordinate to the good of the family, and
the traditional African could not act without involving his entire family.
The extended-family concept is the most crucial of the cultural barriers to
labor and labor recruitment, both of which, in the West, imply freedom of
movement for the individual, with slight, if any, consideration of home
ties. This is not usually the case in Africa.

The division of work by sex. In most African societies men have the
arder and heavier tasks, women the lighter and longer. In hoe cultures,
or example, men hunt, build homes, clear the bush in preparation for the
arden, and often do the heavier gardening tasks. These tasks may be
ccomplished individually or corporately by lineages, or men's work groups.
Vomen, in hoe societies, produce children and gardens, prepare the food,
nd care for the home. A Bulu woman in Southeastern Cameroun, working
y herself on a plot measuring fifty square yards, can adequately feed a
amily of four for half a year. Larger plots require aid, but even in areas
there cooperative labor is engaged, the food produced is inadequate. This
; also true among the pastoral, cattle-keeping nomads of French-speak-
ig Africa. Groups such as the Fulbe and the Hausa will do no farm work,
ut make horticulture the responsibility of their former conquered peoples,
ho barely provide enough crops to meet their own needs, let alone the
eeds of their former masters.

A problem related to the division of work is property ownership.
Throughout West Africa, property is communally owned. (It is believed
nat the land is in fact owned by one's familial ancestors.) The village
hiefs allocate land to hut-families for their kitchen gardens. If the land is
sed, the right (usufruct) to it remains in a particular family, but if it is
ot used it is returned to the local societal authority for redistribution, a
ractice that prevents individual ownership of land. A man may bequeath
grove, of, say, cocoa trees to his son or sister's son, but not the land
pon which the trees grow.

The lineage/clan family principles of land tenure are so deeply ingrained
nat, as Senghor suggests, they might be the basis for an African "com-
nunalism" upon which new African nations could be built.[1] Whether or
ot this is possible is debatable, for it is not clear how a laborer would
etain his family and culturally oriented responsibilities while at the same
me maintaining independence and mobility.

African attitudes toward manual labor. Many French-speaking Africans
ssociate manual labor with slave labor, for, in the pre-White period, only
laves worked for other men, and, after the coming of the White man,
onscripted labor, wagon-pulling, and the carrying of sedan chairs with
Vhite occupants in them, became almost synonymous with "slave" labor.
his impression was further reinforced by the fact that most Europeans in
Africa did not perform physical work. The African began to feel that, al-
nough he received trade goods and money in return for his services, "work-
ig" for the White man was not very different from being his slave. Thus,
raditional attitudes toward manual labor constitute another major barrier
 labor recruitment in French-speaking Africa. The Inter-African Labour

Institute has the following to say of work and manual labor in Africa:

1. Work must be considered in its relation to the basic institution, the family or clan. It becomes a "Social apostasy" as soon as it ceases to be performed on behalf of the clan. Within the family framework it is divided on a basis of sex and age.

2. The idea of work is bound up with religious rites.

3. The African measures his efforts to the needs of this "subsistence economy" of his village and tribe and knows nothing of the "profit-economy" which gives a totally different character to the imperatives of production.

4. Work requires neither foresight nor planning.

5. The idea of *work* does not include any notion of *time*—the tribal worker sets himself no time-limit for a given task.

6. There is no division of labor, or specialization; each man carries out the whole series of operations from start to finish.

7. For men, work is episodic. When a job has to be done, the men do it often without a break until the object has been attained. But the intervals of inactivity are long and frequent.

8. A man hardly ever works alone.

9. Work, in tribal conditions, is not felt as an imposition but as an integral part of the condition of adult manhood. The atmosphere in which it is carried out is usually gay: either a "hunting party" or a "work party," resembling in many ways a collective leisure activity in a modern society.

New incentives to work: Cash and family solidarity. Money had been introduced to all areas of French-speaking Africa before 1920. Most Africans thought of it as another commodity, but one that could be obtained by working for Europeans in the administrative-commercial centers, or by growing crops for cash. Africans were willing to cross from a traditional economy to a European economy to gain those things that cash readily procured. Cash, the African found, could be used as bridewealth, and for replacing sheep and iron hoes, etc. It could also acquire for him such articles of consumption as canned milk, meat, aluminum sheeting, and phonographs and records. And, he could pay his taxes with it, rather than pay them by doing conscription labor. The desire for cash forced men to leave rural villages to work in urban centers where they could obtain it.

In 1956 alone, approximately 29,000 Bamiléké of the Cameroun between the ages of fifteen and forty left their villages and migrated to Douala. After working for a number of years, they returned to their families with wealth and higher status. Relatively few remained at the urban centers.

A man who goes to an urban center looking for work is not necessarily a free agent. Soon after he arrives he must look up members of his extended family. He lives with this group and shares in the cost of running the house hold. He sends a portion of his salary back to his home family. As Balandier points out:

A "real organic unity" is maintained very often between a section of the extended family living in the town and the rural section. This is especially true of the Bacongo families, who may send members in the town to earn money to augment family income, assisting in their establishment in the town and maintaining a fairly close control over them.[4]

Such a relationship is well known and common to all of French-speaking Africa.

Professor J. Némo, in a study of Palimé, Togo, describes the social relationship that develops in the urban center—a relationship that functions like the traditional extended family, which by analogy, is similar to the apprentice system of the Middle Ages. In the urban center, young men, often with their families, "join" a man, who in the role of "father" (*patron*) is responsible for them. They (the *clientèle*) are not necessarily from his lineage or clan, or even his "tribe," but they join him and are loyal to him. Such young men do not share their income with their compatriots or send it home to their families, but give it, either in part or in total, to their *patron*. The *patron* becomes "chief" in the traditional role sense, and respect and deference are paid him by the young men of his "family."[5] The character of the customary family is retained in this way.

Zalinger, in a study of African students in America, noted:

They display a high degree of effective involvement in the norms and customs of the traditional family, and express considerable approval for the cohesion, mutual aid, respect for elders, and other personal relationships which characterize the traditional family.

However, one African reported by Zalinger pointed up the problem this way:

Our family obligations place too much strain on successful individuals. My father had to cater to so many people that he was not able to do much for himself. . . . It isn't the close ties that I object to, but the dependency. . . . There are a lot of people in Ibadan who don't work because they know they can go and live with relatives. This is why you can't amass wealth. . . . I will not help such people.[6]

Money gained from salaries tends to reinforce the traditional family structure not only for the reasons cited above, but because working away from home is considered, at best, a temporary condition. Most French-speaking West Africans are psychologically village-family oriented. Less than 10 per cent plan to live permanently away from the context of their family. Some who stay away during their working years plan to retire in their villages. This kind of "permanency" is found chiefly among school-teachers and government *fonctionnaires*. Even they look forward to retirement in home villages.

Although the number of wage earners in Africa has risen in recent years[7] causing a flow of workers from rural districts to urban centers, this should not be viewed as the kind of population shift that the United States has undergone during the past century—a century in which the economy changed from an agricultural one to an industrial one. Although this is a possibility in Africa's future, family ties and responsibilities are still strong enough to prevent its early realization in French-speaking Africa.

Cash-cropping is a compartively easy and quick way to earn money and to achieve readily either traditional or modern goals. However, cash cropping has commercialized neither land nor labor. Cash has been used to replace traditional commodities—spears, hoes, pots, sheep, cattle—in almost every traditional cultural sector, particularly in marriage. In 1913, for example, no cash was included in the Bulu bridewealth. But today traditional Bulu bridewealth may amount to from 50,000 to 100,000 CFA francs.[8]

The strength of traditionally oriented culture in French-speaking Africa can best be noted in Table 1, which lists the French-speaking African countries, their estimated populations, the estimated percentage of each country's population "employed in the rural sector," and the prevailing economy.

The phrase "employed in the rural sector" needs some explanation because it is somewhat misleading. In the French economists' frame of reference, "employed" in the rural sector means the percentage of the total population working at agricultural food production. The phrase suggests the commercialization of both land and labor. Actually, this is not the case. Translated into local terms, the phrase means the precentage of population engaged in the traditional and culturally oriented production of cash crops and subsistence foods. Cash crops have reinforced the family structure and solidarity. Instead of becoming a factor in the modernization of the rural economy, they have strengthened the traditional ways of life. Cash remains, by analogy, the icing on the cultural cake, since cash derived from the sale of these crops or cattle is used to serve marginal rather than basic needs: It buys phonographs and records; aluminum roofing; bicycles; dry goods and sewing machines; trucks; canned milk; and so forth. As St. Clair Drake points out:

At least seven out of every ten inhabitants of Africa have their roots down deep in the village or cattle camps and are engaged in some combination of agriculture, pastoralism, fishing and hunting. No more than one African in five works for wages. . . . The great forces of urbanization and industrializa-

TABLE 1. THE STRENGTH OF TRADITIONALLY ORIENTED CULTURE
IN FRENCH-SPEAKING AFRICA

Country	Estimated population (1960)	Percentage of population employed in the rural sector	Basis of economy
Cameroun[a]	4,100,000 (1963)	80	Agriculture
Central African Republic[b]	1,170,000	90	Agriculture
Chad[e]	2,640,000	87	Agriculture
Congo Republic[d]	750,000	76	Agriculture
Dahomey[e]	2,070,000	92	Agriculture
Gabon[f]	400,000	62	Agriculture
Guinea[g]	4,000,000 (1963)	90	Agriculture
Ivory Coast[h]	1,100,000	90	Agriculture
Mali[i]	3,680,000 (1963)	95	Agriculture
Mauritania[j]	750,000	93	Cattle
Niger[k]	3,000,000	90	Agriculture
Senegal[l]	3,100,000	80	Agriculture
Togo[m]	1,500,000	80	Agriculture
Upper Volta[n]	4,370,000	94	Cattle

SOURCES: [a] U.S. Department of Agriculture, Foreign Agriculture Service, M64, September, 1959.
[b] *Plan triennal provisoire de développement, économique et social,* 1960, 1961, 1962, Vols. I and II.
[e] through [f] France, Ministry of Cooperation, *Economie et plan de développement,* October, 1960, issued separately for each country.
[g] *Africa Report,* VIII (June, 1964), No. 10.
[h], [i], [j], [l], [m], [n] France, Ministry of Cooperation, *op. cit.*
[k] République du Niger, *Comptes économiques,* January, 1961.

tion have barely touched the majority of people, and even those involved have not all been alienated from the traditional way of life.[9]

Cash income, although a modernizing factor, has not modernized the French-speaking African labor force.

New ways to work and new work roles. Through the incentive of gaining and using cash, a vast variety of new ways to work has been opened to the tribal African by Westerners. The bureaucratic nature of governmental administration itself opened many specialized ways of work. "Factories" and other commercial establishments and missions and their specialized religious groups also offered many types of employment.

In *Tropical Africa,* I classified these new work roles in sociological categories, as follows:[10]

1. The élite class, composed of government officials, rich and educated, store owners, directors of schools, pastors, priests, etc.

2. The *évolué* class, consisting of lesser school and government *fonctionnaires*, clerks in commercial employ, carpenters, masons, truck drivers, domestic workers ("boys"), specialists in ivory, ebony, and wood handicrafts, tailors and educated women.

3. The great mass of non-salaried, uneducated, non-literate, literate or pre-literate villagers—all those living where there are no schools, or where schools have been started too recently to produce a literate class.

Except for a few of the elite class, the remaining Africans do not yet think in "class" terms. It is only an interesting academic classification. Cash-cropping by men and the sale of kitchen-garden produce by women in agricultural areas have also provided new ways to work and, for the male, the new work roles of "producer" and "seller." The male has acquired the role of *planteur*, as well as such roles as buyer, transporter, truck-owner, driver, etc.

It is relevant to note that land allocated to the *planteur* for his picking-crop does not become his land in the sense that he owns it. The land remains in the custody of the lineage or clan group. The *planteur* owns the bushes or trees. Here another new role is introduced, for the care of the crop is the responsibility of the male, a change from the traditional role when a male did no cultivation. However, this does not change the basic cultural concept that economic provisioning is a male responsibility, even though in the cash-crop instance he has to assume the role of cultivator in order to discharge that responsibility.[11] The cash received from the sale of the crop belongs to the owner-producer of the crop. Thus, it was necessary for the male to prevent women from owning these cash-crops. To prevent this, he had to change his traditional role and become a cultivator.

In recruiting a labor force in rural areas, one must bear in mind that there are two important social groups: seasonal and migratory labor groups, and associational and credit groups.

Seasonal and migratory labor groups have a history in French-speaking Africa that antedates the coming of White men. The White men introduced forced labor, and compelled persons or even whole ethnic groups to move from plantation to plantation, or from construction site to construction site.

The Labor Code of 1952 did away with forced labor and gave individual Africans the freedom and right to work, to form labor unions, etc. However, the image of his former servitude has never been completely erased from the African's memory.

Although the pattern of forced labor was broken, workers continued their migratory ways, and moved about the rural areas almost as migrant workers do in America. The difference is that, in Africa, the individuals return to their home village whenever they have earned enough money for bridewealth or to pay off debts or taxes. They do not wait for the jobs to be completed.

The mass of African labor potential lives in rural areas. In the Ivory Coast 90 per cent of the potential "wage earners" are "employed" (sic) in subsistence agriculture.[12]

Rural-urban centers—which in fact are administrative-commercial centers—attract cross sections of local ethnic groups who come to work as unskilled laborers. In each of these commercial-administrative centers, each ethnic group lives in its own section. J. P. Lebeuf reports that Fort Lamy has the following ethnic populations: Arabs, 6,000; Hausa, 3,000; Kenembou, 1,700; Fulani, 2,600; and Sara, 5,000. Lebeuf points out to illustrate the traditional orientation of the above groups that one section of the city, "Quartier des Evolués," is reserved for the trained elite, the *fonctionnaires* of the administration and commerce. These men and their families live in buildings of European construction and have European amenities.[13] Although each section has a permanency, few individuals remain for long periods of time, they come and go according to seasonal or personal needs. This is also true of the administrators and commercial *fonctionnaires*.

In a survey of a group of plantations at Agboville, Ivory Coast, it was noted that there is a correlation between the length of time a worker remains at his job and his daily pay, lodgings, rations, and bonus (if any). (See Table 2.)

TABLE 2. CORRELATION BETWEEN DURATION OF SERVICE AND WAGES, LODGINGS, RATIONS, AND BONUS

Daily pay	Lodgings	Rations	Bonus	Length of time workers stayed
100 Fr.	Poor	Cost-price	No	About 2 months
70 Fr.	Good	Excellent	Yes	5–6 months
125 Fr.	Very Good	None	Yes	Completed contracts

As long as the rural worker can satisfy his cultural needs in short-term employment, crossing at will from the traditional labor base to a Western-oriented labor base, the use of such manpower will be ineffective and will continue to constitute a barrier toward the modernization of the labor force. It will also hamper the training of a skilled labor force, for which there is an immediate demand.

The underpopulation of rural areas because of migration toward urban centers is considered "one of the most serious problems confronting us today." The producers have turned themselves into consumers. The swell in the size of town centers is, in the majority of cases, due also to the easy recruitment of persons from rural milieux at a time when hundreds of long-standing town residents are without work. It is high time the rural exodus be reversed, and heads of state have recently recommended that all townsmen who are new arrivals to the cities return to the land.[14]

Certain areas of French-speaking West Africa suffer from overpopulation. To ease this pressure one famous pilot project was tried some years ago in Togo. It was called the "transfer of labor," and referred to the transfer of populations from villages, such as Lama-Kara, with a population density of 70 per square kilometer, and Pya and Kodjéné, with a density of 200 per square kilometer, to a middle-Togo area that had been deserted.[15] This labor transfer relieved population pressure. The area succeeded in becoming the "granary of mid-Togo," feeding not only itself, but populations adjacent to it—a feat it accomplished by the traditional subsistence techniques.

Mutual-aid groups, work groups, and agricultural cooperatives all basically operate in about the same way: as cooperatives for the promotion of mutual help. They are found in both rural and urban centers, and among unskilled and skilled workers.

Since 1950, mutual-aid groups have multiplied both in variety and members. In Nigeria, for example, there are more than a thousand such societies with a membership of more than 66,000.[16] There is no sharp demarcation between these three groups, only an arbitrary one. Men who form temporary mutual-aid groups technically form a "savings" group too. For example, a group of men who want to purchase a bicycle or a commodity priced higher than any one of them can afford individually will form a mutual-aid group, pool each month's salary, and, in turn, give it to one of the group, who will make his purchase. This continues until each of the members has purchased the same commodity at the same price. At the end of the year each man will have a bicycle and the group will then break up. Note that *all* of the monthly salary is contributed to the pool. This practice is most common in rural-urban centers, and it is not uncommon for the family to be the loser. (It is also common for the last man to be cheated out of his bicycle by the others!)

Work groups are more complex; like the mutual-aid groups, they function mostly in rural areas. They are volunteer associations composed of semiskilled or skilled workers who travel from village to village, within tribal boundaries, as construction or repair men. Such associations are formed by age level, educational level, kin groups, such as a father and sons, or men of an extended family.

The stigma of one African "working" for another does not carry over to working ensemble. In the work groups, wages are, in some instances, paid on individual piecework—e.g., the number of bricks laid in a day—or, in some cases, by group agreement—e.g., the group contracts to finish a specific job at a specific date, with the usual overtime penalties for failing to do so. The men are sometimes salaried workers, receiving a rate figured on speed and a salary base established by the government.

Such work groups are conscious attempts to modernize a local labor force—to get around the male African's distaste for working for a "brother" and the idea of being a slave. These work groups also resemble the traditional "work parties," while providing manpower to meet new needs. The system of "apprentices" trains unskilled young men in carpentry, masonry, electricity, etc.

Agricultural cooperatives were begun by independent growers to aid in the production and transportation of agricultural products. One cooperative, if not the earliest, was begun in 1947, in Senegal. By 1951, in the same area there were 200 cooperatives, each independent of the others, but all growing and transporting the same cash crop, peanuts.[17] Over the years various types of cooperative societies have evolved, including the Sociétés de Prévoyance, Les Mutuelles Vivrières du Niger, and the important Centres Fédéraux de Formation Coopérative, located at Sikasso in the Sudan and Bongouanou in the Ivory Coast.

In each former French territory agricultural credit banks, Caisses Centrales de Crédit Agricole, were established from which short- and long-term loans could be borrowed. One is struck by the relatively few among the local agricultural population, in proportion to the number who joined the bank when it was first formed, who take advantage of their credit opportunities. Because the present organization is too complex and too far removed from its grass-roots origin, it may have become a barrier to modernization, preventing the cooperativeness it sought to establish.

The barriers to modernization of labor in French-speaking Africa are, then, the tenacity of traditional land tenure; the persistence of custom (even when hidden under Western garments and language); and the solidarity of the family. These factors seem to be stronger now than ever before.

These problems remain so crucial that most of the governments are directing their energies to overcoming them, if possible within the next ten years. Education, with its focus on the technical and vocational training of the manpower potential, is the present hope.

PART

FOREIGN
RELATIONS

12

Characteristics of Developing Foreign Policies

I. WILLIAM ZARTMAN

THIS CHAPTER will discuss a number of salient characteristics of foreign policy in the developing states of former French West Africa (AOF) and the Maghreb.[1] Each characteristic is expected to stand by itself, without any primary attempt at linear development from one point to another. It is hoped, however, that the characteristics that *do* interact and overlap can be seen to be related, if not always interdependent.

One final preliminary comment is needed to clear the air. The question may arise, What is it that distinguishes "former French" Africa from any other Africa as far as foreign-policy characteristics are concerned? Briefly, the differences are: First, in former French West Africa, there is the lingering memory of past governmental (AOF) and party (RDA) unity. Second, in the same area, the step-by-step creation of the Parti du Régroupement Africain (PRA) in 1958 to save the AOF by challenging the Rassemblement Démocratique Africain (RDA) began the process of counteralliance that continued after 1958. Third, in North Africa, aspirations toward Maghreb unity created forces all their own. Fourth, both areas have had their own peculiar process of attaining independence— in Black Africa, an *"indépendance octroyée,"* in part due to the influence of North Africa's *"indépendance arrachée."* Fifth, former French Africa strongly feels the impression of French administrative, intellectual, political, and cultural ways. Sixth, whether reacting against it or profiting from it, former French Africa is still within the French sphere of influence, i.e., French interest, aid, and understanding are generally predominant in the area.

The problem of examining foreign policy development in former French Africa requires the invention of new concepts to deal with the bases, units, and interests of these policies. Studies of foreign policies in established states assume the coincidence of three units of interest and identification, the territorial (state), the popular (nation), and the organizational (party-government).[2] In the former French Africa, the noncoincidence of these three units is typical; one of the meanings of development is the gradual overcoming of this anomaly. One aspect—achieving coincidence of the nation and the state—has been termed nation-building and has received much attention; another—achieving coincidence of party-government and nation—gives rise to the term "mobilization regime." Of importance for foreign policy also is the development of coincidence between party-government and state, which involves the extension of government services and control throughout the territory of the country and the replacement of the frontier region or march concept with the notion of boundary lines and limits.

The order of development of the three units is also important. Among modern African institutions, the party antedates all others and legitimizes the government and the state, which then creates the nation—quite the reverse of the "normal" Western experience. This leaves us with a state-nation—like a state religion or state economy—and not a nation-state. In former French Africa, with the sole exception of the historic Moroccan and Tunisian states, the organizational unit existed before the territorial and popular units were ever developed. West African protostates were not set up until the *Loi Cadre* of 1956, and Algeria was not finally defined as a territorial entity until 1961. In all the areas, ideas of national identification were inchoate, and notions of national interest unborn; traditional nations—tribes—did exist but without modern relevance. To the extent that government was controlled by the colonial power, it was conducted in the interests of France and not of the local units. The only modern native unit that was a going concern was the party, and it was sometimes in partial control of AOF governments. It carried out its own policies in its own interest, which can be summarized as the attainment of control over the territorial and popular units. At independence—again with the exception of Morocco—the party and its charismatic leader became the legitimizer of the new regime; it made its own rules of operation, followed its own aims and interests, and set about to develop the state and nation in the image of its dreams.

In a world of logical abstractions, it would seem that at independence, the "second string" or the "civilians" should take over and exercise the governing power that the "first string" or "militaries" had won.[3] The world being no more logical than it is abstract, the organizational unit not only retained the power it had won, but made its consolidation one of its major interests; in other ways, its patterns of action were merely a continuation of those of the pre-independence period. Since even before independence these parties maintained active foreign relations among themselves (including alliances and subversion), with France (including negotiations and aid), and with the external world (including attendance at international conferences and the U.N.), the conduct of foreign policy was no exception to the practice of continuation. Many of the anomalies of former French African foreign policy, from the special relation with France to the incidence of subversion, can be understood only in the light of the organizational unit's past practices, its attempt to consolidate control over the territorial and popular units, and its tendency to view intra-African relations as an interparty affair.

The developing nature of former French African foreign policies means that there is an incomplete awareness of the ideas of national interest as policy criteria. Although there is still little consensus over what constitutes national interest, it is agreed that it involves "national" (i.e., not class, regional, or party) considerations known as "interests" (i.e., not sentiments or ideologies). Beyond these limitations on the concept, it is agreed only that national interest involves a search for security of the national "self," the exact appreciation of "security" and "self" being properly a function of the national leaders' perception.

Obviously, national interest cannot exist as a guiding concept until the coincidence of national, state, and party-government units is well on its way to achievement. It is equally evident that as long as party interests, such as the conquest and maintenance of power by a specific political elite, remain the criteria for policy, national interest remains secondary; and, corollarily, as long as the nation and the state are still in the process of being defined, other interests that are already formulated have first call, particularly insofar as they are not specifically incompatible with efforts at national and state consolidation. Finally, if threats to the security of the national "self" are absent, distant, or ill perceived, other interests rise in importance or, alternatively, threats to security are defined in vaguer ideological or sentimental terms. All of these conditions exist in former French Africa, and their combined effect is that of posing foreign-policy criteria for the most part either on the level of subnational interests or on the level of international sentiments and ideologies or on no conscious level at all.

Strangely enough, there are few cases of foreign-policy actions on the basis of regional or tribal interests. Representatives of the Constantine region of Algeria, Oujda province of Morocco, Nema in Mauritania, Kayes in Mali—to cite just one series of examples—exercised little or no pressure on their central governments to change foreign policies that separated these vulnerable regions from neighboring countries by means of closed frontiers;[4] in fact, pressure toward nation-building required these regions to be "more nationalist than the nation" and to lead the support for the foreign policy. Similarly, class interests have not been of major importance. Again, to cite one example, labor unions in Morocco, Tunisia, and Niger have not protested the evacuation of foreign bases, which gave their members steady employment, for reasons of ideological solidarity similar to those involved in the lack of regional pressures. Another explanation may be that subnational interests have not yet been organized in developing Africa, except as party auxiliaries under government control.

On the other hand, governing elites have sometimes adopted foreign policies to consolidate their domestic power, as in the case of Morocco's sponsorship of the radical Casablanca Group in 1961 at a time of activist pressure at home; Algeria's vigorous response to the Moroccan border war in 1963 at the time of the Kabyle revolt; Houphouet-Boigny's switch to the independence bandwagon as home pressure rose in 1960; and Maga's 1959 decision to bring Dahomey into the Council of the Entente. It is noteworthy that, whether the reasoning was true or not, all such actions have been justified in terms of national interest.

International sentiments and ideologies are more important as foreign-policy criteria. This is explicable not only by the negative reasons already cited but also by other positive factors from the past. In the struggle for independence, the mobilization of slogans was one of the very few sources of power open to the nationalist movements. Since political action accomplished a rather stupendous task in crumbling the walls of the major world empires mainly by blowing on ideological trumpets, there is a continued tendency to believe in the power of slogans and ideas. Because there has been some doubt over what the new nation of Africa really is— the state, AOF, Maghreb, Black Africa, or the whole continent—there is a tendency in some countries to justify action in the name of Africa and African unity rather than on the basis of national interest. Finally, there is also the practice, extending far beyond former French Africa, of perceiving the "self" as inseparable from its ideological content, whose defense is more important than even defense of the land and people. Algeria justified its action in the Algero-Moroccan border war of 1963 in strongly ideological terms, when a simple defense of the national territory and national security would have sufficed. Where, in fact, does national interest stop, and sentiment and ideology begin?

The question cannot be answered in this short study, and may have no answer at all. It does contain a number of lessons, however. First, the conflicting criterion of national interest versus sentiment does give some guide in distinguishing realist from idealist regimes. Second, there are some evident principles of national interest that affect certain states. Mali, Upper

Volta, and Niger—the interior states—need good relations with a maritime neighbor. Mauritania, Togo, and Dahomey—threatened weaker states—need good relations with a protecting neighbor or a counterbalancing neighbor of the threatening state.[5] Senegal, Guinea, Ivory Coast, Dahomey, and Togo—port states—need good relations with a hinterland area. States of the Maghreb, the Entente, or the Senegal river basin—natural complementary areas—need to coordinate negotiating policies for the best use of foreign aid. Thus, Tunisia's policy of the Ejele pipeline in 1958 (as opposed to Morocco's on Gara Jebilet), Ivory Coast's policy on the Entente in 1959 or on shipments to Mali after the breakup of the Mali Federation in 1960, and Mauritania's membership in the African and Malagasy Union (UAM) can all be considered as examples of national-interest policy. These two points will be relevant to the consideration of other characteristics of foreign policy discussed later on. Finally, some policy actions can be taken on the basis of no apparent interest at all, for other reasons to be discussed below.

A major characteristic of former French African foreign policy is its kaleidoscopic nature: A slight turn of events brings dramatic new patterns. There are several ingredients to this extreme mobility: the lack of technical intelligence, the highly political nature of African foreign policy, and the importance of circumstantial incidents and emotion. Each of these ingredients will be examined in turn.

Given the size of the foreign ministries in former French African governments, it is easy to see that basic economic and political information on operations areas is woefully lacking. Added to this is the penchant of African heads of governments personally to handle foreign policy, thereby inviting all the dangers of misinformation on detail that are inherent in summitry. Compounding these dangers is the tendency of any observer to interpret facts in the light of his own experience, a frame of reference foreign to many external policy problems. The size of the foreign-affairs staffs allows these personal reactions to prevail. The lack of technical intelligence is institutionalized by the habit of calling conferences without adequate technical and political preparation; of all the African conferences in which former French African states took part between 1956 and 1964, only the Conference of Independent African States of 1958, the Addis Ababa Conference of 1963, and several of the Brazzaville and Monrovia conferences in between had any serious preparation.

This ingredient in turn reinforces others. Without an awareness of national interest foreign policy becomes an exercise in pure politics—a struggle for influence for its own sake; at worst, given the personal nature of presidential foreign-policy leadership, it descends to a level of whim, emotion, and accident. Contrary to most writings on the subject, it is held here that former French African foreign policy is anything but "domestic policy pursued by other means . . . carried beyond the boundaries of the state."[6] Only if "policy" is understood as "ideology" may this be true; for the most part, much intra-African and extra-African foreign policy has little to do with domestic needs or purposes. Pronouncements and interventions in Cold War conflicts deal with problems remote to African states, and in which they have no direct interest. Groups, constellations, and alliances tend to pass away rapidly under the impact of real economic problems or basic political differences, or remain in rather sterile existence only by avoiding contact with these problems and differences.

Instead, emotion and accident both play important roles. Bad blood between Mali and Senegal (1960–63), Guinea and Ivory Coast (1958–62), Upper Volta and Ivory Coast (1961), Morocco and Tunisia (1960–63), and Morocco and Algeria (1963) was either caused or prolonged by simple reactions of pride or anger, usually personally felt by the head of state. Similarly, continuing solidarity or *rapprochement* among the leaders of former AOF territories depends on tenacious personal friendships developed at the William Ponty School (a high school in Dakar), in the RDA, or in the labor movement.

Perhaps most remarkable is the role of accident, of which three types must be distinguished. The first is the accident of events, a fortuitous happening that triggers an important reaction. The second type is the accident of attendance, which, more than any negotiated decisions, has shaped the various groups and alliances of former French Africa. Finally, there is the accident of excuse, of the "African U-2 incident." Senghor's ousting of Dia in 1962, which had little to do with Mali, was nevertheless seized on by Dakar and Bamako alike as a cause for *rapprochement;* the assassination of Olympio in 1963, which had nothing to do with the Casablanca Group or the UAS, was seized on by Touré as a cause of rupture with Ghana. In this type of accident, the desire is present and only the excuse is awaited, whereas in the other two types the importance of the accident as the fundamental cause for the foreign-policy action is much greater. In either case, there is little control over policy or events, and frequently little purpose evident in the policy action.

Former French African foreign policy has shared in the general African susceptibility to appeals for African unity, although frequently for its own reasons. The basis for the general attractiveness of this appeal is beyond the scope of this chapter; suffice it to add that former French West Africa is particularly sensitive to these appeals because of its own history of federation under colonial rule, and the Maghreb is also susceptible, for inverse reasons, because the presence of strong cultural ties among the three states has been paralleled by the absence of political unity.

Within these generalizations, the value attached to "unity" has differed among the component states of former French Africa. Throughout the revolutionary war, the FLN gave great emphasis to African unity as evidence of encouraging solidarity behind the Algerian causes;[7] after independence, except for a brief interregnum in 1962–63, which included Nasser's trip to Algiers and Khemisti's, Boumedienne's, and Khider's trips to Cairo and ended with the Addis Ababa Conference, Ben Bella has considered Africa as the proper framework for exercising Algerian foreign-policy slogans, but has also shown interest in providing French-speaking Africa with a development model and aid. Morocco's Pan-Africanism has been blocked by her ambitions toward Mauritania, and her invocations of Maghreb unity—except during the 1958 Tangier Conference—have been largely propagandistic. Mali and Guinea place African unity high on their list of slogans and in their ideological hierarchy, while Senegal's attachment to the principle of unity has been more modest, more pragmatic, and more strongly influenced by the failure of the Mali Federation. Most of the other states are—perhaps paradoxically—too small and too poor to look far beyond their boundaries, except Ivory Coast, which, after following a firm stand against the idea of African unity, made a verbal *volte-face* in the first Lagos Conference of the Monrovia Group and was instrumental in the drafting and acceptance of the Monrovia-Lagos and Addis Ababa charters.

The search for an agreeable definition of unity has provided a major impetus in former French African foreign policies, and even Houphouet-Boigny's position was an integral part of this evolution. The search was sparked by two events, one narrow, one broad. One was the injection of the topic itself into newly independent African foreign policy by Ghana, beginning in 1957 and continuing in 1958. The other was the somewhat inexplicable compulsion to overcome the isolation felt by all states of the AOF, dating from their attainment of autonomy in late 1958. It may be hypothesized that their individual powerlessness, the chain-reaction necessity of countermeasures to their neighbors' selective search in the same direction, and nostalgia for the former AOF, all combined to make isolation the major fear to be overcome by the new states' foreign policies; this situation then provided the basis for the aforementioned characteristic of kaleidoscopic alignments. It may also be hypothesized that the sudden loneliness imposed by independence, the breakup of common services formerly taken for granted, and the back-turning process toward neighbors implicit in nation-building increased the fear of isolation. In this situation, former French African states found allies where they could. It was less a question of reviving colonial patterns of relations, as critics claimed, than in accepting the most easily attainable allies, according to the dictates of ideology, history, economy, geography, and politics.

All the while, there was an attempt to devise an agreeable definition of

African unity. This search was made difficult by three factors: The at tempt to overcome isolation was a search for ideologically compatible allies the very words "African unity" implied universality; and, since colonial ism was identified with "divide-and-conquer" tactics, unity was equated with anticolonialism. The end of this period of search, which began in 1958, cam in 1963 at the Addis Ababa Conference. The summit where the Organiza tion of African Unity (OAU) was created appears in retrospect to have been a turning point in intra-African relations, for by its universality and its modest charter it arrived at a temporarily satisfying definition and in stitutionalization of the elusive ideological slogan.[8] Paradoxically, both the role it was given in handling the Algero-Moroccan border war and the plodding way in which it has taken up this charge have prolonged its life.

The accent in this historical summary, however, is on "temporarily." Addis Ababa and the OAU have not brought African unity into permanen being. From the point of view of former French states as well as other African states, its continued good health can be interrupted in certain specific situations: first, if the definition of African unity is no longer universally and minimally satisfying, i.e., if a state such as Guinea or Mal feels that the time has come for closer ties that the OAU majority refuses second, if the OAU fails to handle the problems given it, i.e., if Morocco goes to war again to impress Algeria with the need for a border settlemen following a breakdown of arbitration and conciliation; third, if universality no longer provides ideologically compatible allies, i.e., if Algeria feels the need to seize the leadership and accelerate the pace of the continenta liberation movement; and fourth, if a new trigger incident occurs in a situation when kaleidoscopic characteristics are particularly strong, i.e., i the Congolese Government falls apart again, its divisions being reflected in the positions of other African states.[9] These situation types are similar but their differences show the broad potentiality of future weakness in African unity, even as now modestly defined.

In this fluid situation, how can the effects of African unity on former French African foreign policy be characterized? African unity seems to have five separate utilities: First, it is useful to African statesmen as a justifying slogan by which policies can be sold to their parties and people and to other state leaders; that is, depending on the audience and the mo tives of the user, it can be used as the real reason or a good reason. The power of the slogan was largely responsible for the turnout at Addis Ababa, just as it was used, by inverse logic, to excuse Casablanca states from going to Monrovia and Lagos, when the exclusion of one member or an other violated African unity. Second, it has power, as a myth, to keep open conflict outside of the rules of the game. According to the colonial- division–African-unity dichotomy, conflict is "un-African" and troublemakers are doing the work of colonialism. Hence political conflict is under strong pressure to remain political or to be solved in the name of African unity before it reaches the military stage. Third, African unity is a notion, important, if only as a label, as a stand-in for yet undefined reality as former French African states join the search for a replacement for the colonial system of international relations. It makes great sense to look at the OAU in this light, as the organization of a regional subsystem, comparable to the OAS, the EEC, and the Arab League. Fourth, it establishes a predisposition in favor of intra-African cooperation. In their search for a definition of unity, French-speaking African states have arrived at a minimal understanding of the term as an invitation to regional economic coordination, collective negotiations with the external world (particularly the Common Market countries), and consultation in the U.N. Finally, African unity retains residual importance as a real alternative open to policy-makers in the face of a serious, sudden, unexpected challenge, or, in partial implementation on a subregional basis, in the face of a serious common need.[10] The chances of unity, in its original sense of unification, do seem quite unlikely but are not to be excluded out of hand. In a specific situation, under certain conditions, the policy alternative is always present; suffice it to recall that postcolonial situations in North and South America and Asia provide historical parallels, although never on a continental level.

Power in former French Africa is low in incidence but highly diffused. In global terms, the new states are weak. Even among themselves, the elements of national power are lacking; leaders have little means of bringing their power to bear on other states; there are no important concentrations of power; and military force—the ultimate sanction behind other types of power—is generally lacking or unusable.[11]

This is, of course, not to say that all states are created equal; Ivory Coast has influence over the Entente states, as Senegal has over Mauritania and Algeria over Tunisia. Further, fear of Algeria and Ghana within former French Africa testifies to these two states' activity and potential— and hence to their relative power. Let us here review quickly the classic elements of power in order to determine what has happened to them in former French Africa. Size, a basic consideration, is especially illusory, since the largest states—Algeria, Niger, Morocco, Mali, Mauritania—are largely desert, and, except for Algeria, poor desert at that. Population is also basic to power considerations, but the current absence of political mobilization and socio-economic modernization reduces its importance; certainly Morocco, the most populous, is not the most powerful, and, conversely, Mauritania and Niger, the smallest, may be among the least powerful. Military strength varies sharply between former French North and

French West Africa, the Maghreb countries having a military population of about five per thousand civilians and the Black African states (except Guinea) all having fewer than one per thousand;[12] the armies, however, are more needed as internal than as external security forces. Geography plays a limited role; states on the coast or states astride transportation-communication lines (rivers or railroads) enjoy a certain strategic advantage, the limits of which are clearly shown in the histories of the Mali Federation and the Entente.

Three elments of power do exist, two of them unusual in the absence of more conventional elements. One is the U.N. vote, in which all states are equal. This situation is particularly agreeable in former French African eyes, for the U.N. corresponds to their general image of optimum world politics: It protects the small, grants aid to the underdeveloped, augments the power of the weak, increases the prestige of the powerless, and serves as a force and forum against colonialism. Participation in U.N. debates and votes on world problems has thus suddenly made these states powers to be reckoned with; unfortunately, it has also tended to divert their attention away from national power and national interest, the basic realities of international relations, toward the idealistic type of policy described below.

Another element of power is activity, the manipulation of slogans. Because former French African states were able to attain independence through the simple use of the mobilized masses and *mots d'ordre,* in the absence of any other source of power, there is the continuing tendency to believe that any goal in foreign (or even domestic) policy can be accomplished by political action. This divorce between slogans and power, accompanied by the paradoxical power of slogans, has come to mean that states can attain a position of considerable influence simply by appropriating, manipulating, and monopolizing slogans. Guinea, Mali, and Algeria have done this with success,[13] although the first two lack the economic base of their neighbors and Algeria suffers from political instability more than the other states of the Maghreb.

The third relevant element of power, and that most directly opposed to the juggling of slogans, is development. The creation of an economically and socially modernized nation does provide a real basis of power for use toward foreign-policy goals, and already there are some differences among former French African states on this account. Senegal and North Africa are strong on intrastructure; Ivory Coast has shown respectable economic growth. However, these are only modest beginnings. There is so much more to be done, for the purpose both of internal welfare and of external power, that realism in both fields suggests the wisdom of concentrating attention on development, leaving the exciting temptations of foreign policy to a later day.

Intra-African foreign relations are carried out in former French Africa within limited extremes: The worst usually possible is the rupture of relations and a flow of vile propaganda (external violence being excluded), the best usually possible is close alliance and economic cooperation (loss of sovereignty through union being excluded). Let us examine first the two exclusions, both of which are usually normal alternatives to be considered in classic international relations.

War, conquest, and external violence are outside of the rules of the game for a number of reasons. External violence is "un-African," for it is associated with colonialism. There is strong pressure among the Africans to solve political differences in the name of African unity, unless one of the parties feels compelled to resort to violence in the name of a higher ideological value. One important tenet of moderate groupings, from Brazzaville to Addis Ababa, has been the peaceful settlement of disputes. Even in the revolutionary states, however, the military is weak, and in no country is it organized either for border defense or aggressive attack. Finally, Africa too benefits from the balance of terror; there is no desire to kindle the spark that might set off an international war, no matter how farfetched this might seem, or to set in motion military conflicts that might invite European participation. French military agreements with many of the moderate states thus help freeze the territorial *status quo*.

By the same token, there have been surprisingly few instances of border claims, territorial disputes, or irredentism, apart from the well-known Moroccan claims. (And it should be pointed out that Morocco's intention was not to conquer territory it claimed, but to move Algeria to action on promises of a border settlement that its representatives had made in early 1962.)[14] Other border disputes have been largely tribal in nature. In addition, two examples of smooth and mature liquidation of border problems are available in the infomal Guinea-Liberia settlement of 1958 and the Mali-Mauritanian negotiations that ended in 1963.[15] Considering the miles of borders and their frequently mentioned artificial nature, this is a significantly small number. In fact, its smallness may refute the idea of the borders' artificiality, for it is not the boundary that is artificial but the nation. In terms of an earlier point, the coincidence of the popular, territorial, and organizational units—the nation, state, and government—has not yet been achieved. As the development process continues inside each state, the boundaries develop their character as the natural limits of the state— natural in human and political terms, far more important than the geopolitical notion of geographic naturalness. In the meantime, boundaries have seldom been questioned, no doubt for fear of opening a Pandora's box. If any boundary is seriously questioned, why should not all boundaries in former French Africa be questioned? And then what is "natural"?

The alternative of union is more quickly dealt with. It is unlikely that political elites who have struggled to attain independence for their state would want to give up this independence, and their inherited situation as well, in a political merger (the Guinea constitution notwithstanding, as the abortive Guinea-Ghana Union shows). If and when states turn to regional economic cooperation based on their real needs, a new era in former French African relations may open, with the possibility of a functional approach to integration as the end result.

With war and union excluded, what is left? The question posed in this fashion leaves only three natural answers: alliance, economic cooperation, and political warfare. The first two have been mentioned above; a few words can be said to clarify the latter. The manipulation of slogans and the torrents of propaganda that accompany bad relations between two former French African states are examples of modern technique of political communications. This tendency, however, is further aggravated by the fact, already alluded to, that intra-African relations were carried out among organizational units—political parties—in North and West Africa before independence. The continuing tendency to make use of party auxiliaries—labor unions, women's and youth groups—as instruments of foreign policy perpetuates political warfare, but it is worth noting that those states of former French Africa that either harbored and aided exile foreign groups or intervened indirectly in others' internal affairs—Morocco, Algeria, Mali, Guinea, and, perhaps surprisingly, Ivory Coast[16]—have curtailed their activity vis-à-vis their independent neighbors in recent years.

The developing nature of former French African foreign policy is implied in three salient characteristics: search for policy, *ad hoc* policy-making, and the learning process. Former French Africa is in a stage of political revolt, and this rejection of former ways (including, not too paradoxically, those that are still retained) implies a search for replacements. In foreign policy, the broad framework of this search—as already mentioned—is expressed in the need to find a system of international relations to replace the colonial system and in the attempt to establish a working definition for the myth of African unity. More narrowly, each state searches for new guidelines and policies to clothe its public image, meanwhile insisting—like the Emperor—that it *is* adequately clad. It is significant that every African meeting in which former French states took part since the April, 1958, conferences of Accra and Tangier embodied an attempt to find a formula that would reconcile independent policy and African unity, and every grouping except those that were avowedly regionalistic aspired to universality, no matter how limited their actual membership. It is because of this continual search for policy, patterns, and systems that success or ailure in any one area has such widespread effects and arouses comments ar beyond its apparent importance.

Close to the searching process is the learning process. Former French Africa, like any novice in the field, is only learning some of the basic diplomatic conventions and habits honored elsewhere by established practice. One of these conventions, perhaps the most readily assimilated, is that of compromise; after some two years of obstinate insistence on minor points and on ideological purity, the solution of Addis Ababa showed a willingness to compromise to attain important objectives.[17] Another convention is reciprocity, which covers a range of subjects from noninterference to diplomatic privileges and immunities.[18] Algeria has learned that when it claims it is helpless to control the wave of summary seizures by its citizens, France will claim that it is helpless to ease the limitations on aid imposed by its parliament. A third convention is the observation of treaty engagements. Former French African states have learned only slowly and painfully that in an alliance a state takes on its allies' enemies, that work instead of mere communiqués is needed to accomplish stated aims, and that fellow members are entitled to consider agreements binding.[19] A fourth convention is consultation and the use of diplomatic machinery. The closing of Guinea's embassies in Ivory Coast, Ghana, Mali, and Sierra Leone may be eloquent testimony to the effectiveness of Sékou Touré's summit diplomacy and prestige, but it indicates a misconception of his disposable time, and a previous underemployment of the embassies' diplomatic staffs. On the other hand, it should be noted that all possible diplomatic ways and policies have not necessarily been discovered; in the process of searching and learning it is indeed possible that former French African statesmen may come up with new patterns and solutions more attuned to the modern world and from which other statesmen may learn.

Corollary to searching and learning is the *ad hoc* nature of policymaking. It is a general characteristic of former French Africa that foreign policy is made as problems are posed, with little evaluation of future consequences or estimation of future plans. Decisions are reached most frequently at the summit, where there is pressure for success, and not at lower levels, where sounder and more detailed knowledge is available; this is visible in meetings as disparate as the Keita-ould Daddah meeting at Kayes and the African summit at Addis Ababa, both in early 1963. Policy is thus made by a series of decisions and pronouncements; acts and statements do not issue from a studied policy.[20] Much of this is explained by the fact that foreign policy is still in the dream stage; it still has to be worked down through the principles stage to the stage of policy. As leaders become aware of the limits of foreign policy, and of their own needs and interests, they will be able, to a far greater degree, to weigh goals, envisage alternatives, and plan responses.

The meaningful distinction between foreign-policy schools in former French Africa is not best posed between *status quo* and revisionists, between radicals and moderates, or between activists and nonactivists, but between realists and idealists. The difference is more than one of terminology; it helps re-establish foreign-policy attitudes on levels comparable with those of other countries and in already accepted terms.

The useful, if somewhat unwieldy, distinction between *status quo* and revisionist states has been sharpened by a distinction between territorial and ideological status and revision.[21] All former French African states are revisionist in their basic approach to global policy and in their anticolonialist bent, although in the short run their neutralism and nonalignment logically implies a cold-war stalemate that suggests a *status quo* approach.[22] The inconsistency tends to be discomfiting. In intra-African relations, as seen, former French states have almost unanimously adopted a *status quo* policy on territorial questions, and an ambiguous policy on ideological questions, composed of *status quo* actions and revisionist hopes. Mali and Senegal, Guinea and Ivory Coast, Algeria and Morocco have all told each other that history is on *our* side and in the long run *your* side will cave in. Thus an understanding of the *status quo* and revisionist approaches helps to understand the similarities, but not the differences, among former French African states.

The more frequently used terms "radicalism" and "moderation" are useful, but they are relative, value-charged, and often as hard to transpose as the terms "left" and "right."[23] Moreover, they have more meaning in terms of domestic policy in reference to the time element, radical regimes being distinguishable from moderate regimes largely by the fact that they are in a greater hurry, although the goals may frequently be the same.

There is also the attempt to divide former French African states into the activist and the nonactivist, for want of a better name. Activism does have an apparent meaning with reference to sloganistic or diplomatic activity, already discussed. But it is misleading if it signifies that nonactivist states are not active; Tunisia and Ivory Coast have been as energetic in their policies as Algeria and Guinea, and perhaps more successful in terms of more limited goals, and yet they are rarely included among the activists. The term is rejected, not as meaningless, but as not providing sufficient distinctions.

"Idealist" and "realist" are the terms preferred here, and they are terms already in use in discussions of international relations. Furthermore, the link between revolutionary regimes—regimes that seek a rapid socio-economic upheaval—and idealist policies has already been noted.[24]

If the characteristic of revolt against the colonial heritage is a feature of all former French Africa, then, as the new nations seek to establish their own identity and manage their own political affairs, one difference between realist and idealist policies can be seen in the amount of rejection that the regime proclaims. This difference is evident in the very language of former French African politics, visible in a comparison of Senghor's assertive negritude with Gologo's accusative negritude, of Touré's policy pronouncements with Houphouet's statements, of Ben Bella's speeches with Bourguiba's talks. In addition, the elements of purism and compromise also distinguish idealist from realist foreign-policy views. Max Weber has written of the purist ethics of "ultimate ends" and the compromising ethics of "responsibility." To the idealist, ideological goals are high on the list of policy criteria and must be kept untainted; to the realist, the necessity of making discrete choices for immediate needs involves pushing ideological criteria into the background in order to gain real advantages. This second distinction can be sharpened to include yet a third, the difference between local and universalist nationalism. Idealist foreign policy involves not only an overestimation of the role open to African states in the Cold War, but also an aspiration to speak in the name of all Africa. The universalism inherent in Guinean, Malian, and Algerian policy statements clearly sets aside their idealist views from those of many of their neighbors.[25]

There is a value judgment implied in this distinction, however, and it is preferable that it be voiced rather than remain hidden. This author feels that, given their powerlessness, their developing nature, and their immense needs, former French African states would be safer from repercussive frustrations and surer of needed success if they emphasized the elements of realism in their foreign policy. The states need to be aware of attainable foreign-policy goals, through a development of thinking along the lines of national interest. They need to amass the means of attaining these goals, through primary attention to their own internal development and the construction of the rudiments of power. They need to learn to live in active cooperation—more than in harmony—with their neighbors, without whom the solution of many of their problems of underdevelopment is impossible. They need to devote the majority of the attention that they do give to foreign policy to the problem of working out a system of international relations in Africa that will be successful in handling their own conflicts without disruptive violence.

These prescriptions are stated humbly. The world can learn much from former French Africa's experiences with such problems. Non-African states have often faced the same problems, and have not always dealt with them successfully. Moreover, these prescriptions do reflect recent developments. Particularly in the case of Guinea and Mali, recent years have shown the beginnings of greater realism among the idealist champions of former French Africa. This is inevitable in the long run, or at least until new evolutionary causes and pressures appear.

13

United States Policy: An American View

VICTOR C. FERKISS

IT IS NOT, or at least should not be, possible to speak of American foreig policy toward any area of the world except in the context of the basic ol jectives of American foreign policy generally: world peace, freedom, pros perity, and the security of the United States. This is especially true c American policy toward Africa, and above all of our policy toward Frenck speaking Africa. In perhaps no other area of the globe are American aim less direct and specific and more simply a function and exemplificatio of the general ends of United States foreign policy than in French-speakin Africa. But this very lack of specificity, which has in the past meant th: the formulation of American policy toward French-speaking Africa pose little problem for the policy-maker, is almost certain to make it a difficu problem in the future, for the general propositions about Africa—an(indeed, about the world—on which past American policy relating t Africa has been based are now increasingly shaky.

In order to understand why this is so it is necessary to review the bas: assumptions underlying American policy toward Africa generally. First— though this may offend the sensibilities both of Africans and of America specialists on Africa—it must be admitted that for American foreign polic Africa was and is an area of only peripheral importance. The Africa continent produces little in the way of raw materials important to Ame: ica's economy or military technology. It is not the site of any power (major importance in world political or military affairs; nor is it—at lea at present—a field of major operations of any such powers. In this nucle age it has little strategic importance to the United States. America's intere in Africa therefore has been simply a special case of its general interest i

194

he world at large. The hope of the United States has been that such
esources as Africa has would not be denied to America and its allies or
urned over to its enemies in the Communist bloc. The hope has been also
hat the peoples of Africa would increasingly live under governments of
heir own choosing and in conditions of increasing material prosperity.

This was no more and no less than what America has hoped for in any
nderdeveloped area where it has no specific vital interests. American
olicy toward Africa generally and French-speaking Africa in particular
as been, as we all know, largely the story of the conflict between these
ighly general aims. This conflict has arisen from the fact that, for a pe-
iod of time, it was believed that in order to secure the first objective—that
, keeping the resources, material and human, of Africa in the "Western"
amp—it might be necessary to accept the continuance of a colonialism
hat frustrated the second objective—i.e., enabling Africans to choose
heir own governments and to proceed with economic development.

The one major exception to U.S. policy toward Africa was her policy
oward North Africa. There was a limited period of time when—prior
o the fuller development of intercontinental ballistic missiles and a nuclear
trategy based upon them—the United States was engaged in ringing the
oviet Union with bases for manned bomber aircraft as part of the Ameri-
an strategy of containment and deterrence. North Africa was the site of
wo important base complexes implementing this strategy. One, in Libya,
oes not concern us here; the other, in Morocco, does. The United States
as a unique interest in Morocco. The Moroccan bases were doomed—
nd the United States soon realized this—to be sacrificed to the desire of
Moroccans and of Africans generally for nonalignment in the Cold War.
ut the United States calculated that it could hang on to these bases as
ong as they were of major strategic importance, and sought, in large meas-
re, successfully to do so. The bases were evacuated in 1953, after they
ad mainly fulfilled their function. But during the years prior to 1963, in
rder to keep them available for as long a period as possible after Moroc-
an independence in 1956, the United States was forced to make economic
nd other concessions to Morocco and to adopt a policy not always com-
letely to the liking of the government of France. The United States, there-
ore, had a Moroccan and, by extension, a North African policy, but only
ecause special circumstances caused it to diverge from its generally passive
ole in French-speaking Africa as a whole.

American policy toward Morocco's embattled neighbor, Algeria, was
imply an extension of the general policy of trying to please both sides in
he struggle between colonialist and anticolonialist forces. How successful
 was in achieving this objective is debatable. Some commentators have
ven speculated that America's North African policy in the late 1950's

is the root of much of her difficulty with Gaullist France today. The sphinx of Colombey-les-Deux-Eglises tends to keep his basic motivations to himself, but the suspicion that he regarded French withdrawal from Algeria as a regrettable necessity rather than as something intrinsically desirable is not too farfetched. Can one then, as some have, trace De Gaulle's current pique with the United States and his attempts to sabotage American foreign policy in Southeast Asia to a special resentment of the moral support certain important elements in America gave the Algerian rebels? Can the fact that the then Senator John F. Kennedy was in the forefront of those calling for Algerian independence be one source of De Gaulle's resentment toward the United States?

This seems unlikely. Certainly, official United States Government support for Algerian independence was never more than lukewarm. The United States supported the De Gaulle offers of a French-supervised Algerian referendum in September, 1959, and publicly expressed the hope that the United Nations—then pressed to condemn France over Algeria—would do nothing to prejudice these efforts at conciliation. Although the U.S. angered France in 1960 by voting for a U.N. resolution recognizing the Algerian "right to . . . independence," in general, she has allowed the French full choice of means to this goal in Algeria.

In Tunisia, as in Algeria, the United States sought to conciliate both sides, leaning, when necessary, in the direction of her NATO ally. Though long friendly to Tunisian leadership in Arab politics, the United States equivocated in the bitter 1961 dispute between France and Tunisia over Bizerte and abstained in the United Nations on a resolution condemning France for her harsh military reaction to Tunisian pressure.

The only major clash between France and the United States in North Africa came over an issue that on the surface appears minor, but that is a universal and perennial one coloring the whole relationship of the United States to French-speaking Africa—the issue of cultural relations.

It is virtually axiomatic that no nation in modern history has used cultural contact as a means to national prestige and power for as long or as assiduously and as significantly as has France. Long before the contemporary vogue for educational exchanges and information services in other countries, the French Government officially sponsored the study of French language and culture abroad, even in the United States. Part of France's political and economic strength was based on the ties and prestige created through such means. What was true in the past is even more true today when France, smaller in relative demographic and territorial terms than before, hopes to gain both economic customers and political followers from those who look to Paris for styles in food, dress, machinery, and ideas.

Accordingly, the French Government has not only gone to great expense to subsidize French culture abroad but has bitterly resented and often fought—albeit frequently clandestinely—attempts to spread and encourage the teaching of other languages in former French territories. This first became evident in North Africa, where American attempts to support English-language teaching in Morocco and Tunisia were opposed by France; this conflict is still an important strand in the relations between France, the United States, and French-speaking Africa, especially the former French territories: If the Americans want to build dams and highways, well, all right, this is a fit role for philistines. But when it comes to things of the mind, the spread of American cultural influence in Africa is one issue that Frenchmen of the right and the left—and many former French subjects of the *tiers monde* as well—can readily join in opposing.

The existence of this "cultural curtain," while sometimes a source of friction between the United States and France, paradoxically has been a source of unity as well. It does much to explain why in Black Africa, where the United States had specific strategic interests, she was happy to follow the leadership of and support the French and, *mutatis mutandis,* the Belgians. French-speaking Africa was *terra incognita* to Americans, as was perhaps no other area of the world. American trade with the area was negligible, and therefore so too were consular relations. There could not, of course, be any direct political relations during the colonial era. American missionaries were active to a limited extent in Equatorial Africa and the Congo, but not nearly so active as in other parts of the "heathen" world. American academic specialists on the area were virtually nonexistent. Save for the well-publicized Dr. Schweitzer, and the benighted pygmies and Watutsi, French-speaking Africa might as well have been on another planet, as far as the United States was concerned.

Thus when independence began to come to the peoples of this area the United States not only had no specific interests in the area but also little knowledge concerning it. Preoccupied with the problems arising from her relations with the Soviet Union and China, it was the path of least resistance for the United States to delegate to France and Belgium the problem of keeping the emerging African nations on what the Western alliance regarded as the right path in world affairs. So much was this the case that one could argue that the United States did not really believe in the fact of the independence of the former French colonies and was treating their freedom as an elaborate charade.

The only important opposition within the United States to this idea that France and Belgium should be allowed a virtually free hand in their colonies and former colonies came from those with a principled—sometimes over-rationalized, sometimes visceral—opposition to colonialism per se. French colonialism, with its autocratic internal structure, its centralization, and its assimilationist policies, was deemed as bad as British, if not worse. In the Belgian Congo, the special position of the Catholic Church and economic exploitations by big business afforded additional horrors to the anticolonialists in America, who, though not dominant in the State Department or the military establishment, were prevalent in the foreign-aid organizations. In recent years, anticolonialist sentiment has become more specific and vocal as American academics and intellectuals have come into closer contact with their counterparts in French-speaking Africa. The "anticolonialists," sympathetic to the cause of independence for the African nations, have, in the postindependence period, increasingly identified with the left-wing opposition within the states of French-speaking Africa.

Whether the American policy toward a particular country in French-speaking Africa favored maintaining the *status quo* or installing new leadership was largely determined by the course of events in the nation in question and in the world in general. The case of Guinea is illustrative. Initially, American policy followed the French line of "freezing out" Sékou Touré after Guinea opted for independence in 1958. This policy was influenced in large measure by pressures from the American Embassy in Paris, eager to remain on the best possible terms with French officialdom. When Guinea perforce developed increasingly important ties to the Communist bloc, desperate attempts were made to repair the damage and establish ties of assistance and sympathy between Guinea and the United States—a task more congenial to what might be called the "Africanist" or "liberal" bloc in American bureaucratic politics.

So strong was the American desire to wean Guinea away from the nations toward which, it was now felt, French intransigence had pushed her, that the new friendship survived even the clash of policy between the United States and Guinea over United Nations operations in the Congo. The same strategy was adopted with regard to the other so-called Casablanca Powers—Ghana, Morocco, Mali, and the U.A.R. For instance, at a time when relations between this group and the United States over Congo policy were at their lowest ebb, the United States was widely reported to be giving military assistance to Mali.

Actually, the matter of American relations with the Casablanca Powers is of some significance in illuminating the factors conditioning American policy toward the former French colonies. Although American diplomatic representatives in these areas may have a sophisticated understanding of day-to-day events in these nations and definite ideas about desirable American policy toward them, the government personnel responsible for formulating that policy see the situation in a different light and often feel a need to formulate a policy applicable to a wide variety of situations. Insofar as government policy reflects general public understanding of forces and events, this need to categorize and generalize is strengthened. The exist-ence of such groupings as the Casablanca Powers and the Union Africaine et Malgache (UAM) was a great boon to American statecraft, since it seemed to provide a simple basis for classifying nations in terms of their stance in international politics.

Indeed, it is not completely fantastic to suggest that disappointment at being unable to fathom the political wiles of French-speaking Africans might lead the United States to return to its earlier posture of considering these states a French sphere of influence and letting it go at that, were it not for two factors: One, of course, is the pressure from American officials in these nations to gain a hearing for the problems and interests of the countries in which they serve, a pressure that did not exist in the pre-independence period. The other and more important factor in keeping the United States from following the French lead in Africa is France herself.

De Gaulle's apparent aspiration to lead the nonaligned nations politically and economically in directions in which the United States does not want them to go has occasioned specific policy clashes from Southeast Asia to Latin America and has American policy-makers deeply worried. The United States must be prepared to regard French diplomacy as hostile to her specific aims, and must be prepared to counter it. This applies to the various nations of Africa, and especially to the former French colonies. Whether she likes it or not, here too the United States must stand diplo-matically on her own. But in Africa, the United States suffers a double handicap, for not only does she lack France's background of expertise and local contacts, but she also lacks a precise idea of what France—meaning, in the present context, General de Gaulle—is attempting to do, assuming De Gaulle himself is sure. For those policy-makers long accus-tomed to seeing the world in terms of an East-West dichotomy, and also to seeing France and French influence as on the same side as the United States, the situation must be difficult indeed.

Let us take North Africa as an example. De Gaulle has continued to support the Bourguiba regime in Tunisia, despite events in Tunisia that have made it difficult for him to do so. Well and good. The United States and France have no policy differences here. Nor in the case of Morocco are there any problems. But what of Algeria? Here De Gaulle has taken his biggest gamble for influence in the neutralist *tiers monde*. How much in the way of economic demands and political chaff he is willing to accept from Ben Bella is an indication of how high a price he is willing to pay in order to appear to be in certain respects above the East-West struggle as normally conceived.

The United States has also supported Ben Bella—with food as well as words. Ben Bella, however, continues to strike the United States' rawest nerve—Cuba. Increasing Algerian solidarity with Castro—a position acceptable to De Gaulle despite his support of the basic American position on Cuba during the 1962 missile crisis—is a potent source of hostility and possible conflict between the United States and Algeria (and possibly France). The ambiguous role played by the United States in the Algerian-Moroccan border dispute is an indication of what Algerian relations with Cuba could lead to in the future.

When one turns to sub-Saharan Africa, the American posture of watchful waiting, imposed largely by ignorance of what is going on—an ignorance not necessarily culpable in the confused circumstances—has so far led to no great difficulties. Until De Gaulle makes up his mind as to how much he will tolerate in the way of internal disorder from states that are in some sense tied to France in a client relationship, the United States has little room to maneuver. If the United States gets popular credit for doing what she has not done, for example, allegedly supporting the revolt against President M'ba in Gabon, so much the better. France is faced with a serious decision regarding Black Africa. As the proponents of *Cartierisme* hold, French aid is not only costly but of dubious long-range political effect. Clearly De Gaulle has supported aid to African states in order to obtain political and economic influence. How much aid is he willing to give for how little influence? Suppose in the future he decides that the price is too high?

In my personal opinion the economic relationships between France and its former African colonies are essentially sound. Moreover, given the level of relevant American resources and skills, it would not be in the American interest for these relationships to be terminated and for America to be put in the position of having to replace them. But, at the same time, the United States must be prepared to step in should the Guinea experience be repeated on a widespread and permanent basis. Whether it would be politically feasible for the United States to support forces in these nations, which France was unwilling to do, is another matter. Despite the fact that she favored the relatively conservative UAM prior to its demise, France has shown herself to be more ideologically flexible than the United States and more willing to support so-called leftist regimes than the United States. Whether the United States could take up the slack in the event of French withdrawal from this area is therefore dubious.

One area that I have purposefully put off mentioning until now, and that presents special and vast problems of its own, is the former Belgian Congo and the adjacent nations of Rwanda and Burundi. We are, I fear, witnessing the bankruptcy of American policy in the Congo. In part, this is the result of an American reliance upon a United Nations operation that General de Gaulle regarded as both dubious and illegal from the outset.

Without going into great detail about the tangled American response to an even more tangled internal and external situation, suffice it to say that American policy in the Congo was based on three pillars—pillars that it required no Samson to shake down. These were: freeing the new Congo state from domination by European interests; excluding Eastern bloc influence; and establishing a centralized government of so-called moderates, supported politically and economically by the United Nations and sympathetic to American policy. These objectives were to be accomplished without a major American commitment, either economic, military, or administrative.

As might have been prophesied, the United Nations was too weak to do adequately the job that the United States would not let others do and refused to undertake herself. The Congo, as a result, is in grave and immediate danger of returning to a state of nature, a feudal anarchy in which a few isolated castles of Belgian economic interests will survive behind their guarded moats and drawbridges. At the height of De Gaulle's optimism over extension of French power in Africa, France made attempts to absorb the Congo into the franc zone. Belgium saw the light and has come to a *modus vivendi* with the Congolese Government. In part apparently because of French and Belgian intrigues the government of Adoula collapsed. The American *bêtes noires*—the "conservative" Tshombe and the "radical" Gizenga—returned to political life arm in arm. Whatever plans they have for the Congo, and whatever the outcome internally of their activities, one result is certain: a growing American conviction of the inherent perversity of African politics, a conviction that could have far-reaching results in the future.

I have dwelt at such pessimistic length upon the travails of the Congo not to show that either General de Gaulle on the one hand or President Nkrumah on the other was right, but to highlight certain factors that I believe are determinative for both current and future American policy toward French-speaking Africa in particular and toward the continent in general. In short, the Congo experience could lead American foreign policy-makers to the conclusion that, to be effective, American intervention, in Africa as in Cuba or Viet Nam, must be on a major scale, of an extent and duration adequate to attain the goals intended, or not exist at all. If this is the case, then America will almost necessarily decide to withdraw from large-scale activity in African politics.

The United States will and must continue to maintain diplomatic, cultural, and even economic relations with all nations of the world willing to reciprocate. But, at the same time, American resources of political and economic skill as well as capital are limited, especially in view of the growing realization of the scope of its internal problems, and must therefore be allocated in accordance with a sense of world priorities. In any such scale of priorities Africa, and especially French-speaking Africa, must accept a relatively low place. Massive American activity in this area—on the scale of American commitments in Southeast Asia or in Latin America—is therefore highly unlikely. This is fundamental to any future American policy in any part of Africa. But, this having been said, the fact remains that the United States must have a policy toward French-speaking Africa, one consistent with its policies toward Africa as a whole and with its policies toward all of the Third World. I should like to suggest what some of the broad lines of this policy must be.

First, the United States must unequivocally recognize the independence of the states of French-speaking Africa. I do not mean legally, or even morally, but psychologically. The assumption has always been that most of these states were to some extent French satellites. The United States frequently has treated these states as independent agents whose policies could be brought closer to those of the United States only when French and American interests clashed. The United States, thus, must continue to collaborate with French-speaking African states in exerting international pressures—through the United Nations and otherwise—upon Portugal and the Republic of South Africa, regardless of French policy. The full realization of the implications on the world of the Gaullist "Third Force" policies should serve to liberate the United States from many of its inhibitions in this regard.

What are some of the practical implications of such a policy? I can now only advert to two corollaries. The United States should continue its policy of supporting the UAM's successor economic organization (UAMCE)—American money, it might be noted, helped finance the UAM headquarters building—but it should not react adversely to a gradual breakup of this group and a realignment of its members in terms of other considerations. Insofar as American support for this grouping was a backstop for French influence, based upon the assumption that such influence would serve American interests, it must cease and must exist solely on its own merits, economically and politically.

In addition, the United States must more actively seek to broaden cultural relations with the French-speaking nations of Africa. Few of their overseas students study in the United States. Most go to France, where they become not only anti-French in many cases, but, more important, anti-Western as well. The United States in the past assumed, largely erroneously, that allowing French primacy in this area of cultural relations to go unchallenged was desirable as a means of keeping African students under what it regarded as at least beneficent influences. But even leaving aside Gaullist political adventurism and whatever attraction it might have for French-speaking Africans, it must be recognized that an America and a world seen through the eyes of the Left Bank is one largely seen through a fog of illusion, or disillusion, and America must communicate more directly with the rising generation of French-speaking African leaders. To the extent that sound educational and fiscal policy dictates that students from French-speaking Africa be educated in Africa itself rather than overseas, the United States should seek to ensure an adequate American "presence" in these endeavors.

Second, the United States must face up to the problem of military and physical security in French-speaking Africa—at present the problem in the Congo now that the United Nations has gone. What will happen elsewhere in Africa when the French bases are removed, as in time they must and will be? Who will step into the breach in French-speaking Africa as the British stepped into the breach in East Africa should new military coups or popular rebellions occur in this area? That French arms will return, save to protect French citizens and investments, is unlikely; nor should American approval of such a course be a foregone conclusion. The United States itself could almost certainly never directly intervene militarily. But what can it do to strengthen the ability and willingness of the United Nations and the Organization of African States to act? The alternative to strengthening these agencies is either to allow internal chaos or to permit unilateral intervention by other African states, actions that would make areas of disorder the cockpits of inter-African or even perhaps Great Power struggles.

A clearly related issue is United States policy toward growing armies in these states. Should the policy be to discourage them? How can it do so in the face of the growing need of African states for adequate internal-security forces of their own? It is in most cases very difficult to differentiate necessary internal-security forces from those designed for external adventurism. The United States has in the past helped to build up military forces in Senegal, Morocco, Tunisia, and Mali. Shall it continue to render military assistance to African nations, risking aiding an African arms race?

What, similarly, will it do if *Cartierisme* or pique on the part of De Gaulle triumphs in France and the French-speaking African countries are turned loose economically? The amount of direct assistance the United States can usefully render is limited by its resources and its other commitments. Equally important, the countries of former French Africa are tied to France economically as the Congo is tied to Belgium. Suppose they should lose tariff concessions and other more subtle subventions from France and the Common Market generally? Their products compete in world markets with those of Latin American and Pacific basin nations in which the United States has vital interests, as well as competing with those of many of our own states. Could the United States ever play an economic role in these nations comparable to that now played by France and Europe? It was in answer to this question that the Clay Committee report of 1963 on American foreign aid suggested in effect that the United States allow Africa to remain an area of European economic hegemony. But what would occur if the French drastically reduced or altered the nature of their economic ties to Africa?

Finally, the United States must have a *consistent* policy toward French-speaking Africa. French policy has been inconsistent for many reasons, even if inconsistent only to a limited degree. France is more interested in North Africa than in Black Africa because her financial and strategic interests are greater there. She tolerates a Ben Bella in Algeria, and indeed supports him, for reasons different from those that enable her to remain largely apathetic to apparently growing extremism in Brazzaville. It is still open to conjecture whether French support of the regime in Gabon was reflective of a French determination to hold on to an area of considerable economic interest, to support an unusually pro-French regime, or simply to serve as a warning that coups such as those in Dahomey, Togo, and Brazzaville could not be tolerated indefinitely. Thus far, French policy appears to be dictated by a combination of direct economic and strategic interest, giving it a greater inner consistency than would appear to be the case at first glance.

But the United States can afford—and must have—a broader policy. The United States has no special interests in any French-speaking African area. It is always difficult to speak of foreign policy in general terms, since policies must always be applied in concrete situations and adapted to them. Nevertheless, the United States is free in French-speaking Africa to consistently pursue a general policy of being helpful to those who not only need but who can and will use help, of being friendly to those who are willing to reciprocate friendship, and of respecting the independence and integrity of all. These are the policies that ideally should guide American policy throughout the world. There are regions such as Latin America and the periphery of Communist power in Asia where, on occasion, these policies have had to be modified because of local problems, and the United States has as a result wasted funds, suffered political ignominy, and been untrue to her highest ideals. But this need not be the case anywhere in French-speaking Africa. Here America's lack of special interest can allow a foreign policy conceived and implemented in the highest interests of both America and Africa—a policy based on mutual understanding and respect.

14

The Cameroon Federation:
Political Union Between English-
and French-Speaking Africa

WILLARD R. JOHNSON

*Chrétiennement parlant, tout le monde
reconnaitra que Dieu a crée un seul Cameroun; c'est là le point de départ.*

SIMPLE AND STRAIGHTFORWARD, imbued with a certain idealism, and revealing an extraordinary faith in the persuasiveness of premises, this statement is characteristic of its author, Reuben Um Nyobe, General Secretary
of the Union des Populations du Cameroun (UPC) and the person principally responsible for making "Kamerun reunification" part of the vocabulary of African nationalism. To many people on both sides of the Mungo
River, which, for a goodly portion of its journey southward divides the
former Cameroun Republic and the former Southern Cameroons—the two
states that on October 1, 1961, federated to form the Federal Republic
of Cameroon—the semblance of historic unity under the rule of Imperial
Germany, the existence of certain limited ethnic affinities between them,
and a sense of injustice over their deliberate but arbitrary division between
British and French administration seemed justification enough for the idea
of their reunification. (A German protectorate from 1884 to 1916, the
Cameroun was divided in 1916 into two League of Nations mandates
administered by Great Britain and France.)

The history of the effort to achieve a single political community among
the people who occupy the territory of the former German Kamerun is

205

anything but simple and straightforward, and by no means did it end with the birth of the new Federation. It is not our concern here to analyze the development of the Cameroon reunification movement,[1] but it should be noted that, despite the popularity of this idea (more than 70 per cent of the Southern Cameroon voters favored union with the Cameroon Republic), the leaders of this movement were uneasy with their success.

Following the plebiscite conducted on February 1, 1961, both Prime Minister John N. Foncha, the champion of unification in West (British) Cameroon, and President Ahmadou Ahidjo, his opposite member in East (French) Cameroon, were filled with doubts about the desirability of full union between the two territories. Neither of these political figures had been key leaders in the initial stages of the reunification movement, when the idea was advanced as part of a campaign for achieving a greater measure of home rule. Both represented northern, less-privileged, and less-Westernized areas of their respective states, and emerged as the spokesmen for the partisans of home rule. As late as three months before the plebiscite, Foncha flew to London to demand a continuation of trusteeship for an autonomous Southern Cameroons, possibly for as long as five years. Ahidjo was thought to have preferred no union at all to union with only the Southern Cameroons.

Perhaps each of these leaders considered that the ancient continuities between the two territories were largely irrelevant to the success of a program of broader union. Unlike the justification for union, the means for resolving the problems that would result from it—of merging and accommodating different if not conflicting patterns of administration, law, economic activity, communications, and culture—are often obscure. The Cameroon Federation is something of a testing ground for the practicality of the idea of Pan-Africanism; certainly any future political union involving both English- and French-speaking African territories will have to solve many of the same problems now confronting the leadership of the Federal Republic of Cameroon.

Prime Minister Foncha had been so busy campaigning, first for "secession" from Nigeria, and then for the "white box" (joining the Republic of Cameroon) that he had little time to think of the form that the union might take. Moreover, officials on both sides were reluctant to commit themselves in detail on constitutional arrangements, or were in too weak a position to force acceptance of their views. Foncha could hardly threaten choosing any other alternative should his desire for a very loose federation embodying the institutions of a parliamentary democracy be rejected. Ahidjo, who seems to have preferred a more centralized system, could safely argue that, until it became clear which of the two sections of the British Cameroons (Northern and Southern), if either, would opt for union with the Republic, it was useless to attempt to define too closely the constitutional arrangements that would govern such a union.

Such broad outlines of these arrangements as were decided upon before the plebiscite resulted mainly from pressure from the British and the Plebiscite Commissioner.[2] After several meetings in the late summer and winter of 1960, the two leaders signed an agreement covering, in vague outline, their principal proposals for the Federal Constitution.[3] Both parties had come to use the language of federalism despite the fact that during the early period of the reunification movement its partisans spoke in terms of a unitary system for a "United Kamerun." In keeping with Foncha's current predilections, the agreement signed by him with Ahidjo alloted a minimum number and orthodox cluster of powers to the central government. However, the way for later additions to the list of federal powers was left open by the agreement, no doubt at Ahidjo's insistence.

It is difficult to judge whether Foncha was particularly disturbed or even fully aware of the breadth of the disparity between his view of the federation and that held by President Ahidjo. Despite the fact that he had already secretly received the Yaoundé government's proposals, Foncha called an all-party conference in Bamenda to discuss only those of his own party, the Kamerun National Democratic Party (KNDP). These proposals generally failed to take into account the nature of the conflict between the positions of the two governments.[4] Foncha's proposals contain a curious mixture of provisions, some of which were designed to make it a weak federation, and some that seemed appropriate to the strong federation Ahidjo wanted. Features obviously designed to make it a weak union included: dual federal-state nationality laws; a government responsible to parliament; a prime minister required to rule in accordance with the advice of his own ministers; a bicameral legislature with only enumerated powers; and limiting federal authority in security matters to the defense of the federation from external attacks only. But Foncha also proposed federal control over the direction of the economy; economic-development planning; fiscal policy; external-trade agreements; technical and financial assistance; customs; and weights and measures.

Prime Minister Foncha seems to have placed great faith in the provision in his agreement with Ahidjo calling for a "second stage" list of federal powers that the states could continue to exercise during an undefined interim period. Into this list (contained in Article 6 of the Federal Constitution), he deposited those powers the federal exercise of which he considered would jeopardize the position of the states, but which the French-speaking Cameroonians seemed bent on making federal. However, without a fixed timetable for this transitional period, these powers actually became federalized rather rapidly.

At the Bamenda Conference, the Foncha regime gave no direct indication that a conflict existed between its own proposals and those that would be presented a month later to the official constitutional conference between representatives of the two federating states. The opposition party, the Cameroon People's National Convention (CPNC), which had favored union with Nigeria, was critical, ironically, of those KNDP proposals that would weaken the union, but it failed to appreciate the nature of the fundamental contradictions in these proposals. Though the CPNC was the only party to state flatly that the ideal constitution for a country the size and with the resources of the Cameroon would be a unitary one, it nevertheless argued for legal provisions for secession and insisted that the plebiscite vote did not permanently commit the territory to union.

The One Kamerun Party (OK), a party generally considered to be an affiliate for the then outlawed UPC and thus bitterly opposed to the Ahidjo regime, was the only party that came close to appreciating the contradictions embodied in Foncha's proposals. Despite their dislike for Ahidjo, the OK delegates at Bamenda favored, on ideological grounds, a stronger federation than any of the other parties wanted. Confused and contradictory as many of their own views were, only the OK delegation attacked the basic problem with the KNDP position:

We hear members of the Government Party threaten that if His Excellency President Ahmadou Ahidjo rejects their proposals they will reject unification. The statement implies that they shall declare the Southern Kamerun (sic) a sovereign state. We would wish to observe that this is both impossible and improbable. We cannot declare sovereignty because we cannot assert it and defend it. . . .

When the Kamerunian people opted for Kamerun reunification . . . it was complete and entire. There can be no going back. The terms of the plebiscite were clear and simple and we chose to achieve independence by joining the Kamerun Republic. There was never a condition attached thereto. . . .[5]

No doubt Prime Minister Foncha considered that there had been a condition attached to the vote for union in the plebiscite, namely his signed agreement with Ahidjo. But this was hardly any safeguard, given the vagueness of the wording of the agreement and the fact that it was signed by the leaders not in their governmental capacities but as heads of their parties. In any case, Foncha did not go into the constitutional conference at Foumban in a position of equality with Ahidjo. The festive grace with which his numerically superior delegation was received at Foumban could not alter that fact. The OK delegate had been right: The Southern Cameroons had no alternative but to carry out the union on any terms. Doing otherwise would have required considerable daring on the part of the Buea officials, or at least an awareness of the real meaning of the Ahidjo proposals and a capacity to appraise the sources and strength of potential opposition to those proposals in East Cameroon. Were they simply to reject the obligations presumed to be imposed by the plebiscite results they surely would have eventually required external support. The most likely source of this support, the United Kingdom, had already indicated that she would not give it.[6]

The federal regime proposed by President Ahidjo at Foumban, and largely represented in the final constitution, was not only more centralized than Foncha wanted to have it, but more so than had been the structures of the First Cameroon Republic. Under the Republic, President Ahidjo had been Head of State only, assisted by a Prime Minister who shared his power with his Council of Ministers, but, under the Federation, the new President (sure to be Ahidjo) was both Head of State and Head of Government. No longer would the Council of Ministers have a constitutional basis, or have to be consulted on the items that previously required its accord, such as the exercise of the regulatory powers, the conduct of foreign affairs, proposed legislation, and the general policies of the government. Now the President rather than the legislature was to author the regulations governing the procedures of the courts, of the hiring and firing of magistrates. The regulations governing the civil service were also placed with the President instead of falling within the competence of the legislature.

Previously, in emergency situations the President had to declare a state of emergency through the Council of Ministers, and then gained only such special powers as were determined by legislative enactment, or in truly exceptional situations he might declare an *état d'exception* and take over the government, but thereby gained only those powers enumerated in special "fundamental" legislation. Emergency powers would not require approval of the Council of Ministers in the new Federation, and though normal emergencies (not *états d'exception*) remained regulated by legislation, it was not "fundamental" legislation, which required a fifteen-day delay before passage. *Etats d'exception,* though requiring consultation by the President with the Prime Ministers, would now confer on the President any and all powers he deemed necessary.

Had Foncha understood these changes to be consequential to the Ahidjo proposals he would have known that they could be expected to draw considerable opposition from the forces in East Cameroon hostile to President Ahidjo. But to capitalize on this latent opposition he would have had to carry his case to the people. This would have meant working with the UPC-influenced elements, which Foncha was probably unwilling to do since he had had his fill of them during their period of exile in Southern Cameroons. Moreover, Foncha was never given the chance to make a public issue out of the constitutional debates.

Ahidjo succeeded in basing the Foumban discussions on his own proposals, which he presented in the form of revisions of the Constitution of the First Cameroon Republic. This had the effect of nullifying the work of the Bamenda Conference and of making Ahidjo the arbiter of the constitutional discussions, and allowed the final changes to be instituted by a vote of the National Assembly, where his party now controlled over two-thirds of the votes. This remarkable feat, a stratagem brilliantly conceived and ably executed, was achieved through a deference to the rhetoric of the long reunification campaign itself. Reuben Um Nyobe had asserted the unity of the "Kamerun Nation." Ahidjo echoed him: "[There is] one sole historic unity—the Cameroon Nation, one sole historic unity—the Cameroon Nation, one sole moral unity—the Cameroon fatherland."[7] But if this were so, there was no denying that the larger, more populous, and, most important, already independent Cameroon Republic was the chief expression of that unity. The Republic already possessed an international juridical personality. Thus the principal representation of the Cameroon Nation must only become transformed to incorporate its long-dormant and estranged fragment, and it must accommodate the particularities of that fragment. The new Federation in Ahidjo's view was to be a new form of the old reality, a creative restoration. Consequently it would not be necessary to enact a new constitution, requiring a national referendum; it was only necessary to amend the old one, requiring only a two-thirds vote of the National Assembly.

Since they were not prepared to discuss the Ahidjo proposals (most of them had not seen them at Bamenda), the West Cameroon delegates spent most of the five days of the Foumban Conference meeting by themselves to study the Yaoundé draft. When they rejoined their colleagues from the East, Ahidjo was in a position to accept only those of their recommendations that he found compatible with his view of the Federation. The rest were rejected by omission.

If one judges the progress of political integration in terms of the emergence of a high-fidelity system of communications among the peoples of the nascent community, a sharpened sensitivity on the part of persons and politically relevant groups to each other's needs, and a willingness and capacity to accommodate those needs, then the process of constitution-making for the Cameroon Federation did not advance the process of political integration between the two uniting communities. West Cameroonians received no response to their felt needs, however inadequately articulated, which could have left them gratified. Only two of Foncha's campaign promises found fulfillment in the Federal Constitution: that the union would be called federal and that those powers that did not go to the central government would remain with the states. Substantively, these were hollow victories.

If, however, one considers the structural problems that have to be faced in effectuating a union—of harmonizing, if not standardizing the disparate patterns of government, and of meeting the tremendous burdens that would be placed upon the central institutions for expanded welfare services, capital development, and increased production—then the multiplicity and strength of the ties that shall bind the two states together do not seem completely inappropriate. Perhaps the structure envisaged will permit the future construction of a real community among the peoples of the Federation, something that was lacking at its birth.

Most of the new African states are faced with a difficult language problem: There is a multiplicity of vernacular languages, and only a small percentage of the population is schooled in the one official language. Cameroon has this problem in the extreme. Bridging the gap between the official languages and the nearly 150 vernacular languages will remain a problem for years to come. The immediate problem is to bridge the gap between the two official ones. In their private discussions, Foncha and Ahidjo are reported to have conversed in pidgin English, a lingua franca in widespread use along the coast of and on the frontier between the two states. The Yaoundé government had been able to produce its constitutional proposals in English, and the official gazette of the Federal Government has appeared in both languages from the start. Some administrative regulations allegedly have been sent out untranslated, however, and, as late as two years after reunification, post offices in West Cameroon were still giving out applications and instruction sheets for postal-savings accounts written in French only.

Merging the broader systems of communication so as to permit national distribution of information pertaining to the values and policies held by politically relevant elements in each state and subnational community constitutes a more complex and fundamental problem. Discontinuities are evident throughout the communications system. Even in more advanced East Cameroon, literacy is low. Though few of the indigenous languages serve wide geographical areas, French is widely spoken in East Cameroon. In West Cameroon, there is no adequate link between the modern political and bureaucratic elites and the masses. Either the vernaculars or pidgin English must be used for this purpose. Thus, the few standard-English translations of news and feature items about East Cameroon that get printed or broadcast in West Cameroon fail to really inform these people about their new compatriots. Moreover, the gap between the communities using the official languages is left largely unfilled by the radio and newspaper services. Radio broadcasts are made in both languages in Buea as well as in the principal stations in East Cameroon, but only the major news items are translated into both. English-language broadcasts, whether in Buea or Yaoundé, tend to carry only items about West Cameroon or the English-speaking world, and the reverse is true for the French-language broadcasts. A similar pattern is to be seen in the printed news bulletins, though to a much lesser degree.

Despite West Cameroon's tenuous grasp of standard English, this language is more and more regarded as the foundation of West Cameroon distinctiveness, and its leaders more and more regard its preservation as the safeguard of federalism in the country. This attitude results, in large measure, from their exposure to French-speaking Cameroonians' assumptions of superiority and their view of the process of integration as one of assimilating the West Cameroonians to the ways of the East. Hopelessly outnumbered within the Federation, English-speaking leaders have pointed to the fact that, when one considers the whole of Africa, English is more widespread than French. Some of the West Cameroon leaders have found more than idealistic reasons to be Pan-Africanists.

Close federal supervision and control over the political life of West Cameroon was enhanced by the system of territorial administration instituted by the President shortly after federation.[8] The system provided for six "inspectors of federal administration," one of whom was placed over the federal administrative apparatus is West Cameroon. This system displeased Buea officials greatly because it incorporated into the federal administration officials of the state administration, thus making them the focus of two separate chains of command, with dual federal-state responsibilities. The district officers, for example, were placed in such a situation. The effect was to prohibit an autonomous state administrative apparatus, and thus to vastly augment the federal capacity to control local affairs.

The inspectors supervise and coordinate the functions of the federal departments operating in the six administrative regions. They also serve as a liaison between local administrators and the federal executive. As the direct local representative of the President, the inspector has the authority to make rules within the framework of the executive powers and to enforce these rules with the help of the armed and police forces if necessary. Initially, copies of all correspondence and reports between the Federal ministries and their local branches, and even between the local state administrators and their state superiors, were to be sent to the inspector.

As more and more of the Federal institutions were installed or taken over from state authorities, the district and senior district officers became correspondingly "federalized"; an increasingly greater percentage of their time was spent on coordinating federal rather than state services. One natural consequence, especially given their lack of experience in the administrative procedures used in the East, was that state officials tended to send more and more of their reports and communications directly to the federal authorities; the state administration sometimes got bypassed even on matters within its jurisdiction. Eventually, the local administrators were instructed to refrain from communicating directly with or taking orders from any federal authority, but rather to go through the West Cameroon Prime Minister's office. This is but one evidence of the fact that there has been a great deal of friction created between the state administration and the Federal Government over the role of the inspectors. The system resulted in other instances of friction. The first appointment to this position for West Cameroon stimulated a public outcry in that state because the appointee was an East Cameroonian who spoke no English.[9] The West Cameroon Government claimed also that it had not been adequately consulted about the appointment. A second appointment was made, but even he aroused some opposition because of the extensiveness of his activities, particularly the fact that he tended to operate as if he were a principal political spokesman for the people of West Cameroon.

Providing for the security of the territory was a concern that played an important role in shaping attitudes toward the Federation, both in the preplebiscite campaign and after—a role not so much of avoiding or repelling external aggression, but rather of providing for the maintenance of internal law and order, which concerned the partisans of reunification.

There was widespread fear of disorders resulting from reunification, disorders that might come from two separate sources. On the one hand, the vehemence of the pro-Nigerian (or antireunification) forces in pledging never to accept the results of the plebiscite and in calling for a partition of the territory led to widespread expectations of a repeat of the Congo situation: internal chaos, tribal warfare, and attempts by minority groups to secede. In reality, the Congo crisis exercised a sobering influence on the minority leadership and helped to dampen rather than stimulate local conflict.

On the other hand, there was fear that the disorders and violence that had attended the UPC-directed rebellion in the frontier districts just across the border would spill over into "peaceful" West Cameroon. Many Cameroon Anglophones were convinced that the violence of the "maquis" in the Bamileke, Mungo, and Douala areas was somehow rooted in the French culture that had taken hold there. In any case, fears of a spillover of violence tended to be confirmed by the brutal massacre (presumably by East Cameroon terrorists) of twelve plantation workers at Ebubu on the western side of the internal border just a month and a half before unification.

It was obvious to everyone that the West Cameroon law-enforcement forces needed to be strengthened, especially after it was made plain that British troops would be withdrawn with the termination of the Trusteeship Agreement.[10] The Opposition and Government parties joined in protesting the British action, and called for the raising of a West Cameroon army and a significant expansion of the police forces. But the principal source of security forces would be East Cameroon. Yet, fear of the East Cameroon gendarmes was almost as widespread as was that of the terrorists. Rumors were legion that the gendarmes used brutal methods. Travelers returning from visits to the Republic told of having seen the heads of alleged terrorists impaled on stakes in front of the *gendarmeries*. Many West Cameroonians believe to this day that it was the gendarmes and not the terrorists who were responsible for the massacre at Ebubu.

The opposition party, the CPNC, asserted at the Bamenda consitutional conference that alarm and disorder would result from the introduction into West Cameroon of the East Cameroon gendarmes and army:

It needs little saying to appreciate the extent of harm and chaos that will follow in the wake of any attempt to flood one section of the Federation with armed forces conditioned to training and discipline alien to the place of occupation. Experience has painfully taught people the world over the danger of armies of occupation.

Though West Cameroon has hardly been flooded with gendarmes, serious consequences attended the introduction of these forces into the state, and they have been accused of using brutal methods to gain information or to apprehend suspects and of beating people indiscriminately. Much of the difficulty with the gendarmes resulted from a conflict of jurisdiction between them and the local police. The lack of a clear demarcation of their respective jurisdictions has led to open conflict between them, on one occasion leading to the forcible entry by the gendarmes into a West Cameroon jailhouse to remove a suspect who was then allegedly beaten by them and hospitalized. In the outcry that followed, it was suggested that the police be armed and instructed to defend their own jurisdiction. Others have pointed out that the police have also been guilty of heavyhanded tactics and that perhaps the solution to the conflict of jurisdictions was the centralization of all these forces under federal supervision.

In reality there is a great deal of centralization already, because the new federal administrative system placed certain units of the police under the control of the inspectors or other federal administrative officials, and provided for the automatic federalization of the police whenever actions were taken to protect the security of the federal state. This was an innovation for West Cameroon, because it placed armed forces under the control of civil servants for the first time. The broader problem of conflict between the police and gendarmes and of public hostility to the latter remains unresolved, however, and constitutes one of the really serious challenges to the enthusiasm of West Cameroonians for the Federation and, by association, for Foncha's regime.

Perhaps the source of the most severe criticism of the Federation by West Cameroonians, and the greatest cause of hardship to them, has been the impact of unification on the economic and commercial patterns in the state. This impact was first felt with the replacement, in the spring of 1962, of the Nigerian currency by the CFA franc. Despite the merits of the decimal system, illiterate market women found it difficult to convert their traditional prices into CFA equivalents. Sellers, always anxious to gain the benefit of the doubt, tended to raise prices. Moreover, since the exchange rate (£ = 800 CFA) Nigerian traders found they earned less in sterling from the same sales. They too raised prices. This coupled with stringent licensing requirements instituted in July, 1962, tended to drive the Nigerian traders out of the commercial life of the state and the goods they habitually imported became scarce and prices rose precipitously. To make matters worse, lack of confidence in the CFA franc and lack of understanding of the procedures for conversion resulted in significant hoarding of Nigerian currency, which later found profitable outlets in the black market, augmenting the inflationary pressure on regular markets.

Yet another inflationary pressure and object of bitter criticism resulted from the government's perhaps inadvertent escalation of CFA prices for stamps and fees over their former sterling prices. Many people took this as a guide for CFA-Nigerian-pound exchange rates. Since the formerly six-dime stamp now cost twenty francs instead of seventeen, which would accord with the official rates, all items that formerly cost six dimes were priced at twenty francs. Prices were similarly escalated on up the scale of CFA-pound equivalents. The changeover posed other hazards for West Cameroonians; one person is reported to have commited suicide after being deceived into changing his life's savings of £100 for 100 francs.

In light of the disruptions and criticism produced by the currency changeover, following it with a switch to the metric system of weights and measures seems to have been rather foolhardy. Posters proclaiming the system the "most universal, simplist, and practical" were interpreted as "new equivalents to learn, more equipment to buy, higher prices to pay." After October 1, 1962, no new equipment calibrated in any other than the decimal-metric system was to be imported, and the old instruments marked in the units of the Imperial System were to be adapted "or exported from the Cameroon before the 1st of April 1963."[11] The adaptations made necessary by unification had just about strained the flexibility of West Cameroonians, and the dangers of carrying out the intended change were apparent to the Buea government and to the federal inspector there. The terminal date for the changeover was first postponed by three months and then by six.

The disruptions suffered by West Cameroon in her traditional patterns of external commerce may prove to be the most important and detrimental changes she has had to undergo as a result of federation. Her most important crop, bananas, prior to federation enjoyed free entry into the Commonwealth market, a preference amounting to 7 £ 10/– per ton. The profit margin for the major producer, the Cameroon Development Corporation (CDC), was not much larger than this figure, and that of the independent producer was often less. With the loss of this preference, originally scheduled for October, 1962, but postponed until the end of 1963, the West Cameroon banana crop stood to suffer disaster. Given the ability of other Commonwealth suppliers to expand their production to completely replace the Cameroon crop, and given the apparent inelasticity of the Common Market demand, West Cameroon producers, particularly the independent producers, were threatened with ruin. Some of the latter became so discouraged that they slashed down their trees and let the fruit rot in the fields. Literally by a windfall, however, the 1963 banana crop was sold, and at record prices for many producers: A hurricane in the West Indies destroyed almost the entire crop of this major Commonwealth supplier and Cameroon found a market after all.[12] Only those farmers who had destroyed their crop failed to enjoy a boom year, but the day of reckoning has only been postponed for the others.

Success in achieving an integrated political community may depend, in the long run, on what is done in the field of education, for it is by education that the values that produce complementary patterns of political behavior throughout the national territory can be most easily instilled.

Perhaps in recognition of this fact, Ahidjo insisted that all education above the primary levels be controlled by the Federal Government, and Foncha, in the classic tradition of spokesman for regional interests, demanded that all education, save perhaps a federal university, fall within the jurisdiction of the states. The President's view prevailed.

The first step in accommodating the two educational systems to each other was the introduction of the compulsory study of both English and French in each state. West Cameroon has a special problem to solve in attempting to become bilingual in world languages—too few of its people know English well. For the foreseeable future, the state has opted to introduce French into only the secondary and teacher-training schools, but it will not be available to those "who do not have a solid foundation in English."[13]

A second step in the process of merging the educational systems was the appointment of a federal official to supervise the secondary and technical schools in West Cameroon. This official, the Director of Education in the Ministry of Education of West Cameroon, was appointed Federal Cultural Delegate in Charge of Education. This appointment had the effect of giving the number-two man in the state ministry more responsibilities than the Minister. In July, 1963, the federal budget assumed the burden of the secondary- and technical-education programs.

One of the major differences between the two systems of education before federation concerns the curriculum. Each followed a system peculiar to the territories under the jurisdiction of the administering authority: West Cameroon students prepared for the West African School Certificate or the General Certificate in Education (GCE), and East Cameroonians prepared for the *license* or the *baccalauréat*. This continues to be the pattern, and will remain so for a long while to come, at least until Cameroon can effectuate a merger of the systems and evolve its own examinations and degrees equivalent to those mentioned above.

A start has been made, however, with a reform in the calendar. West Cameroon students used to start primary studies at the age of five and pursued an eight-year primary course. In the East, pupils started at the age of six and followed a six-year course for seven years. In 1965, the primary calendar will be shortened again in West Cameroon and completely synchronized with that now used in East Cameroon.

Another difference between the systems used in the two states is that the West Cameroon Government has been much less involved in the educational program than has that of East Cameroon. In the West, the educational system is almost entirely in the hands of "voluntary agencies," mostly missionary organizations. In mid-1963, only three primary and no secondary schools were run by the Government. The pattern is much different in East Cameroon where the government bears the major burden of education and is in the process of taking over an even greater share from the missionary organizations. Thus, some educational officials in West Cameroon fear that religious instruction may be jeopardized in their system. The Buea government has pledged to continue to permit religious instruction in public schools, something that is not permitted in the government schools of East Cameroon. Missionary officials also fear that government subsidies for their educational programs may not be continued by the Federal Government.

Coordinating the legal systems of each state is proving to be difficult, and little progress in this direction has been achieved. The two systems continue to operate side by side. The Federal Court of Justice will be the first place where a merger of the systems must take place, but so far no cases have been referred to this court, the highest court of appeal in the country. The rules of procedure for this court presumably must accommodate differences between the British system of common law and the French comprehensive code system in, for instance, the admission of hearsay evidence and in certain rules concerning criminal law, such as a difference in the presumption of guilt and in the procedures for trying criminal cases.

Cameroon legal officials have concentrated on the problem of resolving the differences in the rules of each state governing the practice of the legal profession and service on the judicial benches. These procedures are markedly different. In West Cameroon, practicing lawyers must be admitted to the bar (until now this has meant the British bar) usually in addition to their normal legal studies. In East Cameroon, various types of legal studies are sufficient not only to permit legal practice but also to serve on the bench. Years of experience in the courts and in legal practice is normally necessary before a lawyer qualifies to serve on the bench in the common-law system. Efforts to resolve such differences were still in the stage of discussion and negotiation as of the beginning of this year. Achieving even a temporary composite of the two European-inspired legal systems will be difficult, but officials on both sides prefer to work for a genuinely Cameroonian system of law, drawing from the four or more systems that now operate within the Federation (British, French, Moslem, and African customary law, which itself shows great diversity from ethnic group to ethnic group).

Political union of territories with a delicate internal balance of political forces is always likely to produce important political regroupments. In the Cameroon, as would likely be the case in any other such union, the political parties already dominating the government feared their control would be jeopardized by the act of union. This fear came into play even before reunification, and may explain the approaches Foncha and Ahidjo took to the problem of elaborating the constitution. The KNDP officials have often appeared to be more concerned with the threat posed by their own opposition party leadership than with that posed by the federal constitutional arrangements or by the Union Camerounaise, the dominant party in East Cameroon. Despite serious public criticism of many of the changes resulting from federation, the KNDP seems to have weathered the storm, judging by the results of the April, 1964, federal elections in which its list of candidates captured all of the West Cameroon seats in the Federal Assembly.[14]

The progress of the Union Camerounaise toward achieving a one-party state seems to have been somewhat arrested by federation. Shortly after federation, the UC President, Ahidjo, called for a merger of all parties, including the West Cameroon parties, into a single national party. The principal opposition parties in East Cameroon refused to accept the call. These parties were soon swept away, however, by the imprisonment, on charges of subversion, of four of their top leaders. The number of adherents to the UC from these old parties has grown apace. However, the KNDP, despite repeated affirmations of its essential unity with the UC, has so far refused to merge with it. In the face of appeals by the principal West Cameroon opposition leaders for dissolution of both their CPNC and the ruling KNDP and the adherence of their members to the UC, the KNDP has attempted to absorb or demolish its opposition before taking on the problems of union with Ahidjo's party. The KNDP enjoys a position of legitimate autonomous power as the principal political organization of West Cameroon and has been able to resist UC pressures for a union of the parties. None of the East Cameroon parties has such an advantage, and thus one suspects that the political effect of federation has been to retard the emergence of a one-party regime in Cameroon. There is no indication that such a situation has been permanently prohibited, however, as Foncha continues to promise the imminent fusion of the two ruling parties.[15]

Federation of the two states of Cameroon has complicated what would have been a formidable task for either one of them alone—that of evoking a sense of common nationality, of constructing a coherent cluster of political values around national institutions. The process of constitution-making for the Cameroon Federation did not advance this process very much, since it gave expression to the political values of only one side. The structures erected for the central government tend to be authoritarian. Yet it must be admitted that the disparities between the states are very great and centralized authority may be the key to holding the Federation together long enough to permit solution of the initial, agonizing problems consequent to the union.

It is perhaps surprising that despite these many problems a sense of solidarity between the leadership and populace of the two states has been evident throughout the short life of the Federation. For a union that is more of an arranged marriage than one of free choice, with a just-come-of-age bride who had no idea what marriage was all about, the honeymoon was surprisingly real and long. Eventually, if the initial difficulties can be resolved, the superficial sense of solidarity will perhaps precipitate the substance of a real community.

Those interested in promoting future efforts at broader union between African territories of differing colonial backgrounds can look to the Cameroon case for an idea of the problems involved. Though the peculiarities of the Cameroon situation influenced many of the problems we have discussed, all have certain roots in the colonial heritages involved. Of these problems, those arising from the disruptions to economic and commercial life are perhaps the most general and difficult of solution. Much of the success in overcoming them depends on the cooperation and aid received from external sources. The problems relating to the security forces, though involving types of forces and methods of operation distinctive to the French areas, are most influenced by the particular Cameroon situation, by the UPC-led terrorist campaign, for example. In the long run, perhaps the key element in the solution of all the problems examined here is goodwill between the uniting partners and a genuine desire to have the effort succeed.

PART VI

THE THEORETICAL FRAMEWORK

15

Social Change and Modernization in African Societies South of the Sahara

S. N. EISENSTADT

SOCIAL CHANGE in Africa has been studied from various points of view by different social-science disciplines. The original emphasis was generally upon the emergence of new types of social organization that were drifting, so to speak, in new directions not readily discernible, yet not wholly dissimilar to those of other modern, industrial societies. But the establishment of new political structures in Africa has created the possibility—indeed, the necessity—of studying these phenomena in their interrelationships, in what is often called their "global" or "total" setting. Hence, the study of the processes of change has become part of the broad studies of modernization, and the first step in studying African societies is to determine to what extent they develop in the direction of modern societies—i.e., to what extent they develop the major social features and problems of modernity.[1]

The broad sociodemographic and structural corollaries of modernization as they develop in the major institutional spheres are well known. Perhaps the best over-all summary of the sociodemographic indexes of modernization has been coined by Karl Deutsch in the term "social mobilization," which he defines as the "process in which major clusters of old social, economic and psychological commitments are eroded and broken and people become available for new patterns of socialization and behaviour." According to Deutsch, some of the main indexes of social mobilization are exposure to aspects of modern life through demonstrations of machinery, buildings, consumers' goods, etc.; response to mass media; change of residence; urbanization; change from agricultural occupations; literacy, and growth of per capita income.

Similarly, the major structural characteristics of modernization have been identified as the development of a high degree of differentiation; of free resources that are not committed to any fixed, ascriptive (kinship, territorial, etc.) groups; of specialized and diversified types of social organization; and of wide nontraditional "national" or even supernational group identifications. In institutional spheres, these characteristics have been identified as regulative and allocative mechanisms and organizations—such as market mechanisms in economic life, and voting and party activities in politics—and diverse bureaucratic organizations and mechanisms.

But beyond the sociodemographic and structural characteristics of modernity there exists a somewhat larger and, in a way, more crucial problem. Modernization implies not only the development of the various aspects of growing structural differentiation, but also the development of a social system that not only generates continuous change, but, unlike many other types of social systems, is capable of absorbing changes beyond its own initial institutional premises. Hence, the central problem of modernization can be seen as the ability of any system to adapt itself to these changing demands, to absorb them in terms of policy-making, and to assure its own continuity in the face of continuous new demands and forms of political organization.

In other words, modernization creates social, economic, and political problems. The ability to deal with political problems is the crucial test of sustained growth, of development, and of modernization. Research on development and modernization has been guided by frequently implicit assumptions about the conditions of such sustained growth. These assumptions now are being undermined, and the examination of the African may be of special interest for a critical examination of them.

The first such assumption has been the primacy of the economic sphere in development and modernization, of the central importance of the economic solvent for the development of viable modern societies and political regimes. Second has been the assumption that the continuity of modernization, of "sustained growth," of continuous development in any institutional sphere—be it economics, politics, or social organization—was relatively secure after the initial take-off. The third such assumption has been the very close interrelatedness of almost all of the major aspects of "development," or of modernization, in all major institutional spheres of any society.

It may, of course, be claimed that the first assumption—that of the primacy of the economic sphere in development—was discarded relatively early in the game, when some economists discovered that the conditions

)f development and effective functioning of a modern economic system :ould not be understood in economic terms alone, and when the analysis)f the noneconomic preconditions of economic development became one of he major problems of research in this field. However, the very concern vith the preconditions of economic growth tended to reinforce the second issumption that, once initial economic take-off is attained, modernization s more or less assured also in other spheres. Thus, interestingly enough, vhile the literature about the preconditions of economic growth is, and :ontinues to be, abundant, that on the political or social consequences of :conomic growth is only now beginning to emerge.

The second assumption, concerning the assurance of continuous de-'elopment or modernization once the initial take-off stages have been at-ained, can be found with different degrees of explicitness in many :conomic and political analyses—whether in Rostow's *Stages of Economic Growth* or in the first analyses on the development of political institutions n the so-called new nations. Most of these initial analyses were oriented oward the elucidation of the conditions under which parliamentary-constitu-ional regimes can successfully operate in non-Western societies. While it vas usually fully acknowledged that such conditions may not be ripe in nany of these nations, it was often implicitly assumed that, if such polit-cal institutions can be implanted in these countries in the first stages of heir independence, their continuity can perhaps be assured. It was only ater that Rupert Emerson, one of the first students of nationalism and)olitics in Asia, wrote about the "erosion of democracy" in Asian coun-ries;[2] for a relatively long time, Emerson was alone in his theories. Until ecently, we found only a few systematic analyses of the crises and break-lowns of political modernization or economic development after the initial ake-off.

The third assumption, that of the interconnectedness of the various in-.titutional aspects of modernization, held that the process of modernization n the different institutional spheres were so closely interrelated that they vould necessarily coalesce in relatively similar patterns. Although almost ill analysts who dealt with the structural and organizational variety at-endant on modernization stressed that the concrete social and political orms that develop in the new states would somehow differ from those in he West, their assumption of the close interrelationship between the 'arious institutional aspects of modernization was conducive to ignoring hese structural varieties and fostering a "Western-centricity." It also led o a search for conditions under which institutions of the Western type :ould successfully develop and function in the new nations.

Many analyses of processes of modernization that took off from some)f the preceding assumptions often led to or also were based on the—

usually implicit—assumption that the conditions for sustained growth can be found in the continuous extension of these various sociodemographic and/or structural indexes.

For instance, one frequently propounded view has been that the more a society exhibits or develops the basic characteristics of structural specialization, and the higher it is on various indexes of social mobilization, the more modern it is—i.e., by implication, the more easily will it be able to sustain continuous growth and absorb continuous changes.

According to this view, the traditionalism or modernity of a society could be measured by the extent of social mobilization within it and by the extent to which the society's basic principles of allocation and organization were particularistic, diffuse, and ascriptive as against universalistic or achievement- and specificity-oriented. For instance, according to one such study, traditional society tends to be a familistic one, while modern society tends to divest the family unit of most of its functions—the family itself evolves in the direction of the small nuclear family.

Needless to say, such an approach has a great deal of plausibility. However, it is not fully borne out by available evidence. Much recent research indicates that the picture is not so simple or clear-cut. In many cases, we find that the extension of the sociodemographic or structural indexes of modernization may give rise to what may be called "breakdowns" of modernization. In general, it can perhaps be said that, while certain levels of "social mobilization" and of structural differentiation constitute a necessary condition of modernization, the continuous development of these processes does not constitute a sufficient condition of modernization continuity —i.e., in the sense of the creation of an institutional framework capable of continuous absorption of change.

Of special interest here are the implications of the nontenability of the third basic assumption—namely the assurance of continuity of growth after the take-off.[3]

In both the economic and the political spheres it has become quite obvious that there does not exist any assurance of such continuity. The case of Argentina in the economic sphere, and of Burma and Indonesia in the political sphere, are among the most pertinent examples of the possibility of breakdowns after some initial—or even sometimes relatively advanced—stages of modernization.

Contemporary history in general, and contemporary international relations in particular, is a history of breakdowns or of stagnation of political regimes or economic systems that have seemingly "taken-off." But the more paradoxical—and more significant—outcome of these processes was that such breakdowns or stagnations did not necessarily lead to the total collapse of these new regimes or to their return to some traditional social and political form.

These regimes, which evince different degrees of development or modernization in the economic, political, and social spheres, and different types of stagnation, tend to coalesce into some new forms of viable ongoing social and political systems. Such new polities and societies differ in many ways from the "older" (Western) modern ones, and they do not necessarily evolve in the direction of these "older" societies. Yet, they are by no means any longer simply traditional societies. Moreover, however stagnant or unstable these regimes, they evince some capability of reorganization and continuity. They develop various internal and external policies, which aim at the conditions of such continuity.

The conditions that gave rise to such regimes vary, but one such general condition should perhaps be indicated here—namely, their contemporary international setting. This setting, with the Cold War on the one hand and the United Nations drawing together the nations of the world on the other, is of no small importance.

The competition between the great powers for influence in major areas of the world, as well as the desire for ideological legitimation by "independent" regimes, may easily provide crucial resources for initial modernization and for the stabilization of relatively regressive regimes.

The preceding analysis poses two basic problems for the student of the processes of modernization in Africa south of the Sahara. One is the identification of the specific structural characteristics as they develop in African society—as distinct from those of other societies—and of the conditions that explain their development. The other major problem is the indentification of those forces that—within these structural frameworks—facilitate or impede sustained growth and the continuous absorption of change.

It is significant that, for most African states, the emphasis on change, progress, and economic development is one of the main tenets of their political and ideological orientations. But, at the same time, their institutional capacity to absorb changes may be small compared to their aspirations. The ability of the new states to implement desired changes often is limited, frequently, they are barely able even to maintain their own continuity. It is this contradiction that constitutes perhaps the major problem or focus of investigation in the studies of modernization in African societies.

In order to be able to analyze this problem, we have first to go back to the analysis of some of the most important features of modernization as they have crystallized under the colonial regimes in Africa south of the Sahara.[4]

Perhaps the major characteristic of modernization has been its unbalanced process, especially on the "central" and local levels. Most changes introduced by the colonial powers (or by the "traditional" authorities of the independent societies that cooperated with the European powers) have been focused on the central institutions of the society. The most obvious changes were in the broad framework of political and economic institutions. In the political field, the introduction of unitary systems of administration, the standardization or regularization of taxation, the establishment of modern court procedures, and, at later stages, the introduction of limited types of representation, have greatly changed over-all political structures and orientations. These changes have introduced certain universalistic criteria and orientations toward rules and procedures. Even where various forms of indirect rule were practiced, some change necessarily took place in political organization, though this change was much slower than in cases of direct rule.

Similarly, many changes have been effected in the economy, notably the shift to a market economy. In the educational field, change was engendered by endeavoring to provide new types of modern education for selected local elites.

At the same time, however, the colonial powers saw it as part of their task to effect these changes only within the limits set by existing institutions. At the local level, the colonial powers attempted to contain most changes within the confines of traditional groups or even to limit, as much as possible, the extent of any change. Although much change did materialize within local communities, as the literature on detribalization of the family indicates, most of the administrative efforts of the rulers were aimed at strengthening existing organizations and relations, at maintaining peace and order, and at reorganizing local systems of taxation. Thus, while the colonial regime attempted to introduce innovations, it tried to accomplish this within a relatively unchanging social setting, with the implicit goal of confining its efforts to technical matters. Consequently, a basic contradiction tended to develop: On the one hand, attempts were made to establish broad, modern, administrative, political, and economic settings; on the other hand, these efforts were to be limited and based on relatively unchanged subgroups and on the maintenance of traditional attitudes and loyalties.

This situation created a process of disequilibrium or of unbalanced change. In all colonial societies, it gave rise to westernized groups and elites that usually became the spearheads of nationalistic movements. It also greatly influenced some of the basic characteristics and orientation of these movements.

The modernizing orientations of these movements were focused pri narily on the political, rather than the cultural sphere. They sought the reformation of basic internal value-orientations. Consequently, the relations between the rising nationalistic elites and their societies were usually conducted in the political sphere. In most of the nonpolitical economic and cultural spheres, relatively fewer active modernizing groups tended to develop—albeit with great differences between different countries.

Even more problematic was the extent to which the major social groups or strata in these societies were able to develop from within themselves active orientations and resources for modernization, as well as to become integrated into wider frameworks. While all of them underwent processes of social disorganization in various spheres of social life, the extent to which they were able to develop new autonomous orientations and to create the resources for the implementation of such goals was not very great.

With independence, the leaders of the nationalistic groups became the ruling elites and these problems became more acute, for the leaders, bent on the over-all modernization of their countries, were faced with the double problem of establishing new power centers, institutions, and consensus, as well as keeping themselves in power.

It is within the framework of these new power centers that the potential discrepancy between the great emphasis on change and the frequent weakness of the institutional framework to implement change tends to develop. This potential discrepancy could perhaps be best understood by an analysis of the basic structural characteristics of modernization as they tend to develop in contemporary African societies.

Several such characteristics can be discerned in the emerging power centers. First is the development, within the political sphere, of a strong emphasis upon the executive on the one hand, and upon single or dominant parties on the other. The strong emphasis on the executive can be easily discerned in most of the constitutions of the new African states, for they invest the Head of State or of Government with far-reaching constitutional and institutional powers.[5]

The tendency to develop a dominant or single-party system has by now become so widespread in African societies as not to require any special comment. It is important, however, to stress that this tendency is connected with (or to some extent explained by) the differential sequence of modernization in the institutional spheres. Closely related is the great importance of the governmental and political sectors in the modern economy. Government corporations, centrally controlled large-scale cooperatives, and other enterprises run directly by the government or the party form an important part of the African (as distinct from the foreign) modern economic sectors.

The tendency toward single-party systems is also closely connected with the development within modern sectors of African societies of relatively large-scale, highly bureaucratic organization, and of attempts to subsume many "smaller groups like trade-unions or various types of voluntary associations, within the framework of unified political party units."[6]

Against these characteristics there stand out some of the structural characteristics of broader groups. The first such characteristic is the relatively low level of "social mobilization" or differentiation as measured either by sociodemographic indexes or by the extent and scope of social differentiation. The predominance of "primary occupations" in general, of farming in particular, the continuing persistence, even if in changed forms, of various traditional frameworks—all of them attest to this fact, the exact extent of which has, however, yet to be more fully explored.[7]

A second important aspect of the process of modernization of the broader social groups in Africa is the relative sequence of modernization in different institutional spheres—the relatively quick development of the political aspirations of the wider social groups and their over-all political modernization before a concomitant extent of economic, professional, and even educational development. The high level of political modernization, in its turn, usually gives rise to a more rapid development of educational institutions and aspirations—especially of a more generalized and "humanistic" nature—that often outstrip available economic facilities. Closely related to these characteristics is the tendency toward profusion of relatively small-scale, often ephemeral types of social groupings—which are to no small degree connected with the processes of change and with the breakdown of various traditional units.

A third basic characteristic of the modernization of the broader social strata in African societies is the persistence, transformation, and structural recrystallization of various traditional forms and frameworks. Tribal associations or groups within the framework of the broader political parties, trade unions, or various voluntary associations are one important indication of this trend. The continuous recrystallization of traditional symbols, relations, and groupings within more religious frameworks—be they various autochthonous or Islamic and Christian religious organizations—constitutes another such indication.

The synchronization of these different characteristics—of the special temporal sequence of modernization in different spheres, of the relatively low level of differentiation coupled with the tendency to large-scale and monolithic organization—points out the great importance of the processes and structures that bring together the traditional and more modern sectors. Of special importance here are some characteristics of the new emerging system of social stratification, especially as it bears on processes of transition from more traditional to the modern sectors. It has already been pointed out that the range or scope of the modern sector is relatively small, although continually expanding. But this very expansion displays certain distinctive characteristics.

First, it is, on the whole, more heavily concentrated in the administrative and political than in the business or purely economic areas. This is closely connected with the predominance of the government in the economy. Second, the characteristics of mobility to the modern sector and especially to its more predominant or upper positions are of interest here. Usually two channels of mobility—frequently overlapping—seem to be of special importance. One is the educational, the other involves the political party.[8]

Although there is as yet little adequate evidence, what is available seems to indicate that the educational channel is continuously on the rise, and that the more it becomes an important avenue of mobility the greater becomes the pressure on educational facilities and the smaller the return on investment in education. This seems especially important since the modern occupational sector does not expand as rapidly as the educational system or access to it.

There also are very limited data on differential access to educational facilities. But what data do exist seem to indicate that while there is a tendency for sons of the (urban and educated) well-to-do to have greater opportunities for educational advancement, a relatively large extent of accessibility obtains for sons of other (i.e., especially farming) groups.[9]

The process of crystallization of new frameworks or mechanisms that could serve as bridges between the new centers and the periphery has also been evident in the search for new symbols of common cultural identity. Several dimensions of this search stand out. One is that of "traditional-modernity" and the search for those elements in the specific historical heritage that may best contribute to the crystallization of new, more flexible, specifically African symbols of modernity.

A second dimension of this search is focused on the possible crystallization of a meaningful personal and collective identity transcending any given particularistic collectivity. Perhaps the search for an African Personality is the best illustration—if not necessarily solution—of this search.

The last dimension of this search is the incorporation and interpretation of several different historical, religious, and ideological traditions—the divergent historical heritage of these societies, the broad religious orientations of Christianity and Islam and the resistance to them, and the new, modern, national, international, and social ideologies. It is around these varied dimensions that attempts to forge new symbols of collective identity are being focused.[10]

The preceding analysis indicates that the process of modernization will necessarily develop structural forms in African societies that are in many ways different from those of other modern or modernizing societies. But beyond this, it poses also the problem of the extent to which there will develop, within African societies, conditions for sustained growth and modernization. This problem is of crucial importance in African societies.

On the one hand, the crystallization of the various structural character-istics of modernization analyzed above points out some potential weak-nesses of the new emerging centers. Among them, the most important are the (1) possibilities of the crystallization of closed oligarchic elites oriented mainly to self-aggrandizement and to the maintenance of their own posi-tion of power and prestige, and (2) the erosion of commitments to collec-tive and developmental goals.

On the other hand, these elites already face the problems of development and absorption within the new central institutional settings of new social forces that were not initially represented by them, or that are being created by the very impetus of modernization. The most important of these forces are, first, the persistence or opposition of older (even if transformed) tribal or traditional forces; second, the possible emergence in the urban areas of discontented middle-class workers, trade-union leaders, and soldiers and veterans; and, third, the possibility of alienation among younger ele-ments who become discontented with what for them is already an old estab-lishment.

It is out of these varied elements that new orientations of protest, break-down, stagnation, or transformation tend to develop. They create, through their demands, potential splits within the elite and strains on the working of the central institutions. They also tend to raise questions concerning the conditions under which the new centers, with their specific structural charac-teristics, will be able to facilitate continuous and sustained growth and development. Some of the problem areas that should be analyzed are, first, the extent of compatibility or affinity between the modernizing elites and the major social strata. Here of great importance is the general level of development, of "internal modernization" of the different strata that take part in the process of modernization, and the general level of resources that are generated by them in this process. The second problem is the in-terrelationship of different elite groups and especially the extent of harmony or dissociation between the technical, professional, and administrative elites on the one hand and the "solidarity-making" political and cultural elites on the other.

Comparative research on modernization has indicated that, insofar as there exists some affinity between the modernizing elites and the major groups and strata on the one hand and among the major modernizing elites on the other, then the process of political modernization is relatively smooth. Similarly, the stronger and more internally cohesive the major strata, and the more they are able to participate in the process of modernization in various institutional spheres, the greater is the extent of resources that they are able to put at the disposal of various modern institutions and organizations, the greater their ability to regulate through some autonomous mechanism some of the problems attendant on the growing differentiation and modernization, the greater their ability to articulate realistic political demands, and the greater their ability to influence the formulation of major political goals and policies by the elites.

In more general terms, it can be stated that relatively continuous progress and institutionalization of modernization in general, and of political modernization in particular, tend to be greater where modernizing elites are relatively strong and cohesive and are able to mobilize adequate support from different strata without giving rise to new cleavages within the society.[11]

On the basis of the preceding analysis it might perhaps be possible to indicate some of the aspects of the African scene that could be of crucial importance for the development of conditions facilitating sustained growth. In this attempt we must go beyond the description of the structural characteristics of modernization as they develop in African societies and look to those forces that may impede or facilitate the type of interrelation between the modernizing elites and the broader strata that is so crucial for the process of sustained growth.

It is very difficult to delineate and analyze these forces in the African scene, but it might be worthwhile to indicate some areas that should, I think, constitute areas of research interest. It is, of course, very important to analyze sources of economic resources and activities that may be of help in providing the necessary frameworks for economic and sociopolitical development. I would like to emphasize here the importance of identifying those aspects, within the internal structure of African societies, which may serve as important starting points for new and flexible modern frameworks.

Four broad areas seem to be of very great importance from this point of view and may constitute focuses of fruitful research. The first is the examination of possible points of recrystallization within the traditional "tribal" framework. In this context, it is necessary to recognize that all traditional or tribal frameworks are necessarily the most significant determinants of the degree of adjustment or adaptation to modern conditions. Important characteristics seem to be the degree of solidarity of the family and of the community, and flexibility of elites and of systems of stratification. There are probably other factors that are not always directly related, in a one-to-one way, to the basic structural "typological" characteristics of traditional societies. They seem to be more closely related to the cultural differentiation and interrelations between different subgroups that exist with the common framework of these different types of societies than to their over-all structural characteristics.

The processes of religious and ideological transformation that have been taking place is a second important area. Processes of religious reorganization and recrystallization contain, on the one hand, important possibilities for the development of orientations to wider, more flexible, and differentiated activities and goals; on the other hand, they may also contribute to the crystallization of some more flexible and cohesive symbols of collective identity.[12]

Third, the process of political transformation itself, with the strong drive to the center that it implies, offers possibilities of transformation, although, at the same time, it also may offer possibilities of rigidity and breakdowns.

A fourth area, development of which is crucial for sustained growth, is education. We have seen already that education provides one of the most important channels of transition from the traditional to the modern in African societies; hence, it is but natural that its structure and organization can greatly affect the whole process of modernization.

Two aspects of developing educational systems seem to be of greatest importance from this perspective. The first is the extent of heterogeneity and variety of the educational system—the lack of rigid adherence to a narrow "academic" or legalistic schooling system, the development of varied educational programs, and the consequent facilitation by the educational system of the creation of a more flexible and dynamic status order. The other aspect is the nature of the interrelation between educational expansion and the general direction and tempo of economic and social development and modernization.

Educational systems and educational planners are faced here with two basic contradictory possibilities and dilemmas. One is the development of a relatively "conservative," stagnating educational system, geared principally to the needs and self-image of a relatively small, restricted elite—one that loses most of its dynamic innovative and change-oriented potentialities. The other possibility involves an undifferentiated expansion of the educational system outstripping the realistic possibilities of absorption of the new educated cadres in the developing economy, thus creating intensive cleavages, conflicts, and potential breakdowns.[13]

The extent to which the developing educational systems of African societies will be able to overcome these dilemmas may be of crucial importance for their modernization; consequently, the investigation of conditions facilitating educational development certainly constitutes one of the major areas of research in this field.

Of no less importance is the extent to which the processes in these four areas coalesce at the center and create either flexible, "frozen," "rigid" status, political, ideological, or value systems.

The extent of flexibility of the political and status systems—of the mutual openness of various elites and social groups, the extent of interchangeability of different elite tasks (e.g., economic, political, cultural), the extent to which the original "traditional" elites are ready to accept new subgroups, and the extent of common solidarity between the various modern elites and other groups in a society—is crucial for the development of institutional frameworks capable of growth. Insofar as such flexibility tends to develop, it may greatly facilitate the creation of an institutional framework capable of absorbing continuous change. It also will facilitate the development of new elites willing to learn new modern roles in the economic, organizational, and political spheres.

Such new elites (or the members of the old elite who had learned new tasks and patterns of behavior) can often acquire an established place in the structure of the communities, and find some sort of *modus vivendi* with the older elites. The new criteria of status (i.e., of economic achievement and specialization, of participation in a political party or youth movement) may then overlap with many of the older "traditional" ones and with each other without fostering closed groups. In this way it will enable relatively continuous development of varied organizations within a common structure.

Such status-system flexibility also may enable the development of additional status criteria and new groups without great disruption of the older groups. In such cases, the new groups have access not only to existing social positions but to new centers of wealth, power, and prestige.

Status flexibility and the opposite tendency to ascriptive freezing of structural arrangements can be found in all spheres of social organizations —in political parties, in labor organizations, in different areas and channels of mobility—and are not necessarily tied to any specific structural form or level of development.

The development of status flexibility or rigidity is closely related to what may be referred to as value and ideological transformations of society. The major problem here is the extent to which, out of varied searches for new religious and ideological contents and symbols, there may develop what may be called a value and ideological transformation.

In this context, it is very important to distinguish between: (1) those modernized, nationalistic, political, or social elites that, while creating new symbols and political frameworks, are not able to effect any structural transformation within their respective societies that would facilitate continuous growth and; (2) those elites that were relatively more successful in this sphere.

Although it is too early to indicate the exact types of value and ideological orientation that facilitate such transformation, some of their characteristics —as derived from comparative research—can perhaps be tentatively outlined.

The elites that, to some extent, are successful in effecting transformations in the ideological and value spheres aimed at the development of a new, more flexible set of symbols and collective identity could incorporate them into the new symbolic frameworks. They aim at the transformation of the internal values of wider social groups and strata and at the development among these groups of new, more flexible orientations. They tend to develop simultaneous orientations to collective ideological transformation and to concrete tasks and problems in different institutional spheres.

It is, therefore, important to attempt to analyze the developments in this field not only in terms of the manifest content of the new ideologies and religious movements, but also from the point of view of the evolution of these broader orientations and the possibilities for value and ideological transformations that they may imply.

All these formulations are necessarily very preliminary ones; but they attempt to indicate some of the areas and processes the investigation of which seems to be of great importance for the understanding of problems of modernization in African societies. Investigations of the exact ways in which these various processes develop within the new structural frameworks emerging in African societies are still before us. They may constitute one of the major focuses of research in this area.

Notes

PREFACE

(pp. v–x)

1. William H. Friedland and Carl G. Rosberg, Jr. (eds.), *African Socialism* (Stanford, California, 1964).

CHAPTER 1

(pp. 15–41)

1. See Gil Dugué, *Vers les Etats Unis d'Afrique* (Dakar, 1960), for a detailed account of the Cotonou Congress.

2. Gordon Wright, *The Reshaping of French Democracy* (New York), 1948.

3. It is significant that in the French text the word "self-governments" is used for want, apparently, of a French equivalent.

4. Félix Eboué, among the very few Negroes present at the conference, though himself not African-born, was one of the few champions at the conference of the need to recognize the values and the distinctiveness of African culture.

5. René Viard, *La Fin de L'Empire Colonial Francais* (Paris, 1963), p. 25, cited from Louis Merat, *Fictions et Réalités Coloniales* (Paris, 1947).

6. In the recommendations for a federal assembly, the Conference made it clear that such an assembly would be expected to "affirm the indissoluble unity of . . . the Franco-Colonial whole." See Bernard Brown and Roy Macridis, *The De Gaulle Republic* (Chicago, Illinois, 1960), p. 192.

7. The French West African members of the First Constituent Assembly numbered six: Lamine Guèye (Senegal, 1st College, SFIO); Léopold Sédar Senghor (Senegal, 2nd College, SFIO); Félix Houphouet-Boigny (Ivory Coast, 2nd College, PCF); Fily Dabo Sissoko (Sudan, 2nd College, PCF); Yacine Diallo (Guinea, 2nd College, SFIO); and Sourou Mignan Apithy (Togo-Dahomey, 2nd College, PCF). In Ivory Coast, for instance, a Frenchman, Reste, was elected by the citizens with 1,821 out of 2,774 votes on the second count, while Houphouet-Boigny was elected by the noncitizens with 12,980 out of 28,835 votes on the second count. One African with French citizenship, Abdoulaye N'Diaye, stood for the 1st College but gained no votes.

8. Ernest Milcent, *L'AOF entre en Scène* (Paris, 1958), p. 27.

9. Thomas Hodgkin, and Ruth Schachter, *French-Speaking West Africa in Transition* (New York, 1960).

10. "While there were deep divisions among the major political parties and schools of thought in postwar France, a negative consensus existed: all firmly rejected African self-government or independence as a legitimate end of policy." Hodgkin and Schachter, *ibid.*

11. Daniel Boisdon, *Les Institutions de l'Union Française* (Paris, 1949). See, in particular, pp. 41–42.

12. *Journal Officiel,* Debates of the Second Constituent Assembly, 2nd Session, September 18, 1946, p. 3,802.

13. *Ibid.,* September 19, p. 3,849. Houphouet added significantly: "Certainly some of my colleagues ask for independence within the framework of the French Union for the countries which they represent. But that is not contrary to the principles that you yourselves have accepted and often affirmed."

14. *Journal Officiel, op. cit.,* September 18, p. 3,801.

15. *Journal Officiel, op. cit.,* 1st Session, September 18, p. 3,791.

16. *Ibid.,* p. 3,792.

17. *Ibid.,* p. 3,798.

18. *Ibid.,* p. 3,813.

19. *Ibid.,* p. 3,814.

20. *Ibid.,* p. 3,820.

21. *Ibid.,* 2nd Session, September 19, p. 3,850.

22. Majhemout Diop, *Contribution à l'Etude des Problèmes Politiques en Afrique Noire* (Paris, 1959), pp. 134–35.

23. Aimé Césaire, *Lettre Ouverte à Maurice Thorez* (Paris, 1956).

24. David Caute, *Communism and the French Intellectuals* (New York, 1964), p. 208. Algerian resentment of the Communist Party today is partly the result of the hostile position taken by the PCF with regard to Algerian independence.

25. Gabriel d'Arboussier, *Vers l'Unité Africaine* (Paris, 1961), Introduction.

26. Diop, *op. cit.*

27. Even when the SFIO took what were in fact positions hostile to the Overseas Territories in the Assembly.

28. Michael Crowder, *Senegal: A Study in French Assimilation Policy* (London, 1962), p. 36.

29. See Milcent, *op. cit.,* pp. 75–76, where he quotes M. Aujoulat (Cameroun) as saying in his report: "All our efforts are oriented towards the realization of a Franco-African symbiosis which we judge as useful to Africa as to France. You will not find any separatists amongst us. . . . A movement of emancipation is showing itself throughout the world. To want to stem it would be to risk grave catastrophes."

30. James Coleman, *Togoland, International Conciliation,* No. 509 (September, 1956).

31. *Journal Officiel, op. cit.,* 1st Session, March 21, 1956, pp. 1108–12. (Speech of the Minister for Overseas France, M. Gaston Defferre).

32. Cited in Viard, *op. cit.,* p. 71.

33. An excellent analysis of the economic motives behind Houphouet's stand is contained in Elliot J. Berg, "The Economic Base of Political Choice in French West Africa," *American Political Science Review,* LIV. No. 2 (June, 1960).

34. André Blanchet, *L'Itineraire des Partis Politiques depuis Bamako* (Paris, 1958).

35. These difficulties were played up by the French administration at that time. (Personal conversations with French administrators and African leaders, September, 1957–March, 1958.)

36. Kenneth Robinson, "Polling Day in Senegal," *West Africa,* May 10, 1957.

37. Blanchet, *op. cit.,* and "Africa's Youngest Premier—Portrait of Sékou Touré," *West Africa,* May 25, 1957.

38. Blanchet, *L'Itineraire,* pp. 113–17.

39. Cited in Viard, *op. cit.*

40. Viard, *op. cit.*, De Gaulle was reported by *Paris-Presse* as having appeared before the Constitutional Consultative Committee on August 10th, and saying: "One cannot conceive of both an independent territory and a France which continues to aid it." Cited in Marcel Merle, "La Constitution et les Problèmes d'Outre-Mer," *Revue Française de Science Politique*, March, 1959, p. 148.

41. For a full and very useful discussion of this, see Berg, *op. cit.*

42. Immanuel Wallerstein, "How Seven States Were Born in Former French West Africa," *Africa Report*, March, 1961, pp. 3–4, 7, 12, 15.

43. Wallerstein, *ibid.*

44. See Diabate Boubacar, *Porte Ouverte sur la Communauté Franco-Africaine* (Brussels, 1961), where De Gaulle's speech as well as that of Sékou Touré are published in full.

45. See Diabate Boubacar, *ibid.*, for the text of these telegrams. Sékou Touré declared in his speech to the Constituent National Assembly on Independence Day, October 2, 1958: "The Republic of Guinea, in accordance with the terms of Article 88 of the French Constitution, will negotiate the bases of an association with the Republic of France."

46. For a detailed account of the complex maneuvers in Upper Volta and Dahomey, see Dugué, *op. cit.*

47. John Marcum, "French-Speaking Africa at Accra," *Africa Report*, February, 1959.

48. There was very real enthusiasm on the part of Malian leaders from mid-1959 to mid-1960 on the whole possibility of establishing a French-style Commonwealth.

49. Jean Debay, *Evolutions en Afrique Noire* (Paris, 1962), has suggested that France agreed to the Federation of Mali's independence within the framework of the Community and did not cut her off as she had done Guinea, for fear that she might join with Guinea and form a bloc hostile to France.

50. See Berg, *op. cit.*

51. Haut Commissariat de la Republique en Afrique Occidentale Française, *AOF 1957* (Dakar, 1957); and Assemblée Nationale, Constitution du 4 Octobre 1958, Première Legislature, Première Session Ordinaire de 1961–62, *Rapport*, Annexe No. 10, *Coopèration*, No. 1445; and *Avis*, Tome II, *Coopèration*, No. 1459; Sénat, Première Session Ordinaire de 1961–62, *Rapport General*, Tome III, Examen des Crèdits det des Dispositions Speciales, Annexe No. 8, *Coopèration*. Most aid nowadays is channeled through the Ministry of Cooperation, but individual ministries can in fact make provision for aid to the independent French-speaking African states.

52. Today the official French version of the events following Guinea's independence is that De Gaulle foresaw that the other states would want independence and made provision for it in the Constitution of the Fifth Republic. "The Constitution of the Fifth Republic established the procedure for accession to independence on the basis of self-determination. It offered the Overseas Territories, by means of a referendum, the free [sic] choice between immediate independence or membership in the institutional Community," *France Aid and Cooperation* (New York: French Embassy Press and Information Service, 1962), p. 13.

53. Jean Erhard, *Communauté ou Secession?* (Paris, 1959).

54. *West Africa*, October 12, 1957, reported Houphouet as telling a press conference shortly after the Bamako Congress of the RDA that "if we had been colonized by the Anglo-Saxons, there is no doubt that we would have chosen independence even at the cost of economic disadvantages. But in France we think we catch a note of human fraternity. . . . We need France, but we believe that France

likewise needs the advantages of a Franco-African Community of free peoples founded on an absolute equality of rights and duties." Senghor was reported in *West Africa* of September 7, 1957, in a review of *Une Nouvelle Afrique* by Paul-Henri Siriex (Paris, 1957), as telling the National Assembly: "In Africa, when children have grown up, they leave the parents' hut, and build a hut of their own by its side. Believe me, we don't want to leave the French compound. We have grown up in it and it is good to be alive in it. We want simply to build our own huts."

CHAPTER 3

(pp. 58–79)

1. The countries and territories included in this survey are: Angola, Burundi, Cameroon, Central African Republic, Chad, Congo-Brazzaville, Dahomey, Ethiopia, Gabon, Gambia, Ghana, Guinea, the three High Commission Territories, Ivory Coast, Kenya, Liberia, Madagascar, Mali, Mauritania, Mozambique, Niger, Nigeria, Northern Rhodesia, Senegal, Southwest Africa, Spanish Guinea, Sudan, Tanganyika, Togo, Uganda, Upper Volta, Zanzibar.

2. H. L. Nieburg, "Uses of Violence," *Journal of Conflict Resolution,* VII, No. 1 (March, 1963), 43–54.

3. Raymond F. Kent, *From Madagascar to the Malagasy Republic* (New York, 1962), p. 97.

4. Samuel F. Huntington, "Patterns of Violence in World Politics," in Samuel F. Huntington (ed.), *Changing Patterns of Military Politics* (New York, 1962), pp. 22–23.

5. *Ibid.,* p. 20.

6. *Ibid.,* p. 24.

7. *Ibid.,* p. 32.

8. Hodgkin, *African Political Parties: An Introductory Guide* (Baltimore, Md., 1961). The quotations in the paragraph are all from this source, pp. 126–32.

9. Harry Eckstein, "Internal War: The Problem of Anticipation" (Report to the Smithsonian Institute), mimeo. Cited by Andrew C. Janos in his essay, "Authority and Violence: The Political Framework of Internal War," in H. Eckstein (ed.), *Internal War* (New York, 1964), p. 130.

10. Janos, *ibid.;* and William Kornhauser, "Rebellion and Political Development," in Eckstein, *op. cit.,* pp. 142–56. Three other studies of violence, two of them dealing with Africa, are of importance, but are not discussed here because of the limitations of this study: Robert A. LeVine, "Anti-European Violence in Africa: A Comprehensive Analysis," *Journal of Conflict Resolution,* III, No. 4 (December, 1959), 420; Gene Sharp, "A South African Contribution to the Study of Nonviolent Action: A Review [of] Leo Kuper, *Passive Resistance in South Africa,*" *Journal of Conflict Resolution,* V, No. 4 (December, 1961), 395; and Rudolph J. Rummel, "Dimensions of Conflict Behavior Within and Between Nations," in Ludwig von Bertalanffy and Anatol Rapoport (eds.), *General Systems, Yearbook of the Society for General Systems Research,* VIII (1963), 1.

11. Eckstein, *op. cit.,* p. 18.

12. Unless otherwise indicated, the factual data cited hereafter are derived from the following sources: *Africa Report, Africa Digest, Afrique Nouvelle, Neues Afrika, The New York Times, The Sunday Observer, Le Monde, Current History.*

13. It is not unimportant to recall that resolutions adopted by various Pan-African conferences have specifically endorsed the resort to violence if the objectives of the users are anticolonial. One such resolution that came out of the 1958 All-African Peoples' Conference at Accra affirmed "full support for all fighters for freedom in Africa, to all those who resort to peaceful means of non-violence and civil dis-

obedience as well as to all those who are compelled to retaliate against violence to attain national independence and freedom for the people." ("Resolutions of the All-African Peoples' Conference," *Current History*, July 1959.) The Resolution on Decolonization adopted by the Conference at Addis Ababa in May, 1963, specifically established a coordinating committee based in Dar es Salaam to administer a Special Fund to be used to give financial assistance to "national liberation movements," and further "decided" that independent African states would "receive" elements of such "national liberation movements" for training "in all sectors," including presumably, military training. The Resolution also called for the establishment of a "body of volunteers" in each state to assist the "national liberation movements." ("Resolutions adopted by the Conference of Heads of African States and Governments, Addis Ababa, 22–25 May 1963," mimeo.)

14. The difference between assassination and political murder is admittedly a tenuous one; I would contend that it lies in two areas, the role of the killer, and the element of surprise. Assassins are usually hired or delegated, and they generally strike without warning to the victims. As much as is known about Lumumba's death, it appears that it did not come about suddenly or without warning to Lumumba or that its perpetrators were specifically hired for the task.

15. Other theories range from the possibility that the poison Moumié took was meant for someone else to the one explanation that has some currency in the Cameroun itself, namely, that he was removed by his own colleagues because he had become an obstacle in the path of a possible reconciliation between the Ahidjo government and the exiled UPC group. Whatever the case, it is probable that the questions of guilt and motive will remain clouded until the Swiss make public the results of their own investigations. It may be added that the longest account of the affair—and one supporting the "Red Hand" theory—appeared in an unsigned two-part article in a Russian journal: "Zhertvi 'krovavoi ruki' " ("Victims of the 'Bloody Hand' "), *Aziia i Afrika Sevodnia*, No. 6 (1961), pp. 38–41; No. 7 (1961), pp. 49–51. Incidentally, accounts of the Moumié poisoning appearing in Communist publications all call the "Red Hand" the "Bloody Hand," for obvious reasons.

16. République du Sénégal, Ministère de l'Information, de la Presse, et de la Radiodiffusion, *Livre Blanc sur le Coup d'Etat manqué du 19 au 20 août 1960 et la Proclamation de l'Indépendance du Sénégal* (Dakar, probably January, 1961.) For details of the Mamadou Dia coup, see Victor DuBois' excellent coverage for the American Universities Field Staff Reports, "The Trial of Mamadou Dia," West Africa Series, VI, Nos. 6, 7, 8 (July, 1963).

17. Hodgkin, *loc. cit.*

18. Brian Crozier, *The Morning After* (London, 1963).

19. Clifford Geertz, "The Integrative Revolution: Primordial Sentiments and Civil Politics in the New States," in Geertz (ed.), *Old Societies and New States* (New York, 1963), p. 109.

20. *Ibid.*, p. 111.

21. *Ibid.*, p. 125.

22. The point is made by Robert A. LeVine in his contribution to the Geertz volume, "Political Socialization and Culture Change," pp. 280–303.

23. See Hodgkin, *op. cit., passim;* Immanuel Wallerstein, "Ethnicity and National Integration," *Cahiers d'Etudes Africaines*, II, No. 3 (1960), 132–39; Aristide R. Zolberg, *One-Party Government in the Ivory Coast* (Princeton, N.J., 1964), particularly Chapter II, "The Origins of Political Organizations," and Chapter IV, "The Party Militant"; David A. Apter, "The Role of Traditionalism in the Political Modernization of Ghana and Uganda," *World Politics*, XIII, No. 1 (October, 1960), 45–68; and Richard R. Sklar, *Nigerian Political Parties* (Princeton, N.J., 1963), particularly, Chapters I–III. The works cited are only a representative sample of

the growing literature that deals directly or indirectly with the relationship between "primordial" attachments and the modernizing, civil polity.

24. For a presentation of the southern Sudanese side of the conflict, see Joseph Oduho and William Deng, *The Problem of the Southern Sudan* (London, 1963).

25. The fullest reports thus far on the Zanzibari coup have been written by Keith Kyle, "Coup in Zanzibar," *Africa Report* (February, 1964), pp. 18–20; and "How It Happened," *The Spectator* (February 14, 1964), pp. 202–3.

26. Martin Kilson provides a useful summary and appropriate citations in his article, "Single-Party Tendencies in Africa," *World Politics*, XV, No. 2 (January, 1963), 274. Kilson makes the point, on page 273, that "political instability stemming from tribal conflict or unrest has contributed in some measure" to the creation of one-party states.

27. Among those specifically dealing with the passage to independence are Crozier, *op. cit.*; Richard Harris, *Independence and After* (London and New York, 1962); and Lucy Mair, *New Nations* (London and New York, 1963).

28. Immanuel Wallerstein, "The Emergence of Two West African Nations: Ghana and the Ivory Coast," unpublished Ph.D. thesis, Columbia University, 1959.

29. Lucian Pye, "The Roots of Rebellion and the Commencement of Rebellions," in Eckstein, *op. cit.*, p. 163.

30. Although a definitive treatment of the events of 1959–63 has yet to appear, some recent work is relevant: Alan Merriam, *Congo: Background to Conflict* (Evanston, Ill., 1960); Smith Hempstone, *Rebels, Mercenaries, and Dividends* (New York, 1962); Conor Cruise O'Brien, *To Katanga and Back* (London and New York, 1962); King Gordon, *U.N. in the Congo* (New York: Carnegie Endowment Fund, 1962); and René Lemarchand, *Political Awakening in the Congo* (Berkeley, California, 1964). See also the section on the Congo by Eduard Bustin in Gwendolen Carter (ed.), *Five African States* (Ithaca, N.Y., 1964).

31. Dieter Lindenlaub, "Putsch ohne sociale Umbruch," *Neues Afrika*, No. 3 (March, 1964), pp. 87–88. The translation is mine.

32. The roots of the UPC revolt are examined in detail in my sections in Carter, *op. cit.*; and in J. S. Coleman and C. Rosberg (eds.), *Political Parties and National Integration in Africa* (Berkeley, California, 1964).

33. "The Morgan Muddle," *West Africa*, No. 2453 (June 6, 1964), p. 619. See also "Strikebound," *West Africa*, No. 2454 (June 13, 1964), p. 647.

34. Kwame Nkrumah, *Africa Must Unite* (London and New York, 1963), p. 174.

35. A lead article in *The Spark* (Accra) entitled "Dark Clouds Over Africa: Military Plans Endanger Africa's Independence," p. 1, makes this latter point. A map accompanying the article depicts thirteen foreign and NATO airbases, nine naval bases, three rocket sites, nine "strategic ports," eight NATO bases, and six military missions.

36. Accra radio, October 29, 1963.

CHAPTER 4
(pp. 80–91)

1. *Le Monde*, January 30, 1958.

2. For background on the Young Turk influence in early Tunisian nationalism, see Nicola A. Ziadeh, *Origins of Nationalism in Tunisia* (Beirut, 1962), pp. 82–92; and A. Pellegrin, *Histoire de la Tunisie* (Tunis, 1948), pp. 186 ff.

3. There have been several articles dealing with one-party states in sub-Saharan Africa. See Ruth Schachter, "Single-Party Systems in West Africa," *American Political Science Review*, LV, No. 2 (June, 1961), 294–307; Martin L. Kilson, "Authoritarian and Single-Party Tendencies in African Politics," *World Politics*, XV, No. 2

(January, 1962), 262–93; and Immanuel Wallerstein, "What Happened to the Opposition?," *West Africa,* November 21, 1961.

4. *West Africa,* February 23, 1962.

5. Over the past two years a respectable amount of monographic literature has appeared on the Neo-Destour. See Charles Debbasch, *La République Tunisienne* (Paris, 1962); Charles F. Gallagher, Jr., "Tunisia," in Gwendolen Carter (ed.), *African One-Party Systems* (Ithaca, N.Y., 1962), pp. 11–83; Charles Micaud, Leon Carl Brown, and Clement Henry Moore, *Modernization in Tunisia* (New York, 1964); and Clement Henry Moore, "The Neo-Destour Party of Tunisia: A Structure for Democracy?," *World Politics,* XIV, No. 3 (April, 1962), 461–82.

6. The meeting of left and right seems to be easier in Arab countries than in most parts of the world, a dramatic example being Nasser's acceptance of the Muslim Brotherhood. See the treatment of Neo-Islamic and Communist totalitarianism in Manfred Halpern, *The Politics of Social Change in the Middle East and North Africa* (Princeton, N.J., 1963).

7. Although the nature of the conflict varies from country to country, Ben Youssef's demise reminds one of the conflict of equally persuasive personalities in Morocco between Al-Fassi and Wazzani and in Algeria between Ben Bella and Boudaif. The heavily ideological position only won out before independence, i.e., in Morocco, where the split occurred in 1937 in favor of Al-Fassi, while the more nimble tacticians, Ben Bella and Bourguiba, won out in the two postindependence cases.

8. Indiscriminate plundering and murdering was a French colonial technique long before the Algerian revolution. The Cap Bon affair was the prelude to a hardening of French policy throughout North Africa. The most explicit background to the Tunisian resistance movement is in Félix Garas, *Bourguiba et la Naissance d'une Nation* (Paris, 1956), pp. 239–45.

9. *The New York Times,* January 6 and 9, 1955. There was a short-lived resurgence of the original Destour Party, supported by the Bey and aristocratic elements.

10. One manifestation of the "hard-line" political views was the series of trials in 1958 and 1959 to discredit completely remnants of conservative opposition to the party. In addition to two trials of Youssefists involving 180 persons, there were trials of Baccouche and M'Zali, both expremiers under the French. See *The New York Times,* February 24, and April 6, 1959.

11. For details see *Jeune Afrique,* December 13, 1962–January 5, 1963, and January 21–28, 1963. See also Habib Bourguiba, "Analysis of the Plot," Speech of January 18, 1963 (Tunis: Secretary of State for Information, 1963).

12. The complete breakdown of the colonial regime in Morocco dates from the bloody repression of the sympathy strike in Casablanca following Hached's assassination. See Douglas E. Ashford, *Political Change in Morocco* (Princeton, N.J., 1961), pp. 272–73.

13. Early indications of the difference appear in *Petit Matin,* June 3 and 8, and August 21, 1956. In one humorous incident Ben Salah kept referring in a proprietary fashion to the new Maisons de Travail, built with government funds as UGTT labor exchanges. Bourguiba continued to insist they were Bourses de Travail, stressing the relation of labor benefits to government at dedication ceremonies as well.

14. The program appeared as "Rapport Economique," *6ème Congrés National de l'U.G.T.T.* (Tunis, September 20–23, 1956). The basic aims and proposals are repeated in Ben Salah's *Perspectives Décennales* (Tunis: Ministry of Planning and Finance, 1962).

15. See *Petit Matin,* November 10, and December 25, 1956. See also *The New York Times,* December 31, 1956.

16. Garas, *op. cit.,* p. 241. Masmoudi's career is remarkably similar to the capable

intermediary in Moroccan politics, Bouabid, who was also a key figure in negotiating with the French.

17. The government has had to keep on reasonably friendly terms with the business community, and the *Union Tunisienne des Industriels et Commerçants* (UTIC) is regarded as an auxiliary party organization. As the country was being mobilized for development, one of the early controversies was over olive-oil marketing and processing controls. See *Petit Matin*, February 7, 1961.

18. *L'Action Tunisienne*, October 3, 1958. The paper was suspended that month and reappeared, without the party slogan in its title, as *Afrique Action*, later to become *Jeune Afrique*.

19. *Afrique Action*, October 7–18, 1961.

20. *Ibid.*, November 21–27, 1961. See also *Le Monde*, November 18, 1961.

21. *Petit Matin*, November 21, 1961. In this speech and again in the speeches given after the assassination attempt, the President defends himself against charges of neglecting the economy in order to engage in international endeavors. In the later speeches he also spoke publicly in defense of an especially luxurious palace built for himself.

22. *Jeune Afrique*, October 29–November 9, 1962. An interesting commentary on how quickly fortunes change in a developing country is the fact that the president of the Sfax phosphate works had been a UGTT militant. About 6,000 miners struck against UGTT leadership when the government tried to place a levy on their wages to relieve unemployment in other areas.

23. Mestiri replaced Nouira as the Secretary of State for Finance in December, 1958, and was later Ambassador to Moscow. Finance ministries modeled on the French system have been notoriously difficult to adapt to development purposes in North Africa. With Mehiri in the powerful position of the interior, the two "hard-line" officials may have become too efficient in advancing their views. Similar allegations are made for sending Mongi Slim to Washington, where his contacts with the liberal group were cut off.

24. Ladgham, Mestiri, and Mehiri were identified as the *étatiste* group by *Le Monde*, January 1, 1959. None of them joined the interim government of the fall of 1955, although the Neo-Destour officially participated and the liberal leadership group was fully represented.

25. The most complete account of Ladgham's role in this critical period is in Lorna Hahn's *North Africa: Nationalism to Nationhood* (Washington, D.C., 1960), pp. 169–70. It is worth recalling that Ladgham had led the fight against similarly phrased reforms in the Neo-Destour's compromise effort in 1951, which broke down completely. His position in the fall of 1955 is very similar to that of Ben Bella's in the summer of 1962.

26. "Developing" is used here in the simple sense of more intensive government efforts to effect many economic and social changes in a short time. The Neo-Destour's performance during this period in many specialized areas of development is analyzed in the writer's "Local Reform and National Development: The Politics of Integration in Morocco, Tunisia and Pakistan," unpublished ms.

27. The 1959 changes are outlined in Henry Clement Moore, *op. cit.*

28. The National Council was defined in the 1959 party statutes as the Political Bureau, the Commissioners, and a delegate for every cell of 5,000 members. It was seldom convened until difficulties were encountered in mobilizing support for the plan, and later when Bourguiba wanted to explain the coup. In convening the Council in 1963 to consider the party reorganization (before the party congress), youth and other "high Destourians" were co-opted. As the one-party system attempts to follow all the ramifications of a more complex society, the executive bodies take on more general functions. The National Council has become a kind of unofficial con-

gress. In the new organization the Political Bureau will be expanded to some fifty members, and the President will have a "presidium" of five or six as the top executive body. See *Jeune Afrique,* March 11–17, 1963.

29. See, for example, the speeches in *La Presse,* January 19–20, and April 14, 1963.

30. See *The New York Times,* December 28, 1963. In effect, Bourguiba, Jr., was given all the delicate troublespots—supervision of youth and sports, information, and the management of his father's office.

31. Tilili was important to the Neo-Destour as one of the few high officials originating in the south, where the Neo-Destour has had many difficulties. In addition to the strike of late 1961 and general resistance to new agrarian cooperatives, the party suffered a blow in the fall of 1962 when a major flood-control project around Gabès failed to protect the city against unusually heavy rains.

32. Part of the 1963 reorganization involves separating militants from adherents in party cells. The militants will very likely be used in establishing such committees and in arousing popular support for other developmental needs. One of the major weaknesses of the earlier system of highly centralized control was that the party could not fully exploit its membership, although some weaker members were weeded out.

33. See "Accent on Planning," Speech of March 28, 1963, to the UGTT Congress (Tunis: Secretary of State for Information, 1963).

34. The one-party system's reputation for expeditious action has probably been overdone as a result of the sheer chaos many new regimes start from. However, getting a policeman on every streetcorner is not the same as getting peasants to use fertilizer. Bourguiba himself came out strongly for planning and sacrifice on behalf of development in early 1961, and as individuals Tunisians are only today beginning to feel the impact. There was immediate resistance from shopkeepers, who refused to sell goods and foods under price controls, and difficulties in getting peasants to work on cooperative farms or to join cooperative marketing agencies. For Bourguiba's early commitment, see "Neo-Destourian Socialism," Speech of June 21, 1961 (Tunis: Secretary of State for Information, 1961).

35. One of the most interesting common phenomenon among one-party states in Africa is their antipathy to both the Communists and the tribesmen. Neither Marxist students nor paramount chiefs are permitted to disrupt party harmony.

CHAPTER 5

(pp. 95–106)

1. See G. von Grunebaum, "Unity in Diversity" in G. von Grunebaum (ed.), *Unity and Variety in Muslim Civilization* (Chicago, 1955). As von Grunebaum notes, the terminology of "great" and "little" traditions is taken from Robert Redfield.

2. From Abu al Arab, *Classes des Savants de l'Ifriqiya,* cited in Georges Marçais, *La Berberie Musulmane et l'Orient au Moyen Age* (Paris, 1946), pp. 86–87.

3. How much the modern North African idea of the state owes to the Western notion of the nation-state or to the Islamic view of the *umma* is, of course, one of the major points at issue. To avoid prejudging the question, "state," is being used in this paper in the narrowly legal, Austinian sense. Similarly, the argument of the enhanced power and prestige of the state should not be read as implying necessarily the existing political unit in its present geographical boundaries. It is, rather, the idea of the role of the political sovereign that has been radically modified.

4. Malek Bennabi, *Vocation de l'Islam* (Paris, 1954), p. 83.

5. Bennabi also sees how colonization can serve as a catalyst for speeding up the process of eliminating factors making for "colonizability":

D'ailleurs, dans une certaine mesure, la colonisation est l'effet le plus heureux de la colonisabilité parce qu'elle inverse l'évolution sociale qui a engendré l'être colonisable; celui-ci ne prend conscience de sa colonisabilité qu'une fois colonisé. Il se trouve alors dans l'obligation de se "desindigéniser," de devenir incolonisable, et c'est en ce sens qu'on peut comprendre la colonisation comme une "nécessité historique." Ibid., *p. 83.*

6. Ali Belhaouane, *Tunis al Tha 'ira (Revolutionary Tunisia)* (Cairo, 1954), p. 72.

7. Gaston Loth, *La Tunisie et l'Oeuvre du Protectorat Français* (Paris, 1907), p. 60.

8. See the present writer's "The Islamic Reformist Movement in North Africa," *Journal of Modern African Studies,* II, No. 1 (1964); and "The Role of Islam in Modern North Africa," paper presented to the annual meeting of the Middle East Institute, Washington, D.C., May, 1964.

9. Ironically, the stamp of Western training is considered necessary even for Arabic literature and history. A few years ago a young Zitouna professor with an excellent, traditional training in Arabic literature and history but no formal training in French managed to obtain a scholarship for higher studies in France in Arabic language and literature. His pleasure (one might even say relief) resembled that of a man who had received an unexpected pardon.

10. Cited in Charles F. Gallagher, "Language and Identity in North Africa," paper presented to the annual meeting of the Middle East Institute, Washington, D.C., May, 1964.

11. Mahmud Messadi in the Tunisian Arabic language review *Al Mabahith* in 1947.

12. For a general discussion of the attempts in Tunisia to foster national unity, see Charles Micaud, Leon Carl Brown, and Clement Henry Moore, *Tunisia: The Politics of Modernization* (New York, 1964).

13. *Le Peuple* (Algiers), April 6, 1964.

14. Bourguiba speech of October 15, 1959, cited in Pierre Rondot, "Les Musulmans devant la Technique," in *L'Islam, l'Economie et la Technique* (Paris: Cahiers de l'Institut de Science Economique Appliquée, October, 1960), No. 106.

15. Frantz Fanon, *L'An V de la Révolution Algérienne* (Paris, 1959).

16. C.Camilleri, "Les Jeunes Gens Tunisiens Face au Problème de la Mixité," *Confluent,* No. 20, April, 1962.

17. This poem appeared in the Tunisian journal *Al 'Alam al Adabi,* November, 1930.

18. Speech of October 15, 1959, cited in Rondot, *op. cit.*

CHAPTER 6
(pp. 107–118)

1. E. E. Evans-Pritchard, *The Sanusi of Cyrenaica* (Oxford and New York, 1949), p. 59.

2. This is true for instance of the larger groupings of the Ait Bu Gmez tribe of central Morocco, or for the Seksawa, studied in Professor Jacques Berque's *Structures Sociales du Haut-Atlas* (Paris, 1955). The "generalized genealogical" thesis is found, for instance, in Professor G. H. Bousquet's *Les Berberes* (Paris, 1957).

3. Montagne, *Les Berberes et le Makhzen au Sud du Maroc* (Paris, 1930); and *La Vie Sociale et la Vie Politique des Berbers* (Paris, 1931).

4. The area with which Montagne was principally concerned was the Western High Atlas. It is interesting that in the one case in which a subregion of this area was intensively studied since—the region of the Seksawa—the system of *leffs* was found not to apply. See Jacques Berque, *op. cit.*

5. When urban Jews, contemporaries of Ibn Khaldun, claimed affiliation to the tribes of the Old Testament, Ibn Khaldun considered this a kind of sociological fraud: Genealogies or not, town-dwellers could not claim to be tribesmen.

6. Though on occasion this happened, as in the case of the coastal pirate towns of Morocco, founded by Muslim refugees from Spain.

7. Personal communication from Madame J. Favret of the University of Algiers.

8. See comments on this in Professor G. H. Bousquet's study of the customary law of the Ait Haddidou, in *Annales de l'Institut d'Etudes Orientales* (Algiers), 1956.

9. See Vincent Monteil, *Les Officiers* (Paris, 1958).

10. See Professor William Lewis, "Rural Administration in Morocco," *Middle East Journal*, XX, 1960.

11. For instance, I sought out, in 1955, the leader of the senior lineage in Algeria of the religious order whose Moroccan branches I was already studying. He turned out to be a French-speaking minor official in a small municipal office, clearly not a tribal holy man.

12. "Patterns of Rural Rebellion," *European Journal of Sociology*, 1962.

13. Charles F. Gallagher seems to me to exaggerate this trait in his *The United States and North Africa* (Cambridge, Mass., 1963).

14. When the Rif tribesmen rose, their complaint was of being *under*administered —not of being administered at all.

15. Gallagher, *op. cit.*, p. 17.

16. This was illustrated in an interesting way during the French period in Morocco. In Berber regions, the French regime generally underwrote tribal customary law. This relies for its ultimate decision procedure on "collective oath." A tribesman at court needs not jurors convinced of the justice of his case, but *co-jurors*, his own agnates, who will formally stand by him and testify. In the days of anarchy, tribesmen would perform this service for a kinsman in trouble. Under the Pax Gallica, they tended to be reluctant. Why bother? They no longer needed the reciprocated loyalty of the kinsman for their own security, which was now assured.

CHAPTER 7

(pp. 119–129)

1. Lebret, et al., *Rapport Général sur les Perspectives de Développement du Senegal*, Vol. I (Dakar, 1960), pp. 1-5(12)-1-5(14).

2. To my knowledge, Dr. Colot's study has not been published. The translations here and elsewhere in this paper are mine.

3. Lebret, *op. cit.*, Vol. I, pp. 1-5(19).

4. Planning Commission, *Rapport sur le Développement de Madagascar* (Tananarive, 1962), p. 11.

5. Henri Collomb and Henri Ayate, "Une Etude Psychopathologique des Migrants," *Afrique Documents*, No. 67, 1963.

6. Pierre Biarnes, "Note de Conjoncture," *Le Moniteur Africain du Commerce et de l'Industrie*, May, 1961.

7. René Dumont, *L'Afrique Noire Est Mal Partie* (Paris, 1962), p. 72.

8. Lebret, *op. cit.*, Vol. I, p. 1-5(19).

9. This correlation is documented in great detail by Frederick Harbison and Charles A. Myers, in "Education, Manpower, and Economic Growth" (New York, 1964).

10. Lebret, *op. cit.*, Vol. I, pp. 1-7(7).

11. I was given a copy of the resolution and other seminar papers in Cotonou. I do not know if the resolution has been published.

12. The plan was prepared for the French Ministry of Cooperation by the Société d'Études pour le Développement Économique et Social.

13. For an excellent critical view of current theories, see Mary Jean Bowman, "Perspective on Education and Development," in *International Development Review,* September, 1964.

CHAPTER 8

(pp. 130–142)

1. Ruth Schachter, "Political Leaders in French-Speaking West Africa," Paper delivered at the Second Annual Conference of the American Society of African Culture, New York, June 26–29, 1959, p. 1.

2. Edouard Bustin, "The Congo," in Gwendolen Carter (ed.), *Five African States* (Ithaca, N. Y., 1963), p. 108, citing René Lemarchand, "The Rise of Congolese Nationalism: An Enquiry into the Origins and developments of Congolese Political Groups," unpublished doctoral thesis, Columbia University.

3. Schachter, *op. cit.,* p. 1.

4. Herbert Weiss, and Benoit Verhaegen, *Parti Solidaire Africain (PSA) Documents, 1959-1960* (Brussels, 1963), p. 51.

5. The degree of influence that traditional leaders had on the political elite varied in both French-speaking West Africa and the Congo.

6. Helen Kitchen, (ed.), *The Educated African* (New York, 1962), p. 191.

7. Bernard B. Fall, "Education in the Republic of the Congo," *The Journal of Negro Education,* XXX, No. 3 (Summer, 1961).

8. M. Crawford-Young, unpublished doctoral thesis, Harvard University, 1963, pp. 231–32 .

9. Schachter, *op. cit.,* pp. 2–3.

10. Immanuel Wallerstein, "Values of Elites in French-Speaking West Africa," *Journal of Modern African Studies,* forthcoming.

11. Thomas Hodgkin, *African Political Parties: An Introductory Guide* (Baltimore, Md., 1961), p. 29.

12. Bustin, *op. cit.*

13. Hodgkin, *op. cit.,* p. 47.

14. Thomas Hodgkin, and Ruth Schachter, *French-Speaking West Africa in Transition* (New York, 1960), pp. 386–87.

15. In Rwanda and Burundi, Belgium followed a different policy. Indirect rule was a theory not only sometimes expounded, but actually put into practice. The roots of this policy are to be found in the prevailing traditional system and the German colonial period. Another important factor probably causing its retention was the rapid Christianization of the Tutsi, the feudal caste in these two countries.

16. Jean Van Lierde (ed.), *La Pensée Politique de Patrice Lumumba* (Brussels, 1964), p. xiv.

17. This suggests an additional reason why the political elite was drawn almost exclusively from the modern elite.

18. Msgr. A. Huys, "Status du Clergé Indigène," Deuxième Conférence Plénière des Ordinaires des Missions du Congo Belge et du Rwanda-Urundi, Léopoldville, June 16–28, 1936, p. 44.

19. *Ibid.,* p. 43. This picture is somewhat marred by some instances of *de facto* discrimination in the Church, and by such reports as the one of a newly ordained African priest who borrowed the breviary of a European priest in the fear that as an African he had been given a "second-rate" breviary. Ruth Slade, *The Belgian Congo: Some Recent Changes* (London, 1960), p. 35.

20. Huys, *op. cit.* (Pages are indicated at the end of each excerpt.)

21. *Ibid.,* p. 61.

22. Hodgkin and Schachter, *op. cit.,* p. 396.

23. Viz, the Bakongo–"Upper River" conflict in Leopoldville, and the Baluba (Kasai)–Katanga conflict in Elisabethville.

24. Hodgkin and Schachter, *op. cit.,* p. 396.

25. Ruth Schachter, "'Single-Party Systems in West Africa," *American Political Science Review,* LV, No. 2 (June, 1961), 296.

26. Thus, Moise Tshombe's attempted secession of Katanga was probably in part motivated by the conflict between the Balubakat and Conakat. The Baluba secession in South Kasai was much more a breaking away from other Kasai groups, especially from the Lulua, than it was a secession from the Congo.

27. Schachter, "Single-Party Systems in West Africa," pp. 294–96.

28. *Ibid.,* p. 295.

29. *Ibid.*

30. *Ibid.* p. 301.

CHAPTER 9

(pp. 145–153)

1. Ministère d'Etat Chargé de la Réforme Administrative, *La Politique de Coopération avec les Pays en Voie de Développement,* (Paris, 1963).

2. J. A. Schumpeter, *History of Economic Analysis* (New York, 1954), pp. 147–148 n.

3. Baron de Montesquieu, *The Spirit of the Laws* (New York, 1949), Book 21, Chapter 21.

4. S. H. Roberts, *The History of French Colonial Policy* (London, 1929), p. 636.

5. See, for example, H. Brunschwig, *La Colonisation Française* (Paris, 1949), p. 11.

6. Roberts, *op. cit.,* pp. 15–17.

7. Brunschwig, *op. cit.,* p. 65. (The translation is mine.)

8. J. Stern, *The French Colonies* (New York, 1944), p. 263.

9. See, for example, R. Hoffherr, *Coopération Economique Franco-Africaine* (Paris, 1958), pp. 28–29.

10. See H. I. Priestley, *France Overseas* (New York, 1938), p. 80 n.

11. C. Southworth, *The French Colonial Venture* (London, 1931), pp. 175–79.

12. J. J. Poquin, *Les Relations Economiques Extérieures des Pays d'Afrique Noire de l'Union Francaise, 1925-1955* (Paris, 1957), pp. 147–48.

13. Priestley, *op. cit.,* p. 429.

14. See Ministère de la France d'Outre-Mer, *Documents et Statistiques,* No. XIX, June, 1957, pp. 5–14.

CHAPTER 11

(pp. 166–175)

1. Léopold Sédar Senghor, *On African Socialism* (New York, 1964), p. 26.

2. Inter-African Labour Institute, *The Human Factors of Productivity in Africa* (Bamako, June, 1956), pp. 36–37. This material was gathered in former French Equatorial Africa and Madagascar.

3. C. Tardits, *Les Bamilékés de l'Ouest Cameroun* (Paris, 1960), pp. 91–97.

4. G. Balandier, "Sociological Survey of the African Town at Brazzaville," *Social*

NOTES

250

Implications of Industrialization and Urbanization in Africa, South of the Sahara, (Paris: UNESCO, 1956), pp. 108–9.

5. J. Némo, *Etude Socio-Démographique d'une Ville du Togo: Palimé,* in Ministère de la France Outre-Mer Service des Statistiques, *Documents et Statistiques,* No. XXII, Juillet, 1958, pp. 24–25.

6. G. H. T. Kimble, *Tropical Africa,* Vol. II (New York: The Twentieth Century Fund, 1960), p. 374.

7. United Nations, *Enlargement of the Exchange Economy in Tropical Africa,* E/2557, St/ECA/23 (New York, March 12, 1954), p. 37.

8. G. Horner, "The Bulu Response to European Economy," in James B. Bohannon and William D. Dalton (eds.), *Markets in Africa* (Evanston, Ill., 1960), p. 181.

9. St. Clair Drake, "'Social change and Social Problems,'" in Walter Goldschmidt (ed.), *The United States and Africa* (rev. ed.; New York, 1963), pp. 225–26.

10. Kimble, *op. cit.,* p. 67. I have omitted the *planteur* group to fit the salary-nonsalary distinctions made above.

11. Bohannon and Dalton, *op. cit.,* p. 186.

12. U. S. Department of Labor, *Manpower Development in the Ivory Coast* (Washington, D. C., December, 1962), pp. 1–2.

13. Jean-Paul Lebeuf, "Centres Urbains d'Afrique Equatoriale Française," *Africa* (London), XXIII (October, 1955), 288.

14. Inter-African Institute, *Information Sheet* (Brazzaville), VI, No. 2 (April, 1964), 8–9.

15. R. Cornevin, "Un Transfert de Main-d'Oeuvre Réussi: la Colonisation Cabraise au Togo," *Bulletin,* Inter-African Labour Institute, No. 2 (March, 1956), pp. 8–14.

16. C. Meek, *Land Tenure and Land Administration in Nigeria and the Cameroons,* Colonial Office, Colonial Research Studies No. 22 (London, 1957), p. 18.

17. *Annuaire Statistique de l'Afrique Occidentale Française,* Vol. 5, Tomel Direction des Services de la Statistique Générale (1954), pp. 215.

CHAPTER 12

(pp. 179–193)

1. An expanded study of Western African relations incorporating some of these conclusions will be published by Prentice-Hall in 1965. The author is grateful to the Rockefeller Foundation and the University of South Carolina for grants to do research in Western Africa in 1962–63.

2. Party and government are hyphenated to indicate the predominate single-party regime in former French Africa, Morocco excepted. The best review of this situation in Black Africa is found in Jean Buchmann, *L'Afrique Noire Indépendante* (Paris, 1962). For North Africa, see Charles F. Gallagher, *The United States and North Africa* (Cambridge, Mass., 1963); and I. William Zartman, *Government and Politics in Northern Africa* (New York, 1963).

3. This happened to some extent in the three countries of North Africa, and posed political problems. It is now presenting difficulties in Guinea and Mali, and may have been a factor in recent governmental changes in Togo and Dahomey.

4. Boundary problems, between Morocco and Mauritania, Morocco and Algeria, Mali and Mauritania, Dahomey and Niger, and Ivory Coast and Ghana did involve some tribal-regional considerations.

5. Tunisia may fall within this category too, although she has shown no awareness of this need.

6. Robert C. Good, "State-Building as a Determinant of Foreign Policy in the

New States," in Lawrence Martin (ed.), *Neutralism and Nonalignment* (New York, 1962), p. 12, an excellent chapter despite the disagreement on this point.

7. A content analysis of *el-Moudjahid* during the war years would confirm this; surprisingly enough, mentions of African solidarity far outnumber mentions of Arab solidarity.

8. It may be suggested, conversely, that any universal African conference meeting on any terms would have achieved the same position (since that position is qualified as temporary), so strong was the pressure of the slogan. However, this amounts to the same thing, since, in fact, of all the attempted meetings on all conceivable terms, only one did take place.

9. The choice of Tshombe as premier enhances these chances.

10. See Léonard Binder, "The Middle East as a Subordinate International System," in *The Ideological Revolution in the Middle East* (New York, 1964); and Michael Brecher, "International Relations and Asian Studies: The Subordinate State System of Southern Asia," *World Politics*, XV, No. 2 (January, 1963), 213–35.

11. It should be evident that "power," used in an international relations sense, is not equivalent merely to force. Power is relative, and refers to the ability to make decisions and produce intended effects. For a discussion of power, see Harold D. Lasswell and Abraham Kaplan, *Power and Society* (New Haven, Conn., 1950); for a discussion of the elements of national power and the tangible and intangible considerations on which power is based, see Hans J. Morgenthau, *Politics Among Nations* (New York, 1949).

12. For figures, see the special issue of *Africa Report*, IX, No. 9 (January, 1964),

13. Striking examples are found conveniently bound together in Sékou Touré, *The International Policy of the Democratic Party of Guinea*, Vol. 7 (Conakry, n.d.).

14. Similarly, the Tunisian claim against Algeria appears to have been put forward in order to emphasize Tunisia's desire to have a voice in the Saharan settlement, then under discussion between France and the FLN, rather than as a serious territorial demand.

15. On the latter, see the author's "A Disputed Frontier Is Solved," *Africa Report*, VIII, No. 8 (August, 1963), 13–14; and correction, *op. cit.*, IX, No. 3 (March, 1964), 31.

16. Ivory Coast's role in settling political crises in a direction favorable to the establishment of the Entente in 1959 was an example of skillful political warfare.

17. Another way of looking at the problem is to say that Addis Ababa was not possible as a continental summit meeting after 1960 until the independence of Algeria, and that maneuverings between 1960 and 1963 were merely scrimmage. This is basically true. It further suggests that the only states that would want a final summit before Algerian independence would be those that wanted to exclude Algeria, that Casablanca's refusal to join Monrovia was thus basically motivated, that one of the great achievements of the FLN was in early establishing its African membership (whereas, quite surprisingly, Kenya was not able to hold up the summit until its independence, nor were the rest of the still-dependent African states important enough to extend the waiting period beyond 1963), and finally that, given its self-assigned mission, Ghana was born out of time, too early to call a summit that would hold, and too isolated to set up an institution that would gradually incorporate the newcomers.

18. See George Liska, "Tripartism: Dilemmas and Strategies," in Martin, *op. cit.*, p. 212.

19. See Liska, "The 'Third Party': The Rationale of Nonalignment," in *ibid.*, p. 83. Whatever one might think of the issue, the unwillingness of Casablanca states to honor their commitments to Morocco vis-à-vis Mauritania was a sad case.

20. Morocco seemed to realize this in 1957 when she refused to sign a quick

base agreement with the U.S. and have her policy made for her by piecemeal commitments; instead her policy was made by abstract principles laid down in a National Consultative Assembly debate. See the author's *Problems of New Power* (New York, 1964).

21. See Morgenthau, *op. cit.;* and Vernon V. Aspaturian, "Revolutionary Change and the Strategy of the *Status Quo*," in Martin, *op. cit.*

22. This paper has not discussed the tenets of neutralism and nonalignment in former French Africa. That task is aptly enough covered elsewhere, most notably by Francis Low-Beer, "The Concepts of Neutralism," *American Political Science Review* LVIII, No. 2 (June, 1964), 383–91.

23. See Robert Good, "Patterns of African International Relations," (Paper delivered before the meeting of the American Political Science Association, New York, N.Y., Sept., 1963).

24. See Crane Brinton, *The Anatomy of Revolution* (Englewood Cliffs, N.J., 1952).

25. Not all of their neighbors; some, such as Togo or Niger, may have little or no foreign policy at all.

CHAPTER 14

(pp. 205–220)

1. For a detailed analysis of the evolution of the movement for reunification of the Cameroon, see Willard R. Johnson, "Cameroon Reunification: A Case Study in Political Union of Several Africas," unpublished Ph.D. dissertation, Harvard University, Fall, 1964; and Claude Welch, "Political Union Movements in Africa," unpublished Ph.D. dissertation, Oxford University, Spring, 1964. Victor T. LeVine, "Cameroon Mandate to Independence," unpublished Ph.D. dissertation, UCLA, September, 1961, and David Gardinier, *"Cameroon: United Nations Challenge to French Policy,"* (New York, 1963), contain brief references to the reunification movement.

2. *The Two Alternatives,* publication of the Plebiscite Commission, January, 1961.

3. *Ibid.,* pp. 13–15.

4. KNDP, *Constitutional Proposals of the Government Party,* June, 1961; *2nd Draft Revision of the Cameroon Constitution,* June, 1961.

5. Ndeh Ntumazah, President of One Kamerun Movement, opening speech to Conference (Bamenda) on the Constitutional future of the Southern Cameroons, June 26–28, 1961.

6. Representatives of the British Government visited the territory in October, 1961, to explain that they would not support an independent Southern Cameroons. A terminal grant of $1.5 million was given the Southern Cameroon Government. Some observers believe this was done to persuade the Foncha regime to accept the Ahidjo constitution.

7. President Ahidjo explained the logic behind the procedures used to enact the Federal Constitution at the fourth congress of the UC in August, 1962. See the report of that congress, p. 8.

8. Decree 61-DF-15, October 20, 1961.

9. *Cameroon Times,* May 7, 1960.

10. Announced in the House of Commons on February 7, and May 4, 1960.

11. Decree 62-DF-351, December 21, 1962, provided for the switch. Decree 63-DF-110, April 2, 1963 extended the transitional period to June 20, 1963; and Decree 63-DF-213, July 5, 1963, extended it further to December 31, 1963.

12. Cameroon Desk, U.S. Department of State.

13. *Cameroon Times,* July 26, 1963.

14. *L'Unité* (organ of *Union Camerounaise*), No. 179, April 26–May, 1964.

15. Foncha made such a pledge in March 1964, *L'Unité,* No. 174. There are still oppositions in each state, of seven representatives each. These parties probably could not hold out against a UC-KNDP union, and certainly could not win an election run on the basis of a single list, even if the electoral districts followed the administrative inspectorates.

CHAPTER 15

(pp. 223–236)

1. For a further exposition of these points of view, see S. N. Eisenstadt, *Modernization, Diversity and Growth* (Bloomington, Ind., 1963); and Eisenstadt, "Modernization and the Conditions of Sustained Growth," *World Politics,* XVI (July, 1964), 576–95.

2. See Rupert Emerson, "The Erosion of Democracy in the New States," in Harry Eckstein and David E. Apter (eds.), *Comparative Politics* (New York, 1963), pp. 625–44.

3. S. N. Eisenstadt, "Breakdowns of Modernization," *Economic Development and Cultural Change,* XII, No. 4 (July, 1964), 345–67.

4. S. N. Eisenstadt, *Essays on Sociological Aspects of Political and Economic Development* (The Hague, 1961); and Thomas Hodgkin, *Nationalism in Colonial Africa* (London, 1956).

5. See, for instance, Gwendolen Carter (ed.), *African One-Party States* (Ithaca, N.Y., 1962); and R. Schachter, "Single-Party Systems in West Africa," *American Political Science Review,* LV, No. 2 (June, 1961), 294–307.

6. See, for instance, United Nations, *Report on the World Social Situation* (New York, 1963) XIV; and J. Meynaud and A. Selah-Bey, *Le Syndicalisme Africain* (Paris, 1963).

7. *Report on the World Social Situation.*

8. See "Education et Développement," *Tiers-Monde: Problèmes des Pays Sous-développés,* V, No. 17 (January–March, 1964).

9. J. Foster, "Ethnicity and the School in Ghana," in *Comparative Education Review,* VI, No. 2 (October, 1962), 127.

10. Among the many works dealing with the "African Personality," see Ezekiel Mphalele, *The African Image* (New York, 1962); "The First International Conference of Negro Writers," in *Présence Africaine* (Paris), Nos. 8, 9, 10, June–November, 1956; and *The West African Intellectual Community* (Ibadan, 1963). See also Georges Balandier, *Afrique Ambigüe* (Paris, 1957).

11. S. N. Eisenstadt, *Modernization and Conditions of Sustained Growth.*

12. Georges Balandier, *Sociologie Actuelle de l'Afrique Noire* (Paris, 1963).

13. See, for instance, A. Callaway, "School Leavers and the Developing Economy of Nigeria," in R. O. Tilman and T. Cole (eds.), *The Nigerian Political Science* (Durham, N.C., 1962), pp. 220–38; L. Gray Cowan, "British and French Education in Africa: A Critical Appraisal," in Don C. Piper and T. Cole (eds.), *Post Primary Education and Economic Development* (Durham, N.C., 1964), pp. 178–200; and S. N. Eisenstadt, "Education and Political Development," in Piper and Cole, *op. cit.,* pp. 27–48.

Notes on the Contributors

DOUGLAS E. ASHFORD, Associate Professor of Public and International Affairs, Graduate School of Business and Public Administration, Cornell University, has also taught at Johns Hopkins, Indiana, and Princeton universities. He has traveled widely throughout North Africa, most recently in 1961–62; and, in addition to articles on political science and Islamic studies, he has published two books, *Political Change in Morocco* (1961) and *Perspectives of a North African Nationalist* (1964).

LEON CARL BROWN, Assistant Professor of Middle Eastern Studies at Harvard University, spent five years in the Foreign Service before turning to teaching and research. Since 1960 he has been concerned with modern North African history, and he is the co-author of *Tunisia: The Politics of Modernization* (1964).

MICHAEL CROWDER, presently Lecturer in African History, University of California at Berkeley, has served as a freelance journalist specializing in West African affairs, as editor of *Nigeria Magazine*, and as Secretary of the Institute of African Studies, University of Ibadan. He has published widely in magazines and journals, and his published books include the following: *Pagans and Politicians* (1959), *A Short History of Nigeria* (1962), and *Senegal: A Study in French Assimilation Policy* (1962).

SAMUEL N. EISENSTADT is Rose Isaacs Professor of Sociology and Chairman of the Department of Sociology at The Hebrew University, Jerusalem. He studied at the London School of Economics and Political Science and served as a fellow at the Center for Advanced Study in the Behavioral Sciences, Stanford, California. He has also been Visiting Professor at the University of Oslo, the University of Chicago, and the Massachusetts Institute of Technology. He has published widely.

VICTOR C. FERKISS, Associate Professor of Government at Georgetown University, has also taught at Montana State University and St. Mary's College of California. During 1959–60, he served as Field Program Director for the International Cooperation Administration Personnel Training Program of the African Studies Program of Boston University, and in 1961 he served as a consultant on Africa to the Peace Corps. He has contributed articles on political affairs to magazines and journals; he is the author of *Communism Today: Belief and Practice* (1962) and the forthcoming *The New Africa in World Affairs*.

ERNEST GELLNER, Professor of Sociology at the London School of Economics, has done field work among the Moroccan Berbers and been Visiting Lecturer at the University of Ghana. He is the author of *Words and Things* (1959) and *Thought and Change* (1965).

DAVID HAPGOOD, formerly on the staff of *The New York Times,* is currently a free-lance writer specializing in Africa, particularly in problems of rural development. He was last in Africa from 1961 to 1963 on a fellowship from the Institute of Current World Affairs, and he now acts as a consultant to the Peace Corps, evaluating programs in French-speaking Africa. He has published articles in several journals and is the author of two books on Africa to be published in 1965.

GEORGE R. HORNER is Professor of Anthropology and Chairman of the Department of Sociology–Anthropology at Eastern Nazarene College, Quincy, Massachusetts. From 1950 to 1953, he did research in the Cameroon; from 1954 to 1960, he served as Research Associate in the African Studies program of Boston University, and he has published articles in various scholarly journals.

WILLARD R. JOHNSON, Assistant Professor of Political Science at Massachusetts Institute of Technology, did his graduate work at Johns Hopkins' School of Advanced International Studies and at Harvard University, where he recently was awarded his Ph.D. in political science.

MARK KARP, Associate Professor of Economics and Research Associate in African Studies, African Studies Program, Boston University, is the author of *The Economics of Trusteeship in Somalia* (1964) and other works dealing with African economic problems.

VICTOR T. LEVINE is Assistant Professor of Political Science at Washington University, St. Louis. He spent fifteen months in field research in Cameroon and West Africa in 1959 and 1960–61; during the spring of 1964, he spent six months in West Africa, studying generational conflict within the political elites of five French-speaking states. In addition to articles in various scholarly journals, he has contributed to *The Educated African* (1962), *Five African States* (1962), and *Political Parties and National Integration in Africa* (1964). He is the author of *The Camerouns: From Mandate to Independence* (1964).

J. GUS LIEBENOW is Associate Professor of Government and Director of the African Studies Program at Indiana University. He has traveled extensively in Europe, Asia, and Latin America and has spent more than three years in Africa. He has published widely in journals of political science and African Studies, and he has contributed to six books on African affairs and international politics, including *African One-Party States* (1962), *Cases in African Political Institutions* (1963), and *Political Parties and National Integration in Tropical Africa* (1964).

WILLIAM H. LEWIS, Associate Professor of History at Georgetown University, also serves as Chief of the Division of Research and Analysis, U.S. Department of State. Of South African parentage, he has lived in North and East Africa and has traveled extensively throughout the continent. He is editor and co-author of *New Forces in Africa* (1963) and *Emerging Africa* (1964); he contributed to *The Modern Middle East and Muslim Africa* (1961), *The Development Revolution in the Middle East and North West Africa* (1964), and *Communism and Revolution* (1964). Dr. Lewis served as the organizer and director of the jointly sponsored institute and international congress that met at Georgetown University to evaluate the political, economic, and social problems confronting French-speaking Africa.

WILLIAM J. MAZZOCCO, Economic Affairs Advisor, United States Information Agency, has had a long career with the U.S. Government. From 1960 to 1962, he served as Director of the United States Agency for International Development's Mission to the Ivory Coast; before that, he served as a trade and finance officer and an international affairs officer in both Latin America and Europe.

HERBERT F. WEISS, recently Visiting Lecturer on Africa at Stanford University, has long been a specialist and observer on French-speaking Africa. In 1958–59, he served with the U.S. Department of State as a research specialist. Thereafter, he joined a survey team, under the auspices of the Massachusetts Institute of Technology, to conduct field research in the Congo. He is a frequent contributor to professional journals and an active participant in inter-university seminars dealing with contemporary African affairs.

I. WILLIAM ZARTMAN, Associate Professor of International Studies at the University of South Carolina, has served on the faculties of Johns Hopkins and Yale universities. He has traveled widely throughout North Africa, and he has written numerous articles and three books on North Africa: *Government and Politics in Northern Africa* (1963), *Morocco: Destiny of a Dynasty* (1964), and *Morocco: Problems of New Power* (1964).